Natural Language Processing for Historical Texts

Synthesis Lectures on Human Language Technologies

Editor
Graeme Hirst, *University of Toronto*

Synthesis Lectures on Human Language Technologies is edited by Graeme Hirst of the University of Toronto. The series consists of 50- to 150-page monographs on topics relating to natural language processing, computational linguistics, information retrieval, and spoken language understanding. Emphasis is on important new techniques, on new applications, and on topics that combine two or more HLT subfields.

Natural Language Processing for Historical Texts
Michael Piotrowski

ISBN: 978-3-031-01018-7   paperback
ISBN: 978-3-031-02146-6   ebook

DOI 10.1007/978-3-031-02146-6

A Publication in the Springer series
SYNTHESIS LECTURES ON HUMAN LANGUAGE TECHNOLOGIES

Lecture #17
Series Editor: Graeme Hirst, *University of Toronto*
Series ISSN
Synthesis Lectures on Human Language Technologies
Print 1947-4040   Electronic 1947-4059

Natural Language Processing for Historical Texts

Michael Piotrowski
Leibniz Institute of European History

SYNTHESIS LECTURES ON HUMAN LANGUAGE TECHNOLOGIES #17

ABSTRACT

More and more historical texts are becoming available in digital form. Digitization of paper documents is motivated by the aim of preserving cultural heritage and making it more accessible, both to laypeople and scholars. As digital images cannot be searched for text, digitization projects increasingly strive to create digital text, which can be searched and otherwise automatically processed, in addition to facsimiles. Indeed, the emerging field of digital humanities heavily relies on the availability of digital text for its studies.

Together with the increasing availability of historical texts in digital form, there is a growing interest in applying natural language processing (NLP) methods and tools to historical texts. However, the specific linguistic properties of historical texts—the lack of standardized orthography in particular—pose special challenges for NLP.

This book aims to give an introduction to NLP for historical texts and an overview of the state of the art in this field. The book starts with an overview of methods for the acquisition of historical texts (scanning and OCR), discusses text encoding and annotation schemes, and presents examples of corpora of historical texts in a variety of languages. The book then discusses specific methods, such as creating part-of-speech taggers for historical languages or handling spelling variation. A final chapter analyzes the relationship between NLP and the digital humanities.

Certain recently emerging textual genres, such as SMS, social media, and chat messages, or newsgroup and forum postings share a number of properties with historical texts, for example, non-standard orthography and grammar, and profuse use of abbreviations. The methods and techniques required for the effective processing of historical texts are thus also of interest for research in other domains.

KEYWORDS

computational linguistics, natural language processing, cultural heritage, historical texts, digitization, digital humanities

Contents

Acknowledgments

This book aims to give an overview of the state of the art in natural language processing for historical texts; thus, I would first like to acknowledge the work done by all the researchers working in this field—without their work, there would be no state of the art. I would also like to thank Graeme Hirst, the series editor, and Mike Morgan, the publisher—without their work, there would be no published book.

The digitization of the Collection of Swiss Law Sources is what got me into this exciting field in the first place. I am therefore grateful to Pascale Sutter, head of the Law Sources Foundation of the Swiss Lawyers Society, for piquing my interest in historical texts. I also have to thank her for her expertise in history and paleography, and for endorsing this book project.

I would like to thank Martin Volk (Institute of Computational Linguistics, University of Zurich) for the cooperation in the area of digital humanities and for supporting my research on NLP for historical texts in many ways.

I would also like to thank the two anonymous reviewers for their very thorough reading of the manuscript and their helpful comments and suggestions. I am grateful to Sarah Ebling for reading a draft of this book on short notice, for spotting inconsistencies and typographical imperfections, and for offering numerous valuable comments.

Some of the material presented in this book is based on courses I have taught at the University of Zurich and on a course I have given at the 6th DGfS-CL Fall School 2011 in Zurich. I would like to thank my students for their interest in the field, for their enthusiasm, and for their feedback.

Finally, and most importantly, I would like to thank Cerstin Mahlow. I would not have started this project without her, and I would not have finished it without her. As always, her support and encouragement have been invaluable.

Michael Piotrowski
July 2012

CHAPTER 1

Introduction

This book is about natural language processing (NLP) for historical texts. For the purpose of NLP, historical texts may be defined as texts written in historical languages. Defining the term *historical language* is actually harder than it may seem at first. One of the definitions for *historical* given by the *New Oxford American Dictionary* is "belonging to the past, not the present." Latin, Ancient Greek, or Biblical Hebrew would clearly fit that description. Old English, Old German, or Old French are obviously also historical languages, as texts written in these languages are not understandable to today's speakers of English, German, or French.

The problem is, however, that present and past are moving targets: today's present will be tomorrow's past. Historical linguists have defined *language stages* with conventional start and end dates; for example, Old English is said to have been used up to 1150, Middle English from 1150 to 1470, and modern English since about 1500. Should we thus consider only English texts from before 1500 as "historical?" Certainly not. The language of Shakespeare's (1564–1616) plays also clearly differs from today's language, and while a modern English speaker can understand a large portion of it, a glossary is required for many words that have fallen out of use. Abraham Lincoln's Gettysburg Address, given on November 18, 1863, is even more recent, but even though it is relatively easy to understand for educated modern speakers of English, it differs notably in style from modern English texts—today, nobody would say *four score and seven years* to mean 87.

In their preface to a special issue of the journal *Traitement Automatique des Langues*, Denooz and Rosmorduc suggest that "the best delimitation of ancient languages might be in terms of scholarly community" (Denooz and Rosmorduc, 2009, p. 13). Even though somewhat self-referential, this can be a useful definition, as these communities (e.g., historical linguists, medievalists, or Egyptologists) will both use and inform NLP for historical languages.

We can see that it is not easy to define what historical languages are, even though it is obvious that they exist. However, for natural language processing as an engineering discipline, perhaps we do not need a scholarly definition. Instead, we could look where standard NLP tools and techniques— aimed at current languages—are having problems when applied to older texts. This may give us a number of features that characterize historical languages—and thus define the requirements for NLP for historical languages.

1.1 HISTORICAL LANGUAGES AND MODERN LANGUAGES

Historical languages are human languages; as such, they are not fundamentally different from the languages we speak and write today. For NLP of historical texts this means that one is likely to encounter the same challenges as when processing modern texts, for example homonymy and polysemy, i.e., words that are spelled the same but have different meanings. The usual example is the word *bank*, which can refer to (inter alia) the land alongside a river, an array of similar objects, or a financial institution.

Language is used for many different purposes, so we may encounter different domains, genres, and styles. Most NLP is currently done for newspaper texts. When applying tools designed for and trained on newspaper texts to texts from a different domain or different genre, performance degrades, as other domains may differ in vocabulary (each domain has its own terminology), syntax (e.g., different subcategorization frames may be preferred (see Eumeridou et al., 2004)), and semantics (e.g., the meaning of *argument* in mathematics differs from its meaning in "general" language).

However, in addition to these challenges that apply to all NLP, historical languages exhibit a number of differences with modern languages that have a significant impact on natural language processing. First, here are some properties of *modern languages*, i.e., the languages that are commonly targeted by NLP research and applications, such as English, German, French, Spanish, Modern Standard Arabic, or Japanese.

- Modern languages have *standard variants* that are used for writing and supraregional communication. These are typically the languages taught in schools and learned by non-native speakers. They are thus well documented by dictionaries and grammars. In some cases there are even national bodies, such as the Académie française for French, that are officially tasked with regulating the language. In any case, the "boundaries" of the languages are (relatively) well defined, which makes it possible to develop NLP tools and resources that target specific languages, and to evaluate NLP tools with respect to the standard.

- Modern languages have *standard orthographies* and the majority of published texts adhere to the orthographic norms. Writers can check dictionaries to find out how a word is spelled correctly, and both rule-based and statistical NLP tools can rely on the fact that, in most cases, each lexical item has a small finite number of surface forms that can appear in texts. The existence of a standard orthography also makes it possible to correct misspellings.

- For several modern languages, large amounts of text—in standard orthography—are electronically available and can be used for developing NLP tools and resources. Obviously, the number of texts available in, say, Maltese, is much smaller than the number of texts available in English, as the Maltese language community is much smaller. However, even for smaller languages enough newspaper and government texts are generally available in electronic form to get started with NLP development without first having to digitize texts.

- For "larger" languages, such as English, German, French, or Spanish, there already exist many NLP resources and tools—machine-readable dictionaries, corpora, treebanks, part-of-speech (POS) taggers, parsers, etc.—that can either be used directly or on which further development can be based. For "smaller" languages, there may at least exist some resources, such as word lists for spell-checking.

Most or even all of these points do not apply to historical languages. Why is this a problem? As an example, let us take the absence of standardized orthography, which is perhaps one of the most visible problems (we will discuss this topic in more detail in chapters 3 and 6). Historical texts often differ markedly from modern texts in their spelling, and the spelling varies even between documents written in the same language and from the same period; in fact, a word is often spelled in different ways by the same author in the same text.

Many aspects of conventional NLP critically rely on the assumption that the text to be processed is written in a single language with a standardized orthography. Without a standardized spelling, how do you construct a dictionary if every word can be spelled in numerous ways? What do you do when two words may sometimes (but not always) be spelled in the same way? Which spelling do you use to represent a word internally? For statistical methods, if a word may occur in a variety of spellings, each of the spellings is obviously less frequent. This leads to problems of data sparseness, for example, due to the size of the training corpus, only spelling A may occur in some context, even though spellings B and C are in fact equally likely. Spelling variation also affects simple analysis and processing methods, such as stemming, which is based on a list of suffixes. Spelling variation not only increases the size of the suffix list, but it also makes collisions between actual suffixes and other strings more likely.

There is also spelling variation in modern languages; in English, for example, there are American and British spellings (*color* vs. *colour*) or variation with respect to the spelling of compound words (*spellchecker* vs. *spell-checker* vs. *spell checker*). However, spelling variation is much rarer than in historical texts that predate standardized orthography. In some applications, for example, Web search, spelling variation in the form of spelling errors is a significant issue, though. Productive word formation (e.g., derivation and compounding) and the creation of neologisms are different phenomena, but have similar effects on NLP; thus, NLP for modern languages also has to deal with correctly spelled, but unknown words.

Web search engines are designed to handle some amount of variation to cope with spelling mistakes, but they still make the assumption that there is one "correct" form for each word. As these assumptions do not hold for historical texts, one of the main problems for processing and retrieval of historical documents is the handling of spelling variation. The problems are exacerbated in historical document collections covering longer periods of time, since language and conventions also change over time.

When considering information retrieval (IR), further complications are related to search strategies. For example, when doing a Web search one typically knows which *terms* are likely to occur in documents that discuss the *concept* one is looking for—at least when searching in one's native language. When searching a collection of historical documents, the situation is rather like searching in a foreign language: One may have some ideas about which words may be used, but one is not sure. When searching historical documents, these words may also be spelled in many different ways; words may have undergone meaning shifts (e.g., the meaning of *gentle* changed from describing a higher social status—the meaning preserved in *gentleman*—to *kind*); finally, historical texts often also mix languages, so the term one is looking for may actually occur in, say, Latin in some of the relevant documents. For many applications—in particular those targeting casual users—it may thus be desirable that users can enter their search queries in modern language and spelling. To make this possible, an IR application requires natural language processing in order to be able to match modern-language queries to the historical forms found in the document collection.

One of the characteristics of most historical texts is—at the moment—that they were not born digital, i.e., they were not originally created in the digital medium. Thus, the original may have been printed on paper, written on parchment, chiseled into marble, or impressed on clay tablets, and must first be transferred into the digital medium. Note, however, that in the future many historical texts will be born digital.

1.2 INTENDED AUDIENCE

This book is intended both for readers with a background in NLP, who need to process historical text, and for readers with a humanities background, who would like to learn about the state of the art in NLP for historical texts. Quite often, we will therefore first take a higher-level perspective in order to get a general understanding of the challenges and issues involved, and we will then present specific approaches and discuss the results obtained using these approaches.

1.3 OUTLINE

In Chapter 2, we will discuss the relationship between NLP and the emerging field of digital humanities. This relationship is important, because most NLP for historical texts is somehow situated in this field. In Chapter 3, we will give an overview of spelling issues encountered in historical texts; spelling is one of the main problems in NLP for historical texts. After this, in Chapter 4, we will look into the digitization of historical texts and discuss scanning and techniques such as OCR and double-keying. In Chapter 5, we will cover the encoding of historical texts on the character level (using Unicode) and on higher levels (using TEI). Then, in Chapter 6, we will present approaches for tackling the problem of spelling differences and variation encountered in historical texts. Chapter 7 gives an overview of NLP tools that have been developed for processing historical texts, and Chapter 8 lists selected historical corpora for various languages. Chapter 9 concludes the book with some thoughts on the state of the art and the outlook of the field.

CHAPTER 2

NLP and Digital Humanities

Unlike, say, sentiment analysis or biomedical text mining, NLP for historical texts is usually not motivated by potential commercial applications, but rather by research questions from the humanities. This chapter outlines the motivation for automatic processing of historical texts and tries to situate NLP for historical texts with respect to the emerging field of digital humanities.

2.1 ORIGINS OF DIGITAL HUMANITIES

Libraries, archives, and museums hold large collections of historical documents, such as books, journals, letters, charters, treaties, or bulls, but also diaries, laboratory notes, or ethnographic recordings. In many countries there are ongoing efforts to digitize such documents in order to help their preservation and to improve their accessibility for scholars and the general public. These efforts include large-scale digitization projects, which aim to digitize millions of documents. Some of these projects are publicly funded, some are privately funded, and some are partnerships of public institutions with private corporations. Particularly, the public–private partnerships have received much attention from the media; for example, institutions such as Stanford University, the New York Public Library, the Bavarian State Library, and the University Library of Lausanne are cooperating with Google, Inc. in the Google Books Library Project.[1]

When digitizing documents, the first step is generally to scan or photograph the documents to create digital images or facsimiles (see Chapter 4). When the images are annotated with metadata (e.g., author, date, document type, summary) and made available online, access to these historical documents becomes faster and easier than ever before. Collections of historical documents can now be browsed by anyone, from anywhere, and at any time; even fragile documents can be made available without posing any risks to the sensitive originals. While historical documents have been photographed, reproduced, and published before (e.g., in books), the possibilities offered by digital media significantly surpass what was available before: electronic metadata can be searched, digital images can be zoomed into, comments can be attached, and so on.

For documents that are primarily textual, the next step is to convert their full textual content into digital text, which then opens up possibilities that go significantly beyond those offered by facsimiles—including the application of NLP tools and techniques. In principle, everything that can be done with modern texts can also be done with historical texts: full-text search, concordancing, lemmatization, morphological and syntactic analysis, text mining, machine translation, and so on.

---

[1]http://books.google.com/googlebooks/partners.html (accessed 2012-05-25)

The emerging field of *digital humanities* aims to exploit the possibilities offered by digital data for humanities research. The digital humanities combine traditional qualitative methods with quantitative, computer-based methods and tools, such as information retrieval, text analytics, data mining, visualization, and geographic information systems (GIS).

There are currently a number of large international initiatives that aim to create common infrastructure for the digital humanities, including NLP resources and tools. Noteworthy initiatives are the EU-funded CLARIN[2] (Common Language Resources and Technology Infrastructure) and DARIAH[3] (Digital Research Infrastructure for the Arts and Humanities) projects, Project Bamboo[4] (funded by the Andrew W. Mellon Foundation), and the German TextGrid[5] project.[6] Some of the projects mostly coordinate existing activities, while others aim to create new resources. Furthermore, so-called *digital humanities centers*[7] have been established at many institutions, which combine competencies in computing and the humanities and provide support for digital humanities projects.

However, computer processing of historical texts is not a completely new application; on the contrary, it has a history that is at least as old as that of machine translation, if not older (see Schreibman et al., 2004, Chapter 1). However, despite the seemingly obvious connections between humanities computing and computational linguistics, there has been surprisingly little communication and collaboration between these fields. Of course, there has been some computational linguistics work in humanities computing and vice versa, but, by and large, these fields have remained separate, with separate societies, journals, and conferences. One reason certainly lies in the different origins of the two fields: philology and literature on the one side, computer science and formal linguistics on the other. Consequently, humanities computing has often been concerned with higher-level aspects of texts that require human judgment, so that it often required semiautomatic approaches or focused on the automatic evaluation of manually collected data, whereas computational linguistics generally tries to avoid human intervention and manual work as much as possible.

The field now called digital humanities has its roots in humanities computing, but it nevertheless represents a new development. Digital humanities is, we think, not just a new label for an old field; rather, it marks the beginning of a paradigm shift. Whereas humanities computing often had a purely supportive role in otherwise traditional humanities research, quantitative methods are beginning to be regarded as being on par with qualitative methods. Despite the use of computers, the final output still used to be books; digital humanities projects are no longer tied to the restrictions of the printed medium. Two good examples are the *The Proceedings of the Old Bailey, 1674-1913*[8] and the edition

---

[2]http://www.clarin.eu/ (accessed 2012-05-28)

[3]http://www.dariah.eu/ (accessed 2012-05-28)

[4]http://www.projectbamboo.org/ (accessed 2012-05-28)

[5]http://www.textgrid.de/ (accessed 2012-05-28)

[6]See also the Coalition of Humanities and Arts Infrastructures (CHAIN): http://www.arts-humanities.net/chain (accessed 2012-05-28)

[7]For an overview see: http://digitalhumanities.org/centernet/ (accessed 2012-05-28)

[8]The Old Bailey was the central criminal court of London; see http://www.oldbaileyonline.org/ (accessed 2012-06-06) for the proceedings.

of the letters written by and to Alfred Escher,[9] which both make use of the possibilities offered by the Web for interlinking historical text with geographical and biographical data, images, and other related information, and which offer readers different ways for accessing the data—not only from a table of contents, but also via maps, timelines, and other visualizations. Many projects—including these two—also provide the full texts of the documents in digital form and thus go beyond digital facsimiles.

There used to be, however, relatively little work in the digital humanities where NLP methods and tools were used. Much of the quantitative information stems from what could be described as metadata, or from simple counts of word forms.

2.2   CONVERGENCE OF NLP AND DIGITAL HUMANITIES

On the NLP side, the interest in genres other than newspaper and news wire texts is growing, and besides biomedical texts, forum posts, and Twitter messages, computational linguists have discovered historical texts and other types texts of interest to humanities and the social sciences. At the moment, however, much of the work is still concerned with basic problems, such as searching historical text collections using modern query terms and mapping historical word forms to modern word forms, so that NLP tools designed or trained for modern language can be used. Both problems are mostly treated as spelling correction tasks, and other issues, such as usage changes or meaning shifts, are typically not taken into account. We will discuss the issues of historical spelling and the NLP approaches in chapters 3 and 6).

Nevertheless, the developments indicate the beginning of a partial convergence of humanities computing and computational linguistics, in particular in the area of cultural heritage. We are already beginning to see research that combines methods and techniques from both areas. We will cite just a few examples.

In his dissertation, Boschetti (2010) combines research on improving OCR of critical editions of classical Greek works (see also Section 4.3.1), on automatic extraction of conjectures[10] from the apparatuses of the digitized editions, automatic alignment of these conjectures with the source text and with each other, and the use of this quantitative data to study the semantic spaces of Ancient Greek to discover, for example, meaning shifts, and to evaluate the conjectures made by different scholars.

The work by Hendrickx et al. (2010) on the semantic and pragmatic analysis of historical Portuguese letters combines machine learning techniques for automatically segmenting the letters into parts with different pragmatic functions (opener, formal greeting, conclusion, closer) and for annotating the contents of these parts with semantic labels (based on those used by the UCREL semantic analysis system (Rayson et al., 2004) with scholarly methods for discourse analysis and historical pragmatics to examine the social roles of people.

---

[9]Swiss industrialist, politician, and railroad pioneer (1819–1882); the online edition is found at http://www.briefedition. alfred-escher.ch/ (accessed 2012-06-06).

[10]In textual criticism, a *conjecture* is a reconstructed reading of a text not present in the original source, suggested by scholars on the basis of the surrounding context, previous conjectures, or other indications.

Further examples of fruitful cooperation between computational linguistics and the humanities are the research by Pettersson and Nivre (2011), who extract verb forms from historical Swedish texts to support historians studying the sources of livelihood of the people in early modern Swedish society (1550–1800), and the research done in the context of the German eAqua ("Extraction of structured knowledge from ancient sources for archeology") project[11].

What these examples have in common is that the NLP and humanities portions have equal weight: they are neither humanities projects that employ a programmer nor NLP projects that only have a symbolic relationship to scholarly research. We do not want to say that these are the first projects that combine both fields; browsing back issues of, say, the journal *Literary and Linguistic Computing* will yield many other projects. However, most of these earlier projects are exceptional in the sense that they were often carried out by individuals with strengths in both fields (e.g., scholars with programming skills) or in one-time collaborations between scholars and computer scientists or computational linguists.

How can the state of the art be further advanced? It is clear that most of the humanities disciplines primarily or even exclusively rely on texts. More and more humanities research relies on digital texts and, as more and more text is becoming available in digital form, quantitative methods are now gaining acceptance as complementary to the traditional qualitative methods. NLP offers methods and tools for working with large amounts of texts; thus, it is natural to consider NLP a foundation for digital humanities, if the possibilities digital text offers to scholarly research are to be realized. This is, in fact, not a new insight; the French historian Bautier stated already in 1977:

> L'informatique, par nature, permet de traiter un nombre élevé de documents. Bien plus qu'une exploitation exhaustive d'un nombre limité d'actes, c'est surtout ce traitement massif appliqué à des sources pré-traitées et offrant un texte sûr et critique, qui, même s'il ne donne pas tous les renseignements que certains en attendent, fera avancer de façon décisive la science historique.[12]   (Bautier, 1977, p. 186)

At that time, this was a quite radical view, in particular, as much less text was available in digital form than today. Bautier rightly points out that the main use of computers lies in their ability to process massive amounts of data, which has the potential to provide scholars with new information that will lead to new insights. He also noted that reliable "preprocessed sources" are required. These are, in our view, exactly the two areas to which NLP can contribute: digitization—including methods for checking and correcting texts—and processing of texts. In other words: if the humanities seriously want to base their research on large quantities of text and apply quantitative methods, they will need NLP as a basis for all higher-level analyses. To take one field of digital humanities as an example, for digital historical scholarship, NLP must then be regarded as an auxiliary science of history, similar to archeology, diplomatics, paleography, etc., which are indispensable for evaluating and using historical sources.

---

[11]http://www.eaqua.net/ (accessed 2012-07-01)

[12]"Computers, by their very nature, are able to process large numbers of documents. It is particularly this massive processing of sources (preprocessed and offering a reliable critical text)—not the exhaustive analysis of a limited number of charters—which will decisively advance the historical sciences, even if it may not give all the answers that some may expect." (My translation.)

As such, digital humanities researchers have to get acquainted with the methods and tools of NLP; to cite another French historian, Froger noted in 1970:

> Il n'est pas indispensable que le philologue établisse lui-même le programme, encore que ce soit infiniment souhaitable ; il devrait au moins connaître assez le langage de programmation pour contrôler le travail du technicien ; en effet, l'expérience m'a appris qu'il ne faut pas s'en remettre les yeux fermés aux électroniciens, mal préparés par leur formation mathématique à se faire une idée juste de problèmes concrets qui se posent dans la domaine de la philologie. [13]   (Froger, 1970, p. 213)

We believe that this is still true today, which means that NLP also has its place in any digital humanities curriculum, so that students—future scholars—have a good understanding of NLP methods and tools and their utility—and limits—in the context of their own research.

NLP can also benefit from the humanities applications and from the humanities themselves. Since most of the NLP work up to now has been done on newspaper texts, what NLP currently lacks is a conceptual model of spelling variation, genre differences, and language change. For example, the approaches to spelling normalization described in Chapter 6 are useful but, by their very nature, superficial: there is no underlying computational model that describes how synchronic and diachronic variants relate to each other and—possibly—to some shared meaning or some kind of prototype that represents the relatedness of the variants. At the moment, all we have are edit distances. The problem is even more pressing when one wants to process languages—whether modern or historical—without fixed orthography (Strunk, 2003) and without a modern variant with standardized orthography that can serve as a reference.

It is well known that applying NLP tools trained and tested on newspaper texts to other domains and genres results in a sharp drop in performance—even for contemporary language—and that the tools must be adapted to different domains and genres. It has been shown that such adaptation can improve performance (see, e.g., Foster, 2010; Foster et al., 2011). However, we also do not yet have a good conceptual model for domain and genre differences; it is fairly obvious that there are lexical and syntactic differences, but how do they relate? Could we determine similarity of genres for NLP purposes? Would this relate to, say, literary criteria?

Many of these questions are not only of interest for historical text processing and other digital humanities applications but also for any application out of the domain of newspaper texts, in particular for SMS messages, forum posts, chats, and social media texts, which share many characteristics with historical texts, including non-standard spelling and grammar. See Gouws et al. (2011) for an investigation into the writing conventions in these so-called *microtexts*; Han and Baldwin (2011); Liu et al. (2011); Xue et al. (2011) present approaches for spelling normalization; and Kaufmann and Kalita (2010); Foster (2010); Foster et al. (2011) discuss syntactic normalization and parsing of such texts. In fact, Barthélemy (2007) compares the writing system of (French) SMS messages to cuneiform writing and finds several parallels—both systems are heterogeneous writing

---

[13]"It is not absolutely necessary that the philologist writes the program himself, even though it would be extremely desirable; but he must at least know the programming language, so that he is able to check the work of the technician; in fact, experience has taught me that one should not blindly rely on the electronics people, whose mathematical training has hardly prepared them for fully understanding the concrete problems encountered in the domain of philology." (My translation.)

systems comprising syllabic, phonetic, and ideographic elements—prompting him to suggest a similar approach for transcribing SMS messages into standard orthography as is used for transcribing cuneiform writings.

2.3   SUMMARY

In this chapter we have argued that NLP—and NLP for historical texts in particular—should be considered a foundation for the emerging discipline of digital humanities. NLP researchers are becoming aware of the requirements of humanities research, and humanities scholars are becoming aware of the tools and techniques NLP has to offer; there are already projects that combine both NLP and humanities methods, but they are still relatively rare. However, we think that both the humanities and NLP could very much benefit from increased collaboration.

Just like computational linguistics are not linguistics with a little bit of programming, digital humanities are not humanities with a little bit of programming. What is needed are scholars with a deeper understanding of algorithms, data structures, and abstraction and computational linguists (or computer scientists) with a deeper understanding of the humanities.

CHAPTER 3

Spelling in Historical Texts

Spelling differences and variation in spelling are some of the most obvious properties of historical texts and a substantial obstacle to NLP. In this chapter we will discuss the importance of orthography for NLP in general, and examine how historical texts differ from modern texts in this respect.

3.1 THE ROLE OF ORTHOGRAPHY IN NLP

When discussing orthography, one first thinks of the spelling of individual words. It should be noted, however, that spelling also concerns issues such as punctuation, abbreviations, hyphenation, and the separation of words. The latter is a critical issue for NLP, as it affects tokenization—typically the first processing step—which consequently influences all further processing steps.

Natural language processing methods—including information retrieval—generally assume that the text to process adheres to a consistent orthography. This is because, at some point, most NLP techniques need to consult lexical resources to obtain information (e.g., part of speech, case, or number) about the word forms encountered in the text, and the word form serves as key for accessing this information. This is regardless of whether the lexical resources were constructed manually (such as traditional machine-readable dictionaries) or extracted automatically from texts. For example, WordNet (Fellbaum, 1998) contains much information on *book*, but a search for, say, *boke* or *booke* will return no results.

This also applies to statistical methods: statistical models are based on the assumption that parameters learned from training data (say, a manually tagged corpus) are applicable to other data as well. Again, as surface forms are the starting point for NLP, the spelling of words is one important parameter. The strength of statistical methods is that they can draw inferences from sparse training data, for example, a POS tagger can predict (i.e., guess) the part of speech of a word form it has never seen before. This requires, however, that enough contextual information in the form of known word forms is available; the higher the number of unknown word forms, the lower the reliability of the tagger. Clearly, the number of unknown word forms increases if the spelling of the input text differs from the training data. Another source of information are affixes (usually suffixes); in English, for example, an unknown word form ending in *-ion* is likely to be a noun. Of course, the same problem arises here as well: If an affix is spelled in different ways, the tagger cannot relate the variants to each other.

Information retrieval is another application that critically depends on standardized orthography. Standard IR methods assume that document authors and information seekers use the same terms to describe concepts. This effectively means that they use the same words and spell them in the same way. Modern search engines are able to cope with spelling errors in queries (see Manning et al. (2008, Chapter 3) for an overview of methods for "tolerant retrieval"), but this can only work if the document collection (mostly) uses a consistent spelling. Query expansion can cope with possible (morphological, terminological, lexical, etc.) variation in phrasing a certain query, but the rules for such variation (e.g., inflection patterns) have to be determined beforehand.

3.2 SPELLING AND HISTORICAL TEXTS

With respect to spelling, historical texts exhibit three basic characteristics. First, *spelling difference*, i.e., their spelling may differ from the spelling used today. Spelling conventions change over time, and many orthographies are officially reformed from time to time; well-known recent examples—sometimes the subject of much dispute in the respective language communities—are the German spelling reform of 1996, the Dutch spelling reform of 1995, and the 1990 *rectifications* (spelling amendments) in French.

The simplification of Chinese characters in the People's Republic of China in the 1950s is an example of a spelling reform in a language not written using the Latin script. Some languages, for example Turkish, Korean, or Mongolian, changed at some point in time to a completely different script; such changes obviously go beyond a mere reform of the orthography.[1] The spelling and spelling conventions found in older texts often differ from those of newer texts; in diachronic historical corpora, which cover longer periods of time, one will typically find several different historical spellings.

Second, nationally or even supranationally standardized orthographies are a relatively recent development. For example, German orthography was formally regulated as late as 1901 and Portuguese orthography in 1911. Spelling was not completely arbitrary before these standardization efforts, but in the absence of a standard, there existed no concept of "correct" spelling. Instead, there were typically different "schools" of spelling or *written dialects* and a much wider range of acceptable spellings, often reflecting regional pronunciations. This means that the spelling in older texts—even from the same period—is often highly variable; it is not rare that a single author spells a single word in a single text in different ways. We may call this phenomenon *spelling variance*.

In linguistic terms, the two issues of spelling difference and spelling variance are related to *diachronic* and *synchronic variation*, respectively. Figure 3.1 illustrates these two dimensions: it shows the percentages of occurrences of spelling variants of the German word form *wird* 'becomes' (3rd person singular indicative present) in a diachronic corpus. One can see, for example, that around 1530, all four spellings occurred; this is synchronic variation. On the time axis one can see that eventually the spelling *wird* became generally accepted; this is diachronic variation.[2]

---

[1]Turkish changed its writing system in 1928 from the Arabic to the Latin script. Hangul, the native Korean script, was created in the 15th century, but the move from Hanja (Chinese characters) to Hangul took place gradually until the early 20th century; today Hangul has almost completely replaced Hanja. The traditional Mongolian script is related to the Arabic script, but is written vertically; in the 1930s, the Latin script was introduced, but replaced by Cyrillic in 1941.

[2]One may argue that *wirdet* actually reflects a different pronunciation and is thus not a spelling variant. Indeed, Ruge (2005) notes that during the transitional period between Middle High German and New High German, the explicit form *wirdet* and the contracted form *wird* were still competing. However, the contracted form already appeared in Middle High German (loss of

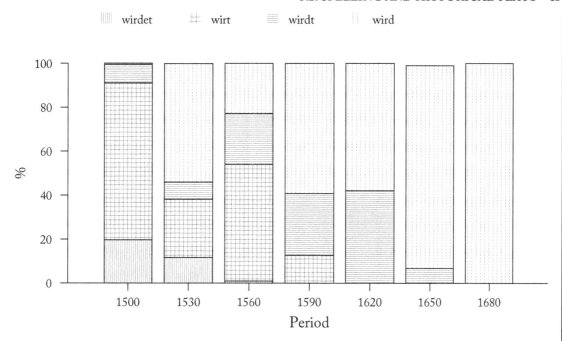

Figure 3.1: Synchronic and diachronic variation of spelling: percentage distribution over time of spelling variants of German *wird* 'becomes' (data from Ruge, 2005).

The third issue is *uncertainty*. In NLP one is working with digital texts, but most historical texts were not created in digital form, so they first need to be digitized, i.e., transcribed into the new medium. The transcription can be performed automatically (by OCR) or manually. We discuss the technical aspects in Chapter 4; the important points here are that *any* transcription (1) entails interpretation and (2) may introduce errors and artifacts. Thus, when applying NLP to historical texts, one never works with the "original" text but with some (possibly erroneous) interpretation of it.

These three issues are characteristic for historical documents. However, the extent of these issues depends on many factors, including the language (or languages) of the text, age of the text, type of document (manuscript, typescript, book, etc.), writer, intended audience, etc. The amount of digitization errors depends on physical properties of the original document, typefaces, and handwriting, but also to the digitization procedures used, which may not be under the control of the computational linguist or NLP researcher (see Chapter 4). We will now discuss these three issues in some more detail with the help of some concrete examples.

---

unaccented vowels); Wright (1917, p. 10) writes: "The **e**, when not preceded by a nasal, was sometimes dropped in verbal forms ending in **t**. This was especially the case in **wirst**, **wirt** older **wirdes(t)**, **wirdet**." Given this strong tendency, one may assume that at least some of the explicit spellings are archaisms, i.e., the writers wrote *wirdet* but pronounced it *wird* (compare the verbal ending *-ed* in English). For the purposes of this discussion we therefore believe it is legitimate to treat these forms as spelling variants.

3.2.1   DIFFERENCE: DIACHRONIC SPELLING VARIATION

As an example of diachronic spelling variation, consider William Caxton's[3] preface to his translation of *Eneydos* from 1490, an excerpt of which is given in Figure 3.2(a). Despite its age—and despite some syntactic differences with modern language—most of it is readily understandable to today's speakers of English. The spelling differences with modern English are obvious, though. In order to assess the amount of differences with modern spelling, one may run a modern spell-checker on the text.

From a spell-checker's perspective,[4] the complete preface consists of 1225 tokens; of these, the spell-checker reports 693 (56.6%) of these as known and 532 (43.4%) as unknown. Of the 476 types occurring in the text, 146 (30.7%) are known and 330 (69.3%) are unknown to the spell-checker. This is just an approximation, but it is safe to say that almost half of the tokens and almost 70% of the types differ from modern spelling. For comparison, when running the same spell-checker on the modernized version by Gray (2000, pp. 155–158), of which the beginning is shown in Figure 3.2(b), it reports only 15 of 1097 tokens (1.4%) and 13 of 444 types (2.9%) as unknown, and these are almost exclusively proper names such as Eneydos, Diodorus, and Syculus, and archaisms.

As a rough measure of the impact of spelling difference on NLP, we also ran the TreeTagger[5] part-of-speech tagger (Schmid, 1994) on the texts. For the tagger, the original text consists of 1351 tokens (as it treats punctuation as separate tokens), of which 519 (38.4%) are reported as unknown; however, of the 544 types, 373 (68.6%) are unknown, which is consistent with the results of the spell-checker. Running TreeTagger on the version in modernized spelling (1199 tokens, 472 types) only reports 12 unknown tokens (1.0%) and 10 unknown types (2.1%).

As noted above, spelling also concerns the definition of what constitutes a word and the separation of words; the above experiments with the spell-checker and the POS tagger do not take this issue into account, which is exemplified in Figure 3.2(a) by the spelling *thystorye* 'the history'.

3.2.2   VARIANCE: SYNCHRONIC SPELLING VARIATION

Baron et al. (2009) perform a large-scale analysis to determine the extent of spelling variation in Early Modern English. To this end, they analyzed six different corpora: *ARCHER* (see Section 8.4), a subset of *Early English Books Online*,[6] the *Innsbruck Letter Corpus*,[7] the *Lampeter Corpus*, the *Early Modern English Medical Texts* (EMEMT) corpus (see Section 8.4), and a collection of Shakespeare's works. Together, these corpora cover the entire Early Modern English period from 1410 to 1799, various text types and genres. For their study, Baron et al. take samples from each corpus at intervals

---

[3]William Caxton (ca. 1422–1491) was an English printer; in 1474 he printed the first book in English.

[4]We used Hunspell 1.3.2 (`http://hunspell.sourceforge.net/` (accessed 2012-06-06)) with the official en_US dictionary, which is based on the Spell Checker Oriented Word Lists (SCOWL, `http://wordlist.sourceforge.net/` (accessed 2012-07-01)), version 7.1.

[5]Version 3.2 with the standard English parameter file; `http://www.ims.uni-stuttgart.de/projekte/corplex/TreeTagger/` (accessed 2012-06-27).

[6]`http://www.textcreationpartnership.org/` (accessed 2012-06-30)

[7]`http://www.uibk.ac.at/anglistik/projects/icamet/` (accessed 2012-06-30)

After dyuerse werkes made / translated and achieued / hauyng noo werke in hande. I sittyng in my studye where as laye many dyuerse paunflettis and bookys. happened that to my hande cam a lytyl booke in frenshe. whiche late was translated oute of latyn by some noble clerke of fraūce whiche booke is named Eneydos / made in latyn by that noble poete & grete clerke vyrgyle / whiche booke I sawe ouer and redde therin. How after the generall destruccyon of the grete Troye, Eneas departed berynge his olde fader anchises vpon his sholdres / his lityl son yolus on his honde. his wyfe wyth moche other people folowynge / and how he shypped and departed wyth alle thystorye of his aduentures that he had er he cam to the achieuement of his conquest of ytalye as all a longe shall be shewed in this present boke. In whiche booke I had grete playsyr [...]

(a)

After diverse works made, translated and achieved, having no work in hand, I sitting in my study where lay many different pamphlets and books, there happened to my hand a little book in French, which was late translated out of the Latin by some noble clerk in France, which book is named Eneydos made in Latin by that noble poet and great clerk Virgil, which book I glanced over and read therein. How after the general destruction of the great Troy, Aeneas departed bearing his old father Anchises on his shoulders, his little son Iolus on his hand, his wife with many other people following, and how he shipped and departed with all the history of his adventures before he achieved the conquest of Italy, all of which will be shown in the present book. In that book I had great pleasure [...]

(b)

Figure 3.2: Excerpt from William Caxton's preface to his translation of *Eneydos* from 1490; (a) original spelling, from the edition by Jack Lynch, `http://andromeda.rutgers.edu/~jlynch/Texts/eneydos.html` (accessed 2012-06-06); (b) modernized edition by Gray (2000, pp. 155–158).

of ten years; the number of texts in each sample was chosen on the basis of the size of each corpus. The texts were then selected randomly.

To calculate the spelling variance per corpus and per decade, Baron et al. check for each word form in the historical samples whether it could be found in either the Spell Checker Oriented Word Lists (SCOWL)[8] or the list of word forms from the *British National Corpus* (BNC) with a frequency greater than 5. If a word form was not found in the modern word lists it was considered a spelling variant. This analysis provided a percentage of variant types and tokens per corpus and per decade sample; Figure 3.3 shows the percentages averaged over all corpora. The graphs clearly show the decrease of spelling variation from the beginning to the end of the period; the token graph also shows that English spelling had become mostly uniform and stable by about 1700.

The authors note that the numbers should be taken as approximate, as spelling variation cannot be calculated automatically with absolute precision by comparing isolated word forms (i.e., without

[8]`http://wordlist.sourceforge.net/` (accessed 2012-07-01)

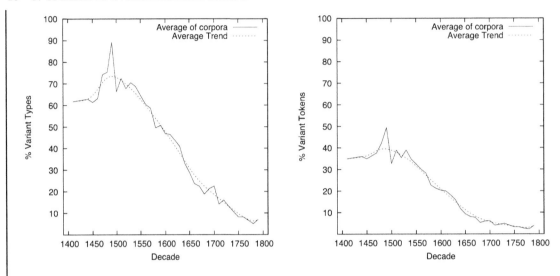

Figure 3.3: Baron et al. (2009) examine the extent of spelling variation in Early Modern English on the basis of six corpora. The left-hand graph shows the average percentage of variant types; the right-hand graph shows the average percentage of variant tokens in the corpora available for each decade (diagrams from Baron et al., 2009, p. 52)

taking the context into account). An obvious problem is that it is impossible to distinguish between spelling variants that coincide with the modern spelling of another word form and word forms that are actually spelled according to today's orthography; examples are *be* and *bee*, *affect* and *effect*, or *pray* and *prey*. In spell-checking, these are known as *real-word errors*, *malapropisms*, or *confusables*. Baron et al. try to quantify the amount of such confusions by analyzing two small manually normalized samples from the *Lampeter Corpus* and from Shakespeare; table 3.1 summarizes the results. The percentage of real-word errors found by Baron et al. is surprisingly low compared to the number of real-word errors reported for modern English texts; Mitton (1996) found 40% of the errors in his error corpus to be real-word errors. Spell-checkers are likely to be one source of real-word errors in modern texts; Hirst and Budanitsky (2005) note that "it is now common for real-word errors to be introduced by auto-correction mechanisms and by conventional spelling checkers." The rightmost column in table 3.1 suggests a further problem when trying to detect spelling variants in isolation, namely word forms that are erroneously marked as spelling variants because they are not contained in the modern word lists; this includes rare and obsolete words, proper names, and foreign-language material (in particular, French and Latin in the context of Early Modern English). Baron et al. conclude that even though their variant rates are approximations, the inaccuracies caused by real-word errors and false positives affect all corpus samples evenly, so that the general trend should not be affected.

The amount of spelling variance and difference also depends on the types of texts. For example, the degree of standardization in printed texts is generally higher than in manuscript texts. As an

Table 3.1: Analysis of variants found in manually normalized Early Modern English texts (Baron et al., 2009). The column "% Variants" lists the percentage of word forms that required normalization (actual variants); "% RWE" gives the percentage of variants that are real-word errors; "% False Pos." gives the percentage of word forms erroneously marked as variants after the text had been normalized.

Sample	Total		% Variants		% RWE		% False Pos.	
	Typ.	Tok.	Typ.	Tok.	Typ.	Tok.	Typ.	Tok.
Lampeter	839	2,726	19.19	9.61	4.35	2.67	12.04	4.37
Shakespeare	897	3,991	63.88	24.03	8.55	5.11	7.80	3.38

example, consider the text excerpts in Figure 3.4. Figure 3.4(a) reproduces the beginning of Immanuel Kant's famous article *Beantwortung der Frage: Was ist Aufklärung?* (in English: *Answering the Question: What Is Enlightenment?*) as it was first printed in 1784. Figure 3.4(b) is a transcription of a manuscript from 1786, a draft for a wine tax by the city council of Rapperswil in Switzerland. The printed text is not normalized[9]; the manuscript text was transcribed according to the guidelines of the Collection of Swiss Law Sources, which require the addition of punctuation and the normalization of capitalization in manuscripts to sentence initials and proper names; deletions and corrections (which are recorded in the edition) are not shown here. In both texts, the long and short forms of *s* are rendered as *s*.

The printed text basically conforms to the current German orthography with respect to spelling conventions (letter-sound correspondences) and capitalization. The only major spelling difference is the use of *th* where *t* is now used (e.g., *Muth* 'courage', *Theil* 'part'). The usage of *ß* conforms to the orthography before the 1996 reform.

The spelling used in the manuscript, however, differs *significantly* from today's orthography and "looks" much older to a modern speaker of German. Some major differences are: *ey* is used instead of *ei*; there are doubled letters and clusters of redundant letters such as *ckh*, *nff*, *sß*; in some words, *ü* is used where now *i* is written (e.g., *würth* 'innkeeper', now spelled *Wirt*), *i* and *j* are still used interchangeably, etc. Not surprisingly, the manuscript also contains more variation (e.g., *weinschenckhen* vs. *weinschenkhen* 'tavern keeper') and errors.

For readers not familiar with German, the number of spelling errors found by a spell-checker for modern German may illustrate these differences between the two texts. Table 3.2 shows the results of running a spell-checker for modern German[10] on the excerpts shown in Figure 3.4: in the printed text only 6% of the running word forms are considered erroneous by the spell-checker (we include Latin words and capitalization differences in the count), but it flags over 45% of the

---

[9]The original was printed in a blackletter typeface that uses a superscript *e* instead of two dots to mark the umlaut, but in this case this is merely a property of the typeface.

[10]We used Hunspell 1.3.2 (`http://hunspell.sourceforge.net/` (accessed 2012-06-06)) with the "frami" dictionary, version 2011-05-05.

Aufklärung ist der Ausgang des Menschen aus seiner selbst verschuldeten Unmündigkeit. Unmündigkeit ist das Unvermögen, sich seines Verstandes ohne Leitung eines anderen zu bedienen. Selbstverschuldet ist diese Unmündigkeit, wenn die Ursache derselben nicht am Mangel des Verstandes, sondern der Entschließung und des Muthes liegt, sich seiner ohne Leitung eines andern zu bedienen. Sapere aude! Habe Muth dich deines eigenen Verstandes zu bedienen! ist also der Wahlspruch der Aufklärung.

Faulheit und Feigheit sind die Ursachen, warum ein so großer Theil der Menschen, nachdem sie die Natur längst von fremder Leitung frei gesprochen (naturaliter majorennes), dennoch gerne Zeitlebens unmündig bleiben; und warum es Anderen so leicht wird, sich zu deren Vormündern aufzuwerfen. Es ist so bequem, unmündig zu sein. Habe ich ein Buch, das für mich Verstand hat, einen Seelsorger, der für mich Gewissen hat, einen Arzt der für mich die Diät beurtheilt, u. s. w. so brauche ich mich ja nicht selbst zu bemühen. Ich habe nicht nöthig zu denken, wenn ich nur bezahlen kann; andere werden das verdrießliche Geschäft schon für mich übernehmen. Daß der bei weitem größte Theil der Menschen (darunter das ganze schöne Geschlecht) den Schritt zur Mündigkeit, außer dem daß er beschwerlich ist, auch für sehr gefährlich halte: dafür sorgen schon jene Vormünder, die die Oberaufsicht über sie gütigst auf sich genommen haben.

(a) Beginning of Immanuel Kant's article *Beantwortung der Frage: Was ist Aufklärung?* (*Answering the Question: What Is Enlightenment?*) from the original publication in the journal *Berlinische Monatsschrift* of December 1784.

Proiectum wegen umbgellts:

1°. Könfftige fronfasten sollen alle würth- und weinschänckhkeller recognosciert werden und beschriben, wie vill wein darin enthalten.

2do. Ein weins inspector, so von m. gn. herren geordnet wirdt, solle bey allem zu wasßer und landt hier ankhommendten wein gegenwärthig seyn, und eines jeden ville und qualitet aufzeichnen, sonderlich zu herbsts zeit, auch auff allen ab hiesiger pottmäsßigkeit von würth- und weinschenckhen einlegendten newen erkaufft old jhnen selbst gewachsenen wein gleiche obsicht halten; desßwegen

3tio. sollen die würth und weinschenkhen bey jhren eydten jhren einlegendten wein dem inspectori gethrüwtlich anzugeben schuldig seyn, und ohne beyseyn der küeffern weder gantz- noch halbe eimer, noch bey der gelten, wein verkäüfflich hinweg geben und darbey wüsßen, daß wasfür wein beym zapfen ohne eingebung desß inspectoris verkaufft wirdt, selbiger nit abgethan, sonder gleich dem bey der masß außschenckhendten solle verumbgeltet werden, zu dem ende die küeffer auch beeydiget und allen durch sie weggehendten wein dem inspectori schrifftlich eingeben, und der inspector solches schrifftlich an denen fronfasten vor denen herren umbgeltnern einbringen solle.

(b) Beginning of a draft for a wine tax by the city council of Rapperswil (Switzerland), dated July 8, 1786.

Figure 3.4: Transcriptions of two 18th-century German-language texts: (a) a printed text (from `http://www.deutschestextarchiv.de/kant/aufklaerung/1784/` (accessed 2012-06-06)), (b) a manuscript (Rechtsquellenstiftung des Schweizerischen Juristenverbandes, 2007, p. 890).

Table 3.2: Results of running a spell-checker for modern German on the 18th-century texts shown in Figure 3.4. The column "Errors" shows the number of supposed spelling errors reported by the spell-checker; the column "Percentage" reports the percentage of "misspelled" word forms. The numbers are given for tokens (running word forms) and types (distinct word forms).

Text	# Word Forms		# Errors		Percentage	
	Tok.	Types	Tok.	Types	Tok.	Types
Printed (Figure 3.4(a))	215	141	13	12	6.0	8.5
Manuscript (Figure 3.4(b))	172	123	78	66	45.3	53.7

running word forms in the manuscript, illustrating that historical texts from the same period may differ widely with respect to spelling difference and variance.

3.2.3   UNCERTAINTY

Uncertainty, as defined above, comes from the fact that digital historical texts are not originals but transcriptions. As an example, Figure 3.5(a) shows a text from the 16th century, a court record from Switzerland, written in Early New High German.[11] Figure 3.5(b) shows a transcription of this text.

Generally speaking, no transcription preserves all features of the original. The amount of information preserved from the original document depends on the *level of transcription*. Greg (1950) introduces the distinction between *substantives*—the text as presumably intended by the author—and *accidentals*, i.e., surface features like spelling, punctuation, or capitalization. It is clear that transcriptions will generally aim to preserve the substantives as much as possible, but they differ in their treatment of accidentals. At one extreme, a strict *diplomatic transcription* may try to render (or annotate) every feature of the original that can be reproduced: pagination, page layout, initials, line breaks, spelling, variant letter forms, down to errors in the original. Driscoll (2006, p. 254) notes that editions so close to the originals are "all but unreadable for those unfamiliar with early palaeographical or typographical conventions, or in any case no easier to read than the originals."

At another extreme, a fully *modernized transcription* (such as that in Figure 3.2(b)) may choose not to record the original pagination, layout, etc., modernize all spellings, and silently correct all scribal errors (such as obviously missing letters). Such editions may be produced for use in schools or for the general public. However, scholars may not consider such a text to be an edition in the technical sense, but rather a translation.

Most transcriptions—such as the one shown in Figure 3.5(b)—are somewhere in between these two extremes. This particular example may be called *semidiplomatic*: it does not attempt to preserve the original layout, but it aims to faithfully reproduce the original *text*, including the spelling. Unlike fully diplomatic transcriptions, semidiplomatic transcriptions allow for some normalization

---

[11] High German is the standard written and spoken form of German, originally used in the southern ("upper") part of the German language area. The development of High German is conventionally divided into the following periods: Old High German (up to 1050), Middle High German (1050–1350), Early New High German (1350–1650), and New High German (since 1650).

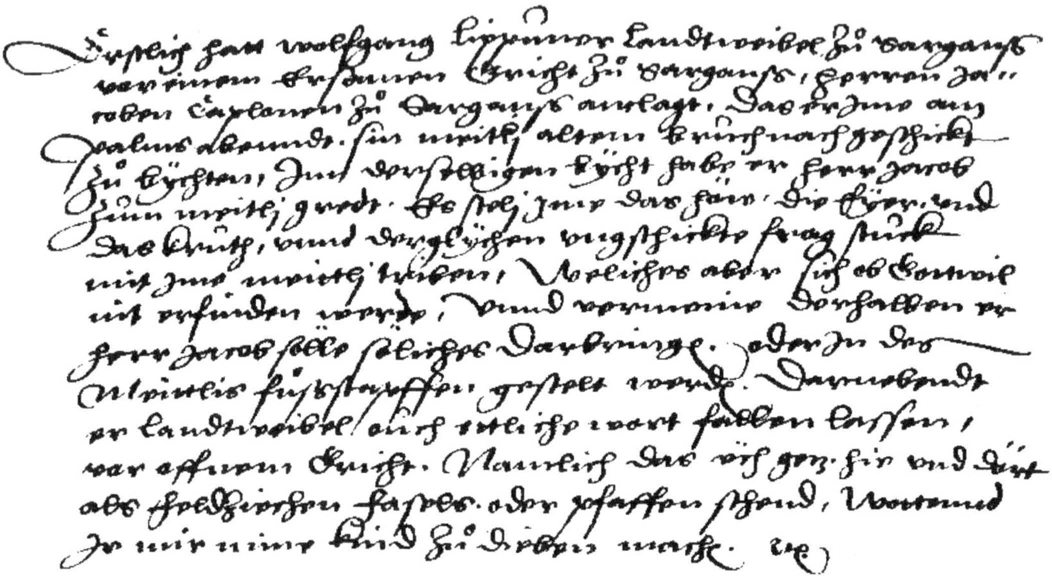

(a)

Erstlich hatt Wolfgang Lippuner, landtweibel zů Sarganß, vor einem ersamen gricht zů
Sarganß herren Jacoben, caplonen zů Sarganß, anclagt, das er ime am palms abenndt sin
meitli altem bruch nach geschickt zů bychten. Inn derselbigen bycht habe er, herr Jacob,
zum meitli gredt, es steli ime das höw, die eyer und das kruth unnd derglychen ungschickte
frag stuck mit ime, meittli, triben. Weliches aber sich, ob gottwil, nit erfinden werde unnd
vermeine derhalben er, herr Jacob, sölle söliches darbringen oder in des meittlis fůßstapffen
gestelt werden. Darnebendt er, landtweibel, ouch ettliche wort fallen lassen vor offnem
gricht, namlich: «Das üch gotz hie und dört als feldziechen, fasels oder pfaffen schend,
wottennd ir mir mine kind zů dieben machen,» etc.

(b)

Figure 3.5: Primary source (a), a 16th century court record of a defamation case (Early New High German; State Archives of Lucerne (StALU), A1 F1, Sch. 395, Mappe Pfarrei Sargans) and its semidiplomatic transcription (b) according to the rules of the Collection of Swiss Law Sources.

in the interest of readability. For example, the transcription rules of the Collection of Swiss Law Sources for German-language texts,[12] which were used in Figure 3.5(b), mandate the capitalization of proper names (regardless of the spelling used in the source) and the addition of punctuation to ease the reading. Furthermore, the two forms of the letter *s* ($\int$ and *s*, usually referred to as *long s*

---

[12] http://ssrq-sds-fds.ch/index.php?id=16 (accessed 2012-05-26)

Table 3.3: Overview of STTS tags occurring in the TreeTagger output shown in Figure 3.6.

STTS Tag	Meaning	STTS Tag	Meaning
ADJA	adjective, attributive	NN	noun
ADJD	adjective, predicative	PPER	personal pronoun, irreflexive
ADV	adverb	PRELS	relative pronoun
APPR	preposition	PRF	personal pronoun, reflexive
APPRART	preposition with article	VAFIN	auxiliary verb, finite form
ART	article	VAINF	auxiliary verb, infinitive
KOKOM	particle of comparison	VVFIN	main verb, finite form
KON	coordinative conjunction	VVIMP	main verb, imperative
KOUS	subordinating conjunction	VVINF	main verb, infinitive
NE	proper noun	VVPP	main verb, past participle

and *round s*) are always transcribed as *s*, and *u* and *v*—which were in earlier times both used for the consonant and the vowel—are transcribed according to their pronunciation.

For a detailed discussion of transcription levels in the context of electronic editions see (Driscoll, 2006). In any case, it is important to note that *any* transcription entails interpretation. Thus, when applying NLP to historical texts, one never works with the "original" text but with some interpretation of it. In some cases—especially for very old texts—an edition may constitute the result of merging different manuscripts, for example, when there is no extant complete manuscript. In such cases, editors may "correct" or modify not only spellings but also word order, inflections, etc. Differing transcription and edition principles may also mean that resources and tools developed on the basis of one type of transcription or edition may not be readily usable for texts that come from the same period, but were transcribed or edited using different principles. For an example of a more complex transcription, see Section 5.2. The volumes by Rehbein et al. (2009) and Fischer et al. (2011) give an overview of the state of the art of digital and computer-aided paleography.

Even though the gist of the text in Figure 3.5(b) should be, by and large, understandable to modern German speakers, there are significant differences in vocabulary. The transcription also shows the other two typical characteristics of historical texts, spelling difference and variance. The spelling in the example text differs from modern German, from other texts from the same period, and it is also internally inconsistent—for example, *meitli* 'girl' is sometimes spelled with one *t* and sometimes with two. Furthermore, the text uses letters and symbols that are now obsolete, for example, the superscript *o* as in *zů*. The last symbol in the last line of Figure 3.5 was transcribed as *etc.*, but even experts are not sure about its actual meaning—this is a further source of uncertainty.

To get an impression of the performance of NLP tools for modern languages on this historical text, we also run TreeTagger on it. The German parameter file available from the TreeTagger Web page was trained on the TüBa-D/Z treebank (Tübinger Baumbank des Deutschen/Schriftsprache) (Telljohann et al., 2009), consisting of newspaper texts from the early 1990s. Since the example text requires Unicode to encode the special characters, we use the UTF-8 version of the parameter file. To keep the example short, we only consider the first sentence here. In modern German, it could be rendered as

> Als erstes hat Wolfgang Lippuner, Landweibel in Sargans, vor dem ehrwürdigen Gericht in Sargans Herrn Jacob, Kaplan in Sargans, angeklagt [und berichtet], dass er ihm am Tag vor dem Palmsonntag sein Mädchen gemäß altem Brauch zum Beichten geschickt habe.

This may be translated into English as follows:

> First, Wolfgang Lippuner, summoner in Sargans, accused Mr. Jacob, chaplain in Sargans, before the honorable court in Sargans, [reporting] that he had sent him his girl on the day before Palm Sunday, according to old custom, in order to confess.

Figure 3.6 shows the tagging result for this first sentence of the example text. In case of tagging errors, we have added the correct tag in the rightmost column. The tagset used is STTS,[13] the de-facto standard for German. Table 3.3 lists the tags that occur in the example together with their meaning.

Examining the output of TreeTagger, we see that 22 of the 39 tokens (56%) are reported as "unknown," i.e., they were not contained in the training data. A closer analysis of the results shows that 22 of the 39 tokens (56%) of the tokens are tagged incorrectly. If we do not count punctuation marks, 22 of 33 tokens (67%) are tagged incorrectly. There are various types of errors, but generally speaking, the low level of accuracy is mostly due to the high number of unknown word forms. This accuracy level is clearly too low to be used for any serious work. As in Caxton's preface (Figure 3.2(a)) we also have differences with modern spelling with respect to tokenization; *palms abenndt* in the first sentence would be spelled *Palmsabend* in modern German (but this word no longer exists); a further example later in the text is *ob gottwil* 'God willing', which would be spelled *so Gott will* in modern German. Particularly when transcribing manuscripts, word separation is a considerable source of uncertainty.

3.3   SUMMARY

In this chapter we discussed the importance of standardized orthography for NLP and the spelling-related challenges presented by historical texts that predate standardized orthography. We identified three main types of problems: difference with modern spelling, variance in spelling due to a lack of standardization, and uncertainty caused by transcriptions, which introduce modifications and errors. In Chapter 6, we present various NLP approaches that aim to handle these problems.

---

[13]`ftp://ftp.ims.uni-stuttgart.de/pub/corpora/stts_guide.pdf` (accessed 2012-05-27); see `http://www.isocat.org/rest/dcs/367` (accessed 2012-05-27) for short descriptions of the tags in English.

Input	Tag	Base Form	Correct Tag
Erstlich	ADJA	\<unknown\>	ADV
hatt	NN	\<unknown\>	VAFIN
Wolfgang	NE	Wolfgang	
Lippuner	NE	\<unknown\>	
,	$,	,	
landtweibel	ADJA	\<unknown\>	NN
zů	ADJA	\<unknown\>	APPR
Sarganß	NN	\<unknown\>	NE
,	$,	,	
vor	APPR	vor	
einem	ART	eine	
ersamen	ADJA	\<unknown\>	
gricht	NN	\<unknown\>	
zů	ADJA	\<unknown\>	APPR
Sarganß	NN	\<unknown\>	NE
herren	VVFIN	\<unknown\>	NN
Jacoben	NN	\<unknown\>	NE
,	$,	,	
caplonen	NN	\<unknown\>	
zů	ADJA	\<unknown\>	APPR
Sarganß	NN	\<unknown\>	NE
,	$,	,	
anclagt	NN	\<unknown\>	VVPP
,	$,	,	
das	PRELS	die	KOUS
er	PPER	er	
ime	VVFIN	\<unknown\>	PPER
am	APPRART	an	
palms	NE	Palm	NN
abenndt	NE	\<unknown\>	NN
sin	VVFIN	\<unknown\>	PPOSAT
meitli	NE	\<unknown\>	NN
altem	ADJA	alt	
bruch	NN	Bruch	
nach	APPR	nach	APPO
geschickt	ADJD	geschickt	VVPP
zů	ADJD	\<unknown\>	PTKZU
bychten	ADJD	\<unknown\>	VVINF
.	$.	.	

Figure 3.6: TreeTagger run on an Early New High German Text (see Figure 3.5(b)). The first column contains the input word form, the second column the assigned tag, and the third column the assigned base form. If the assigned tag is incorrect, the correct tag is shown in the fourth column.

CHAPTER 4

Acquiring Historical Texts

In this chapter we discuss the acquisition of historical texts in electronic form. The topics discussed include scanning, optical character recognition (OCR), and manual transcription and tools for supporting transcribers.

4.1 DIGITIZATION OF HISTORICAL TEXTS

Digital text is an essential prerequisite for natural language processing. However, books on NLP rarely discuss how to acquire texts, since electronic texts in modern languages are easy to obtain today, whether as raw texts or in the form of corpora. If desired, one can also build a corpus automatically from Web texts (Sharoff, 2006).

The situation is different for historical texts. On the one hand, numerous historical documents have already been digitized by heritage institutions such as archives, libraries, and museums, by private non-profit initiatives, and by commercial enterprises. Both the selection of the material to be digitized and the methods of digitization vary. Here are some noteworthy examples of these different types of digitization projects.

HathiTrust[1] and the *Text Creation Partnership* (TCP)[2] are examples of institutional digitization projects. HathiTrust is a partnership of research institutions and libraries with the goal of ensuring that cultural records are preserved and will be accessible long into the future. Currently, HathiTrust comprises about 60 U.S. institutions, but membership is open to institutions worldwide. According to their website, HathiTrust has, at the time of this writing, digitized about 5.5 million books. The TCP is a project jointly funded by more than 150 libraries from all over the world. Its goal is to create XML-encoded electronic editions of early printed English-language books. In the TCP project, the page images of books from ProQuest's Early English Books Online (EEBO), Gale Cengage's Eighteenth Century Collections Online (ECCO), and Readex's Evans Early American Imprints (Evans) are manually transcribed and encoded. The digital texts produced by the TCP will be placed into the public domain.

The *Europeana*[3] is a portal serving as a single point of access to the digitized holdings of many heritage institutions in Europe. It is thus not a digitization project per se, but the results of many publicly funded European digitization projects can be accessed through it.

---

[1] http://www.hathitrust.org/ (accessed 2012-06-03)
[2] http://www.textcreationpartnership.org/ (accessed 2012-06-04)
[3] http://europeana.eu/ (accessed 2012-06-03)

Project Gutenberg[4] is probably the prime example of a private non-profit digitization initiative. Project Gutenberg was founded in 1971 and aims to create freely available electronic books. It focuses on popular out-of-copyright works and relies on volunteers for scanning, typing, and correcting texts. In the beginning, books were keyed in, but today most books are scanned, processed by OCR software, and the resulting text is proofread. For proofreading, a *crowd-sourcing approach* is used (Distributed Proofreaders[5]). Crowd-sourcing means to involve "the public" (typically a specific community) over the Internet to manually solve problems in a distributed fashion that are hard to solve automatically. Each member of the community only contributes a small portion, but, as the Internet makes it possible to reach large numbers of people, the problem can be solved collaboratively. Here, volunteers check out individual pages, correct them, and submit them back, so that many people can work on one book at the same time. We further discuss crowd-sourcing in Section 4.3.3.

Wikisource[6] is another non-profit crowd-sourcing initiative, started in 2003 and run by the Wikimedia Foundation, which is also responsible for Wikipedia. Wikisource was originally conceived as an archive for important historical texts, but has become a general library of electronic texts, similar to Project Gutenberg.

Google Books (see Section 2.1) is a massive commercial digitization project, aiming to make as many books as possible available for searching, using a highly automated scanning and OCR workflow. There has been much controversy surrounding Google Books: Google has been accused of copyright infringement by publishers, of careless and unsystematic scanning and OCR, and of poor metadata by scholars (e.g., Nunberg, 2009). Whether these accusations are justified will not be discussed here, and Google Books has also received much praise. However, as Google Books is the largest book digitization project ever (at the time of this writing, over 20 million books have been scanned (Howard, 2012)), a corresponding number of errors are to be expected, and it is not surprising that it is under public scrutiny. Microsoft had a similar digitization project, Live Search Books, which scanned 750,000 books, but this project was terminated in May 2008.[7]

This list of projects is not intended to be exhaustive; there are many other small-scale and large-scale digitization projects around the world that aim to produce electronic text. Further work has been done in the context of *digital libraries* and *digital preservation*.

Nevertheless, despite all the work that has already been done—including the projects mentioned above—the bulk of historical texts still only exists on paper (or on even older media such as parchment) and has not yet been digitized. Many historical texts thus still need to be digitized before NLP can be applied to them. But digitization of historical texts is not only of interest to us because it provides NLP with the necessary "raw material," but there are two further aspects. First, as the conversion from one medium to another is not lossless and bound to introduce errors, the digitization process and the quality of its results has a direct impact on subsequent natural language processing.

---

[4]http://www.gutenberg.org/ (accessed 2012-06-03)
[5]http://www.pgdp.net/ (accessed 2012-06-04)
[6]http://wikisource.org/ (accessed 2012-06-07)
[7]http://www.bing.com/community/site_blogs/b/search/archive/2008/05/23/book-search-winding-down.aspx (accessed 2012-06-04)

Second, NLP resources and tools may also play a role *during* the acquisition and preparation of historical texts, in particular in OCR and OCR post-processing.

Since historical texts and their intended use differs widely, there is no general recipe for digitization—the best approach depends on the properties of the texts and the needs of the project. If the texts have already been digitized (e.g., in a previous project or for Project Gutenberg), only error checking and correction may be required to achieve the desired quality. For example, Project Gutenberg does not aim to create authoritative editions; in the essay *The History and Philosophy of Project Gutenberg*[8] project founder Michael Hart stated:

> We do not write for the reader who cares whether a certain phrase in Shakespeare has a ":" or a ";" between its clauses. We put our sights on a goal to release etexts that are 99.9% accurate in the eyes of the general reader.

However, as they are freely available, texts prepared by Project Gutenberg may also be interesting as basis for scholarly work, but further work would be required in order to ensure that they meet the requirements of a particular project.

If the texts are only available on paper, parchment, or other media, the choice of digitization technique depends on several factors, most notably on the medium, the type of writing, and the language of the text. In any case, the first step is usually to create a digital image using a scanner or a digital camera. For printed texts typeset in roman type (see Figure 4.2 for examples of typefaces) and printed in good quality, the options are OCR or manual keyboard entry (usually *double-keying*, see Section 4.4). If the texts are printed, but the print quality is low or the texts are set in blackletter types (see Figure 4.2) or other type styles that are not used for modern texts, it depends on the language and the desired output quality whether OCR (with a larger amount of post-processing) is still a viable option. Otherwise, manual keyboarding is likely to be required.

For handwritten texts, manual keying by qualified personnel is generally the only option. There is growing interest in automatic handwriting recognition for historical texts (see Antonacopoulos and Downton, 2007), as this would clearly help to make large collections of manuscripts more accessible, especially when the documents have already been digitized. For example, the Manuscript Division of the Library of Congress holds approximately 60 million manuscript items in 11,000 separate collections.[9] However, the problem of automatically recognizing handwritten text from scans or photographs is a largely unresolved problem and still an active area of research.

There are two major types of handwriting recognition tasks: *online*—during writing, for example, on a tablet computer—and *offline*—from an image of a completed text (for overviews, see Plamondon and Srihari, 2000; Arica and Yarman-Vural, 2001). Handwriting recognition of historical manuscripts is clearly an offline recognition task. Offline recognition is harder than online recognition because it is not possible to utilize temporal information, such as the order of strokes or the length of pauses between them. Recognition for historical manuscripts also has to cope with

---

[8]http://www.gutenberg.org/wiki/Gutenberg:The_History_and_Philosophy_of_Project_Gutenberg_by_Michael_Hart (accessed 2012-06-04)
[9]http://www.loc.gov/rr/mss/ (accessed 2012-06-05)

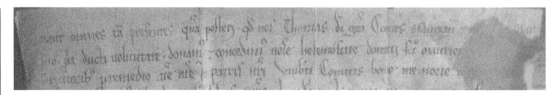

Figure 4.1: The first three lines of a manuscript from Saint-Maurice d'Agaune (Switzerland), dated April 26, 1221. It is written on parchment (heavily damaged) in Latin in a late Carolingian minuscule. Thomas, count of Maurienne, gives an island called "Naveto" as a gift to the Saint-Maurice's Abbey. The Latin text starts with "Sciant omnes tam presentes quam posteri, quod nos Thomas, dei gratia comes Maurianensis et in [Italia] mar/chio [...]" (Original: AASM, CHA 26/5/1)

problems such as damaged media, bleed-through, and fading. Furthermore, manual transcription, which is required for creating training data, is time consuming and expensive.

On the other hand, some types of historical documents also exhibit features beneficial to automatic recognition; for example, the handwriting found in medieval manuscripts is often more regular and shows less variation across writers than modern handwriting, and in the Carolingian minuscule—the script used in Charlemagne's empire and its successor states between approximately 800 and 1200—words and letters are more clearly separated than in modern cursive handwriting. These two features enabled Fischer et al. (2009) to reach a word accuracy of 93.32% for a medieval document (Codex Sangallensis 857), which is significantly better than the word accuracy of 77.12% achieved for unconstrained modern handwriting—using the same system, originally developed for modern handwriting. However, the manuscript is very well preserved. In addition, in order to obtain such a high word accuracy, a perfect segmentation of the document image into words is required. The results obtained by Fischer et al. (2009) are thus promising, but cannot be generalized yet.

Figure 4.1 shows an example of a medieval manuscript, illustrating both helpful and detrimental features: the handwriting is legible, but partly obscured by damages to the parchment. Everything we have said above about digitizing handwritten documents also applies to even older documents such as clay tablets, but these clearly pose even greater challenges.

4.2   SCANNING

If historical documents are to be digitized "from scratch," scanning is generally the first step, regardless of whether text is to be obtained by OCR or by keyboarding. Digital images are required for OCR, but they also have advantages over the original paper documents when keyboarding is used: the originals can be stored safely, digital images are cheaper and easier to ship for keyboarding off site, several people can work on the same document, and digital images make typing easier since they can be displayed on the same screen; service providers also usually charge a lower fee. Even if subsequent work will be done primarily on the digital text, one may want a facsimile for reading or for error checking.

Scanning itself has no relation to NLP. However, it is a prerequisite for practically all further work with historical documents, and as scan quality directly impacts the resulting text quality, all members of a digitization project should have at least a general knowledge of scanning. This section gives a brief overview over some important aspects of scanning; it is not meant to be exhaustive, though, and all digitization projects tend to have their own specific requirements and challenges. We focus on printed books and do not discuss special cases; in particular, when originals are very old, oversized, or damaged, scanning and image processing experts should be consulted to obtain the best possible image quality.

If books are to be scanned, there are two main cases: If the books can be cut open (with a book cutter), sheet-fed scanners can be used, otherwise flat-bed or book scanners with manual or automatic page turning must be used. The decision also depends on the budget and the amount of scan work to do; it also depends on whether the scanning is to be done in-house or outsourced. Sheet-fed scanners are inexpensive, reliable, and provide good image quality; they are thus suitable for in-house use. Specialized scanners, and fully automatic book scanners in particular, are much more expensive and need to be operated at full capacity to amortize their cost; for a single project, it may thus make more sense to contract out the scanning.

When scanning is to be done in-house, a scanner must be selected. Selection criteria for sheet-fed scanners include the scan speed, the automatic document feeder (ADF) capacity, and the *duty cycle*, which is often given in pages per day or per month. If a larger collection of documents is to be digitized, say 50,000 or 100,000 pages, it makes a difference whether 8, 16, or 24 pages per minute can be scanned. For example, if 65,000 pages are to be scanned with a scanner that scans 21 pages per minute, total scanning time is

$$\frac{65000 \text{ pages}}{21 \text{ pages/min}} = 3095.2 \text{ min} = 51.6 \text{ h.}$$

This corresponds to about seven 8-hour days, but additional time is needed for loading the ADF, separating pages that are sticking together, etc.

When comparing scanners, one should note which scan parameters (resolution and depth) were used for the speed measurements given by the vendor. The daily or monthly duty cycle gives an indication of the mechanical quality; not a problem for a few hundred pages, but important when several thousand pages are to be scanned. The mechanical quality also influences the likelihood of jams and double feeds.

The optimal scan parameters depend on the intended use of the images. In general, a higher scan resolution is better, as it captures more details; lower-resolution images can easily be created by scaling down, but the inverse is not possible. Of course, the resolution must actually be provided by the scanner (optical), not interpolated. On the other hand, a higher scan resolution means slower scanning. In practice, books are usually scanned at 300 or 600 dpi.

A topic of frequent discussion is whether text intended for OCR should be scanned in black and white (1 bit per pixel (bpp)), also called *bilevel* or *bitonal*, or in grayscale. OCR software vendors typically recommend to scan in grayscale even though the actual OCR is always done on bilevel

Table 4.1: File sizes (TIFF file format) for a scan of a typical yellowed book page with different resolutions, depths, and compression methods. "Grayscale" here means 8 bits per pixel (bpp), i.e., 256 shades of gray. The column "Resolution" gives the resolution in dots per inch (dpi), file sizes are in megabytes. Group 4 compression can only be applied to bilevel images. Deflate compression can also used with the PNG file format; the file sizes are approximately the same as for TIFF files with Deflate compression.

Resolution	Bilevel		Grayscale	
	Compression Type	Size	Compression Type	Size
300	None	0.86	None	6.96
300	Group 4	0.17	Deflate	4.07
600	None	3.45	None	27.79
600	Group 4	1.08	Deflate	12.03

images. The background for this recommendation is that the OCR software can then apply its own binarization algorithms to produce the bilevel images.

However, it is not certain whether this actually improves OCR quality. Holley (2009a) conducted experiments with historical newspapers for the Australian Newspaper Digitisation Program of the National Library of Australia, comparing the OCR accuracy for grayscale and bilevel scans. Her results show no significant improvement in OCR accuracy between using grayscale or bilevel files; furthermore, there was no consistency in results or overall significant improvement. These results have been confirmed by others (e.g., Powell and Paynter, 2009). Holley concluded that, given the small variation in overall accuracy of results, the use of grayscale files would not lead to uniformly improved OCR accuracy rates on every file, whereas the processing of grayscale files would increase the cost of OCR. Grayscale data results in significantly larger files. Larger files not only need more storage space but are also slower to process for OCR software. Table 4.1 compares typical image file sizes for bilevel and grayscale scans of a book page. It should be kept in mind that difference in size is multiplied when scanning complete books and larger collections. For example, 100,000 bilevel images (of the type as in table 4.1) scanned at 600 dpi and compressed with Group 4 would consume about 105 GB, whereas Deflate-compressed grayscale images would require 1175 GB or 1.1 TB. While this amount of data can easily be stored on today's hard disks, backup, throughput, and general file management are still issues.

We recommend running experiments with test pages from the actual documents. If grayscale images do not yield significant improvements over bilevel data for a particular project, higher-resolution bilevel scans are to be preferred.

As always, special cases require special measures. For example, Bertholdo et al. (2009) compare several approaches to binarization, including their own layout-aware method. Their test data were JPEG images of hastily produced microfilms of Brazilian secret police files; as the original paper files had been incinerated, the microfilms were the only "original."

The preferred file format for bilevel scans is TIFF with Group 4 compression. Even better compression rates can be achieved with JBIG2 compression (ISO/IEC 14492). For example, 50 scanned pages at 600 dpi (4048×6072 pixels), which consume 5.6 MB disk space with Group 4 compression, only occupy 744 KB when compressed with JBIG2. Both compression methods can also be used with images embedded in PDF files, so that no special viewer is required. Unfortunately, support for JBIG2 compression (as opposed to decompression) is not yet widespread, as it requires a relatively sophisticated analysis of the image to be compressed. There are some commercial tools available; Sojka and Hatlapatka (2010) present an open-source solution. For grayscale data, TIFF with Deflate compression or PNG can be used. PNG uses the same compression algorithm, so the file size is approximately the same.[10] The JPEG file format uses a lossy compression algorithm designed for photographs and should not be used for text under any circumstances: not only is the image quality reduced and artifacts are introduced, but the file size is also larger than when suitable compression methods are used.

4.3 OPTICAL CHARACTER RECOGNITION

Given the need to transform paper documents into electronic text, *optical character recognition* (OCR) immediately comes to mind. OCR promises a fully automatic solution for the conversion of printed text: you just have to feed the documents into the scanner and obtain text files on your hard disk. If only a one-time fee for the OCR software and the salary for the scanner operator have to be paid, it is also very cost efficient. And indeed commercial OCR packages today yield very good recognition rates *on modern documents*.

Generally speaking, OCR can be used for printed text in modern typefaces (see Figure 4.2 for examples of typefaces); this also applies to non-Latin scripts, such as Cyrillic or Greek. Best results are achieved if the text uses a simple one- or two-column layout and only few different typefaces. Results are generally worse for italic typefaces (as italic letters tend to overlap) and for typewritten documents (due to the specific problems with typewriter-produced documents, such as individual letters that are too dark, too light, or damaged; the monospaced typewriter fonts also make word identification more difficult). Even though modern OCR software does a good job of visually reconstructing the original layout (e.g., as an HTML document), the text flow is not necessarily correct with complex magazine-like layouts (with images, text boxes, non-rectangular text blocks, etc.), initials, marginals, captions, or footnotes.

The high quality of OCR output on modern documents critically depends on NLP resources, in particular dictionaries. If the pattern recognition engine cannot decide between multiple possible readings, say, between *cunent* and *current*, the dictionary is consulted. In this case, only one of the two hypotheses (*current*) would be found in an English dictionary, so this reading would be preferred. Additional language-specific rules help the OCR software to resolve issues such as capitalization and punctuation. For example, it is difficult for a pattern recognition engine to distinguish between periods and commas—even in a good 300 dpi scan of 12-point text, the difference is at most a dozen

---

[10]This also applies to the file sizes listed in table 4.1.

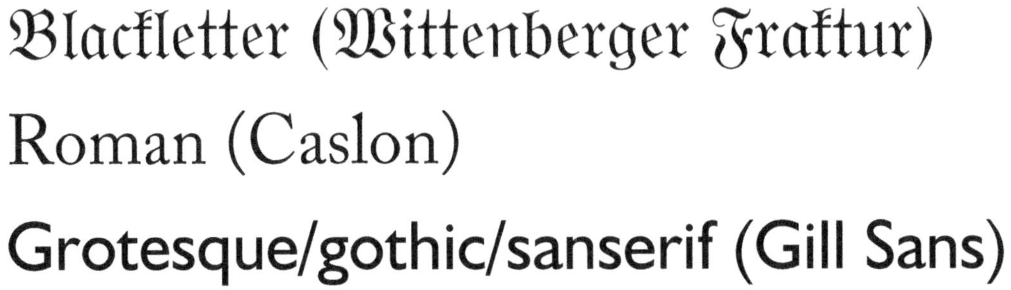

𝕭𝖑𝖆𝖈𝖐𝖑𝖊𝖙𝖙𝖊𝖗 (𝖂𝖎𝖙𝖙𝖊𝖓𝖇𝖊𝖗𝖌𝖊𝖗 𝕱𝖗𝖆𝖐𝖙𝖚𝖗)

Roman (Caslon)

Grotesque/gothic/sanserif (Gill Sans)

Figure 4.2: Examples of the three main typeface styles of the Latin script: blackletter (fraktur), roman, and grotesque (gothic, sanserif).

fade away, so, too, will our current notion of files. In the

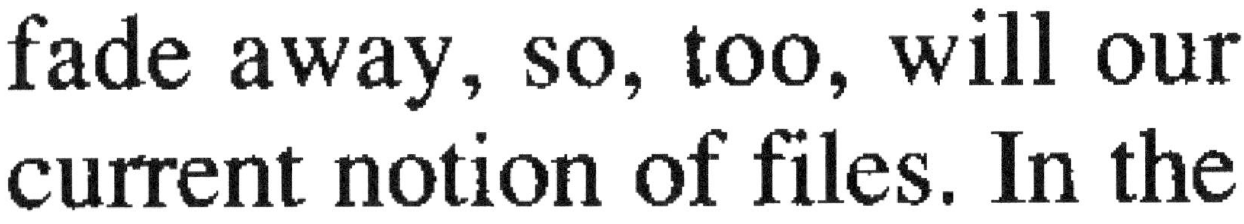

Figure 4.3: Detail of a 300 dpi, 1 bit per pixel scan of modern magazine print.

pixels; see Figure 4.3 for an example. However, if the software has knowledge of the co-occurrence of periods and capital letters, it can decide that the three marks in the first line are most likely to be commas, that the mark in the second line is a period, and that the following character is a capital *I* (hence neither the digit *1* nor the lowercase letter *l*).

For historical languages, however, these resources do not exist and are not easy to create. One issue is, of course, spelling variation, which makes the construction of lexical resources difficult; another issue are the typefaces used in historical prints. For 19th century documents, Abbyy offers a special version of its FineReader OCR system,[11] which supports various blackletter typefaces (see Figure 4.2 for examples of typefaces) and dictionaries for 19th century variants of several languages (including English, German, and French).[12] However, as it focuses on 19th century books, only some projects can benefit from it. Figure 4.4 shows a portion of a 16th century text; the corresponding OCR output is clearly very poor. Figure 4.5 shows further problems: decorated initials—hardly recognizable as letters—various font sizes, a mix of blackletter and roman typefaces, and text shining

---

[11]http://www.frakturschrift.de/ (accessed 2012-06-06)

[12]The explicit mention of a commercial product should not be construed as an endorsement of any kind. Abbyy FineReader is mentioned here because it is currently the only OCR product available that recognizes blackletter fonts without prior training. Also, most academic research on post-correction of blackletter OCR results relies on it.

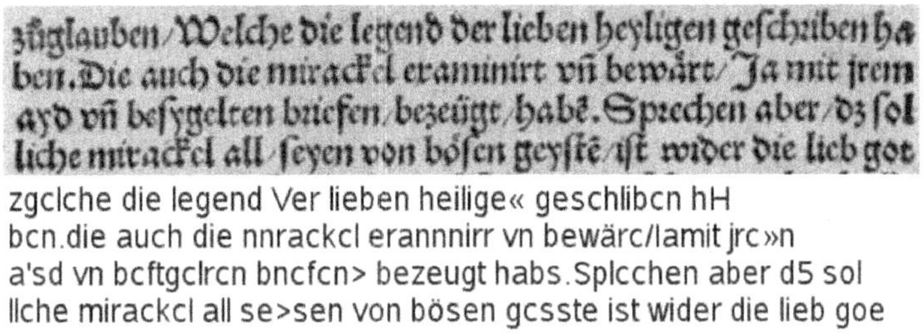

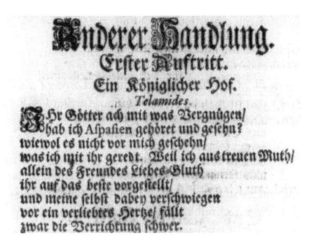

zůglauben/ Welche die legend der lieben heyligen geschriben ha
ben. Die auch die mirackel erannnirt vñ bewärt/ Ja mit jrem
ayd vñ besygelten briefen/ bezeügt/ habē. Sprechen aber/ dz sol
liche mirackel all/ seyen von bösen geystē/ ist wider die lieb got
zgclche die legend Ver lieben heilige« geschlibcn hH
bcn.die auch die nnrackcl erannnirr vn bewärc/Iamit jrc»n
a'sd vn bcftgclrcn bncfcn> bezeugt habs.Splcchen aber d5 sol
llche mirackcl all se>sen von bösen gcsste ist wider die lieb goe

Figure 4.4: A poor 16th century image and the corresponding OCR result (from Gotscharek et al., 2009b, p. 198).

Anderer Handlung.
Erster Auftritt.
Ein Königlicher Hof.
Telamides.
Ihr Götter ach mit was Vergnügen/
hab ich Aspasien gehöret und gesehn?
wiewol es nicht vor mich geschehn/
was ich mit ihr geredt. Weil ich aus treuen Muth/
allein des Freundes Liebes-Gluth
ihr auf das beste vorgestellt/
und meine selbst dabey verschwiegen
vor ein verliebtes Hertze/ fällt
zwar die Verrichtung schwer.

Figure 4.5: A scan of a 17th century page, illustrating various problematic features found in old books (from Bennett et al., 2010, p. 64).

through from the reverse page. This illustrates that there exists no "one-size-fits-all" OCR solution for historical documents.

Based on the Australian National Library's experiences with the digitization of historical newspapers, Holley (2009a) discusses 13 approaches for improving OCR results. Some of the points relate to image processing (e.g., the use of grayscale vs. bilevel files for OCR or the deskewing of images, so that text lines are as horizontal as possible). Points 10 to 13 concern OCR and NLP technology; Holley considers using more than one OCR system and voting to pick the best results, using special dictionaries in the OCR process, manual correction of OCR-produced text, and using language modeling during or after OCR processing. Holley (2009a) evaluates these approaches with respect to the digitization of historical Australian newspapers, but they are, in principle, of interest to any project using OCR. We will present some realizations of these ideas below.

4.3.1   USING MORE THAN ONE OCR SYSTEM

We first look at the idea of using several different OCR systems with some voting scheme to pick the best reading. The rationale behind this is that different OCR systems have different strengths and weaknesses; the hope is thus that when one system makes an error the other (or the others) yield a correct reading. Assuming that the voting scheme is able to pick the correct reading, it should be able to raise the overall OCR quality above that of the individual systems.

This idea was first explored (for modern documents) in the early 1990s, in particular by Handley and Hickey (1991) and Concepcion and D'Amato (1993). Lopresti and Jiangying (1997) use a similar approach, but used a single OCR system with multiple scans: each page was scanned three times, processed by the OCR system, and the OCR outputs were then merged using a consensus sequence voting procedure. Using this approach, Lopresti and Jiangying were able to eliminate between 20% and 50% of the OCR errors. Handley (1998) gives an overview of the research from this period.

In this section we present two recent examples of projects that have evaluated this approach for historical documents. Boschetti et al. (2009) digitize 19th and early 20th century critical editions of classical Greek works. Volk et al. (2011) digitize the yearbooks of the Swiss Alpine Club, also from the 19th and early 20th century. Both projects applied further OCR post-processing, but we focus here on their use of multiple OCR engines.

Digitizing Critical Editions of Classics

The goal of Boschetti et al. (2009) was to evaluate whether OCR could be used to create high-quality digital versions of critical editions of Greek classics for addition to the Perseus digital library[13]. They point out that virtually all digital editions of classical texts are based on previous critical editions but discard the prefaces, apparatuses, indices, etc., which are essential for serious scholarly research. Thus, Boschetti et al. wanted to include this information in the digital version.

Critical editions are particularly challenging for OCR systems due to a variety of special properties. First, critical editions typically consist of at least two different text flows: the historical text and the critical apparatus, which records the editorial decisions, notes peculiarities of the original, and contains the editor's commentary. Some editions have more than these two text flows; for example, several versions of a manuscript may be presented side by side in a *synoptic presentation*, a parallel translation may be given, or glosses or cross-references may be given in marginal notes. The critical apparatus is usually typeset in a smaller font.

Second, critical editions are typically multilingual, as the language of the apparatus usually differs from the language of the edited text; the apparatus itself may also be multilingual, for example, when it contains citations from the edited text or from scholarly texts; the names of cited scholars may come from virtually any language. In the case of the classical Greek editions, the critical apparatus is usually in Latin; prefaces, introductions, translations, indices, etc. are also often in Latin, as well as in modern languages.

---

[13]`http://www.perseus.tufts.edu/hopper/` (accessed 2012-06-06)

Third, the language of the edited text often requires special historical characters; Ancient Greek, in this case, requires a large set of characters to represent the combinations of accents and breathing marks on vowels, which are often hard to distinguish and thus difficult for OCR systems to recognize correctly. Finally, in the case of critical editions from the 19th and early 20th century, as used by Boschetti et al., the pages may be damaged or the typefaces may be unusual.

Boschetti et al. (2009) randomly extracted five pages each from three editions of Athenaeus' *Deipnosophistae* (Meineke, 1858; Kaibel, 1887; Gulick, 1951) and one of Aeschylus' tragedies (Hermann, 1852). The editions used differ with respect to the size of their critical apparatuses, the typefaces, and other parameters. For their experiments Boschetti et al. manually separated the apparatuses from the primary texts.

Boschetti et al. (2009)'s approach consists of several components: three OCR engines, post-processing scripts, a progressive alignment algorithm, a selection algorithm based on a naive Bayes classifier, and a final spell-checking step. The selection algorithm makes use of information gathered during the training of the OCR engines; the spell-checker relies on the alignment of the OCR results from the three engines and considers only alternative readings found in the aligned OCR results to avoid miscorrections.

The following three OCR engines were used by Boschetti et al. (2009): Ideatech Anagnostis 4.1, a system specially optimized for polytonic Greek, Abbyy FineReader 9.0, and OCRopus[14] 0.3 with the Tesseract[15] engine 2.03, an open-source system. All OCR engines were first trained on material from the different editions. FineReader has a built-in model for modern (monotonic) Greek, which can be used in conjunction with the user-trained model; it was found that using the built-in model increases the recognition accuracy for unaccented characters, but decreases the accuracy for characters with diacritics. Thus, FineReader was evaluated both with and without the built-in model. OCR output was then post-processed with two scripts. First, encoding and formatting errors were corrected; these are primarily implausible sequences such as Latin characters inside Greek words, (e.g., when a Greek omicron is replaced by the nearly identical Latin letter *o*) or spaces followed by punctuation marks. Second, a small set of high-frequency errors were detected and corrected with regular expressions. The OCR output of the individual systems for a first set of test pages was aligned with the manually transcribed gold standard in order to determine and record the average accuracy of the systems, which was later needed for the multisystem alignment.

For aligning the output of the three systems and deciding between different readings, Boschetti et al. (2009) use the *progressive multiple sequence alignment* algorithm as described by Spencer and Howe (2004), which is an adaptation of an algorithm for sequence alignment from bioinformatics to the domain of critical editions. *Multiple alignment* means that an alignment of *all* texts is produced, not just pairwise alignments to a base text. Progressive multiple alignment methods generate a multiple sequence alignment by first aligning the most similar sequences and then progressively adding less related sequences or groups of already collated sequences to the alignment until all

---

[14]http://ocropus.org (accessed 2012-06-06)
[15]http://code.google.com/p/tesseract-ocr/ (accessed 2012-06-06)

sequences have been incorporated into the overall alignment. The similarity of sequences—and the order for the progressive multiple alignment— are determined by first performing pairwise alignments and constructing a so-called *guide tree*. Since Boschetti et al. only had to align three texts, they used the average OCR accuracy rating established during training instead of building a guide tree. FineReader had the best accuracy, followed by OCRopus and Anagnostis, so FineReader and OCRopus were aligned first, and the resulting OCRopus string with gap signs was then aligned to Anagnostis. The new gap signs were subsequently propagated to the previously aligned FineReader string. An example result of the triple alignment is shown in Figure 4.6, where the gap signs are represented by underscores.

Clearly, the alignment alone is not yet sufficient to determine the most probable character. If two engines agree on a character, the third, disagreeing, engine may still be right. Even more extreme, the correct character may not be in the output of any of the engines; in this case, all engines may even be in agreement, but nevertheless wrong. However, Boschetti et al. (2009) only considered characters suggested by at least one engine.

The question is thus: What is the probability that the current position on the original printed page e_0 contains the character x when the first engine e_1 suggests the character c_1, the second engine e_2 the character c_2, and the third engine e_3 the character c_3? Formally:

$$P(e_0 = x \mid e_1 = c_1, e_2 = c_2, e_3 = c_3).$$

Boschetti et al. derive these probabilities from the error patterns recorded during the training process. To find the highest probability among the three readings provided by the three engines, Boschetti et al. use a naive Bayes classifier. The final formula for finding the x_0 that has the highest probability is:

$$x_0 = \arg\max \prod_{i=1}^{n} P(e_i = c_i \mid e_0 = x) \cdot P(e_0 = x)^{\frac{1}{n}},$$

where n is the number of OCR engines, e_i is a specific engine, and c_i is the character provided by that engine. As implemented by Boschetti et al. (2009), a triple agreement is not processed, and in the case of a probability equal to zero, the output of the first engine (here: FineReader) is used. The bottom line in Figure 4.6 shows the result of the selection process. The blue and red characters indicate the cases where the correct characters are selected from OCRopus/Anagnostis, despite FineReader having suggested a different character.

As a final step, Boschetti et al. (2009) integrated a spell-checker into the system, which uses information gained from the OCR alignment to avoid miscorrections. They used an Aspell[16] checker based on a list of word forms generated by the Morpheus morphological analyzer/generator (Crane, 1991). The string produced by the naive Bayes classifier is passed to the spell-checker; if a word form is rejected by the spell-checker, its suggested corrections are filtered by a regular

[16]http://aspell.net/ (accessed 2012-06-06)

Figure 4.6: Result of alignment of OCR output from three engines (from Boschetti et al., 2009).

Edition	FineReader w/o Built-In Model	FineReader w/	OCRopus	Anagnostis
Gulick	96.44	94.35	92.63	93.15
Kaibel	93.11	93.15	95.19	92.97
Meineke	94.54	93.79	92.88	91.78
Hermann	97.41	N/A	91.84	78.64

Table 4.2: Single-engine accuracy (in percent; from Boschetti et al., 2009).

expression constructed from the aligned original OCR outputs. The regular expression is constructed as follows. Characters on which all engines agree are copied verbatim; when the engines suggest two or three different characters, they are surrounded by angle brackets (i.e., as a character class); gaps are rendered as question marks, indicating in that the previous character or character class is optional. For example, given the aligned readings πρῶτος and πρῶτος, the constructed regular expression would be πρ[ώῶ]τος. Thus, from the spell-checker's suggestions πρῶτος, πρῶτός, and πρῶτὸς, only πρῶτος would match.

Tables 4.2 and 4.3 summarize the results of Boschetti et al.'s experiments.[17] Table 4.2 lists the accuracy of the individual engines on their test set. Table 4.3 presents the final results for the main text (i.e., without the apparatuses). Triple alignment and constrained spell-checking result in an average gain of 2.49% over the best single engine. According to the authors, the t-test shows that the improvements are always significant, with $p < 0.05$. For the apparatuses, the average accuracy with triple alignment is 92.01%, with an average gain of 3.26% over the best single engine. The improvements are also significant, with $p < 0.05$. In the editions used by Boschetti et al. (2009) the apparatuses comprise, on average, between 5 and 14% of the text on each page.

---

[17] Some experiments were apparently not performed on the Herrmann edition, but no explanation is given by Boschetti et al. (2009).

Table 4.3: Effect of alignment and spell-checking on accuracy (main text only; all numbers are percentages; after Boschetti et al., 2009).

Edition	Best Single Engine	Alignment	Align. + Spell-Checking
Gulick	96.44	98.02	99.01
		+1.58	+2.57
Kaibel	95.19	95.45	98.17
		+0.26	+2.98
Meineke	94.54	96.15	97.46
		+1.61	+2.92
Hermann	97.41	N/A	98.91
		N/A	+1.50

Digitizing Mountaineering Yearbooks

Volk et al. (2011) use two OCR engines to improve the OCR quality for texts from the 19th and early 20th century, namely the yearbooks of the Swiss Alpine Club (SAC). In the "Text+Berg" ("Text and Mountain") project, they digitize all yearbooks from the first edition from 1864 until today.

Like the critical editions tackled by Boschetti et al. (2009), the yearbooks have a number of properties that make them hard to process by OCR. First, figures, illustrations, and footnotes create a non-trivial layout with multiple text flows. Second, the yearbook corpus is multilingual, with articles written in German, French, and Italian, and citations in English and Rhaeto-Romanic and Swiss German dialects. Third, the corpus is characterized by numerous occurrences of proper names, in particular toponyms, including exonyms and historical variants, but also of personal names of mountaineers. Finally, as a diachronic corpus, it contains texts written in different orthographies. Having only been standardized in 1901, German orthography in particular has undergone considerable changes. The last two points are especially challenging for OCR systems, as they are not handled by their standard lexicons.

The Text+Berg corpus is not only intended for linguistic research—where the spelling of proper names is typically of relatively low importance—but also for other fields of research, where it may, for example, be of interest to find the first mention of a particular place; here, spelling is obviously important.

OCR merging, i.e., the use of two OCR engines, is one of several post-processing modules for improving text quality in the pipeline described by Volk et al. (2011), and we will only focus on this module here.

Despite some common aspects, the approach of Volk et al. (2011) differs significantly from that of Boschetti et al. (2009). Volk et al. use the Abbyy FineReader 7 and Nuance OmniPage 17 OCR engines without special training. Like Boschetti et al. (2009), a first post-processing step corrects typical OCR errors such as *ii* for *n*, *u*, *ü*, *li*, or *il*.

Volk et al. avoid the potential complexity of global alignment and proceed page by page and paragraph by paragraph. In case of large differences—which may occur, for example, when the layout recognition fails to identify an image as such and generates random text—the default is to use the output from FineReader, which is considered the primary system. In contrast to Boschetti et al. (2009), alignment is not a separate processing step, but is rather done "on the fly." For each page, their algorithm traverses the two OCR-generated texts linearly until a difference is encountered; the 40-character window starting from this point is then searched for the longest common subsequence. The text up to the start of the longest subsequence is considered the difference region.

Inside the difference region, the algorithm then proceeds on the token level. For each token, not only the readings produced by FineReader and OmniPage are considered, but in addition, all combinations of the differences between the two readings are generated as potential alternatives. For example, if FineReader outputs *Recensione-* and OmniPage outputs *Rccensionen*, the additional variants *Rccensione-* and *Recensionen* are generated; in this case, the last one is in fact the correct reading.

After the alternatives have been generated, a decision must be made for one of them. Volk et al. use a unigram language model trained on the uncorrected output of FineReader. This may be surprising, as the raw output is *known* to contain errors. However, Volk et al. argue that the performance of FineReader on the corpus is already relatively good (above 90% accuracy). Furthermore, the language model is based on 25.7 million running word forms, so that the correct readings should typically outnumber the incorrect readings by a large margin. For example, the frequency of the correct reading *Bergbauer* 'mountain farmer' is more than 20 times higher than that of the incorrect reading *ßergbauer* (47 vs. 2 occurrences). It is interesting to note that the language model is actually language-agnostic, i.e., it is trained on the whole corpus before any language identification is performed.

Since the language model assigns a higher probability to alternatives with fewer tokens—which is undesirable in the case of word forms running together—a second score is calculated that prefers alternatives with a high ratio of known words. The alternatives are then ranked on this score first and on the language model probability second. Table 4.4 shows examples where OmniPage's readings are preferred over the default, i.e., FineReader's reading.

In a manual evaluation of a subset of the test data, 448 changes compared to the FineReader output were examined. In 277 cases, the changes constituted an improvement (see the example marked ⊕ in table 4.4), 89 did not represent an improvement (marked ⊜), and 82 changes introduced errors (marked ⊖). Overall, OCR merging resulted in an improvement of the OCR output quality. The authors state that it is, in fact, the most effective post-correction method in their post-processing pipeline.

Conclusion

We presented two approaches for merging the output from several OCR engines. Boschetti et al. (2009) and Volk et al. (2011) use different methods but both teams achieve an improvement of text

Table 4.4: Examples of OmniPage readings that were chosen over the default FineReader readings during OCR merging (from Volk et al., 2011).

FineReader	OmniPage	Context	Better?
Wunseh,	Wunsch,	… entstand in unseren Herzen der **Wunsch,** …	$\oplus$
East	Rast	… durch die **Rast** neu gestärkt …	$\oplus$
Übergangspunkt,. das	Übergangspunktr das	…ein äußerst lohnender **Übergangspunkt, das** …	$\equiv$
großen. Freude	großen, Freude	… zu meiner **großen Freude** …	$\equiv$
halten	hatten	Wir **halten** es nicht mehr aus …	$\ominus$
là	la	… c'est **là** le rôle principal qu'elle joue …	$\ominus$

accuracy. Nevertheless, OCR merging is still largely experimental, and there are a number of open issues. One problem is that commercial OCR engines combine layout recognition and character recognition; this means that their output not only differs on the level of characters, but text may be missing or in a different order. In their experiment, Boschetti et al. (2009) avoid this problem by manually separating the primary text from the critical apparatus, an approach that would not be feasible for production systems. Volk et al. (2011) explicitly account for this problem and handle it by skipping regions that contain cross-paragraph differences between the OCR output of the two systems.

The open-source OCRopus system [18] (Breuel, 2009a) encapsulates layout analysis and character recognition into separate modules, meaning that different implementations of these modules can be used in various combinations. This architecture would make it possible to combine different OCR engines with the same layout analysis module, thus minimizing differences in OCR output due to differences in layout analysis. OCRopus has been used for OCR of historical texts (e.g., Breuel, 2009b), but to the best of our knowledge, this feature of OCRopus has not yet been used in conjunction with OCR merging, probably due to a lack of suitable open-source OCR engines besides Tesseract. [19]

---

[18] http://ocropus.org (accessed 2012-06-06)
[19] http://code.google.com/p/tesseract-ocr/ (accessed 2012-06-06)

Figure 4.7: Blackletter characters frequently confused by OCR systems. From left to right: ſ (long *s*) and *f*; *u* and *n*; a damaged letter that could be either *u* or *n*; *B* and *V*; *R* and *N* (from Furrer and Volk, 2011, p. 101).

4.3.2 LEXICAL RESOURCES FOR HISTORICAL OCR

IMPACT[20] ("Improving Access to Text") was an EU-funded project to advance the state of the art for mass digitization of historical documents. The project ran from 2008 until the end of 2011, involved 26 partners from 14 countries, and had a total budget of 16.5 million euros.

One of the main objectives of the project was to improve the quality of OCR for historical documents, stating that currently "[n]o commercial or other OCR engine is able to cope satisfactorily with the wide range of printed materials published between the start of the Gutenberg age in the 15th century and the start of the industrial production of books in the middle of the 19th century."[21]

Researchers at the University of Munich, Germany, focused on NLP resources—in particular specialized lexicons—to improve the accuracy of Abbyy FineReader (Abbyy was one of the IMPACT project partners) on historical documents, in particular those typeset in blackletter typefaces. This type of document is important for two reasons. First, practically all printed material from the time of Gutenberg until well into the 17th century (for German until the middle of the 20th century) was typeset in blackletter. Second, the accuracy of OCR for blackletter typefaces is generally much lower than for roman typefaces—regardless of the age of the text—due to the high similarity of several letterforms, some of which are shown in Figure 4.7.

Since FineReader is the only commercially available OCR engine supporting blackletter typefaces, the use of a second engine—as described above—was not a viable approach. The Munich researchers therefore focused on special lexicons for the OCR engine, since lexicons play an important role in OCR accuracy (see Section 4.3). However, unlike for modern languages with standardized orthography, it is not easy to establish the criteria for a lexicon optimized to support OCR on historical documents, due to the high variability in spelling (see Chapter 3). Gotscharek et al. (2009b) thus carry a number of experiments in order to find some answers to this question. For evaluating the effectiveness of various approaches, they build a corpus of historical German documents from before 1500 to 1950, constructed different types of lexicons, and tested them on a set of test documents from different periods.

The *main corpus* consisted of the *Historical Corpus* of the Institute for the German Language (IDS), the *Bonner Frühneuhochdeutschkorpus*, the *GerManC Pilot Corpus*, and 53 German texts

---

[20]http://impact-project.eu/ (accessed 2012-06-06)
[21]http://impact-project.eu/about-the-project/concept/ (accessed 2012-06-06)

(proofread twice) from 1504 to 1904 from Wikisource[22], totaling 2,693,966 running word forms (288,709 unique words). See Section 8.6 for descriptions of these corpora.

Gotscharek et al. use the main corpus to build a lexicon; since the OCR engine only requires a list of words, it is essentially the list of unique word forms contained in the corpus. After cleanup, it contained 204,834 entries. Gotscharek et al. refer to this lexicon as the *witnessed historical dictionary*.

As an alternative to the witnessed dictionary, they also build a *hypothetical dictionary*. The hypothetical dictionary is actually a matching procedure that decides whether a token suggested by the OCR engine is "similar enough" to a modern word form. A historical word form is considered similar if it can be derived from a modern word form by applying certain transformation patterns, for example, $t \mapsto th$. CISLEX (Guenthner, 1996) serves as the modern reference dictionary for the hypothetical historical dictionary.

For the OCR experiments, a *test corpus* was built from pages selected from books from the 16th, 18th, and 19th centuries. The text corresponding to the page images was manually verified against the original and, if necessary, corrected. This corpus contains 25,745 running word forms.

Gotscharek et al. then process the images of the test corpus with Abbyy FineReader, using various combinations of the various lexical resources described above. The test corpus was split by period into three parts: 16th, 18th, and 19th century. The baseline was established by the empty dictionary; in this case, the OCR engine can only rely on its pattern recognition. The theoretical upper bound was established by a dictionary containing the word forms of the gold standard text (the "perfect dictionary").

Gotscharek et al. find that the lexicon has a significant effect on OCR accuracy. However, the results have to be understood in their experimental context; the authors caution that the situation is more complex than the numbers may suggest. First of all, the 16th-century test set only contains documents for which OCR results could be expected to achieve a minimum level of quality. As Gotscharek et al. point out, the OCR results for 16th-century documents are frequently "a complete disaster" (Gotscharek et al., 2009b, p. 198). One issue is that the OCR engine is trained on blackletter typefaces from the 19th century; another major problem is word segmentation, as texts were often set very tightly. Gotscharek et al. therefore look only at word errors when the segmentation was correct. Thus, the word error rates reported for the 16th-century test set cannot be expected to be achieved for random prints from the 16th century, not least due to the wide variability in appearance and quality between documents from this period.

The experimental results are as follows. Using the empty dictionary resulted in a word error rate of 25.94% for the texts from the 16th, 31.10% for the texts from the 18th, and 11.49% for the texts from the 19th century. Using the perfect dictionary resulted in word error rates of 15.02% for the 16th, 14.86% for the 18th, and 3.39% for the 19th century texts. This means that lexical resources can theoretically reduce the error rate by as much as 70.49%. However, since real-world lexicons will rarely have 100% coverage, this rate of improvement cannot be achieved in practice. For the 16th-century test set, the witnessed historical dictionary yielded the best performance, reducing

---

[22] http://www.wikisource.org/ (accessed 2012-06-06)

errors by 28.20%. For the 18th-century test set, the combination of the modern dictionary and the witnessed historical dictionary reduced errors by 42.00%; however, the witnessed historical dictionary alone yielded almost the same increase in accuracy. Finally, the best results for the 19th-century test set were again achieved by combining the witnessed historical and the modern dictionaries, reducing errors by 59.06%.

Even though the results are only generalizable to a limited extent—as discussed above—the results are interesting as they illustrate the importance of adequate NLP resources for OCR. This point is especially exemplified by the effect perfect dictionaries have on recognition accuracy. At the same time, these numbers also show the limits of lexical resources: the different effects a perfect dictionary has for the 16th, 18th, and 19th-century test sets shows that even a perfect dictionary cannot compensate for problems with low-level character recognition. To improve the situation, lexical resources adapted to the language of the documents are required to maximize recognition accuracy.

4.3.3   COLLABORATIVE CORRECTION OF OCR OUTPUT

OCR results always contain errors. Technical measures can help to improve OCR accuracy and correct some errors, but—depending on a project's requirements—one may conclude that, in the end, manual correction of the OCR output is required. However, for large-scale digitization projects, a huge staff would be required for manual correction, possibly nullifying the cost and time-saving of OCR over rekeying.

An interesting idea is thus to use *crowd-sourcing* for correcting OCR output. Crowd-sourcing is becoming increasingly common for all kinds of NLP-related tasks; see, for example, the proceedings of the NAACL HLT 2010 Workshop on Creating Speech and Language Data with Amazon's Mechanical Turk (Callison-Burch and Dredze, 2010) for an overview of some NLP applications of crowd-sourcing.[23]

The Distributed Proofreaders project, volunteer proofreaders collaboratively working on Project Gutenberg texts (see Section 4.1), was established in 2000 by Charles Franks. The use of crowd-sourcing for correcting OCR output in an *institutional* digitization project was first proposed by Holley (2009a); she also led its implementation it for the Australian Newspapers Digitisation Program (ANDP), an ongoing large-scale national project that is digitizing historical Australian newspapers from 1803 onwards.[24] Figure 4.8 shows a screenshot of the Web-based Trove system used by Australian Newspapers: the scanned image is shown on the right-hand side, the recognized text on the left. When hovering the cursor over a line of text, a button "Fix this text" is shown; users can click this button to edit and correct the text. No registration is necessary; unregistered

---

[23]Mechanical Turk is one particular sourcing platform, operated by Amazon in the form of a marketplace for *human intelligence tasks* (HITs) (https://www.mturk.com/ (accessed 2012-06-06)).
[24]http://www.nla.gov.au/ndp/ (accessed 2012-06-06)

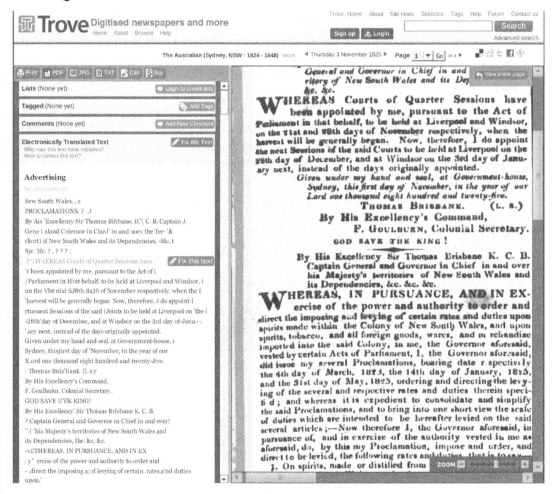

Figure 4.8: The Trove platform allows users to correct OCR errors ("Fix this text").

users who want to correct text only have to respond to a CAPTCHA challenge.[25] Changes to the text are immediately accepted and added to the search index, but prior versions can be restored by administrators. Holley (2009b) reports encouraging results: the service was released to users in August 2008; in November 2009, it contained 8.4 million articles to search and correct; by that time, over 6,000 users had corrected 7 million lines of text in 318,000 articles (see also Holley, 2010, 2011).

---

[25]A *CAPTCHA* ("completely automated public Turing test to tell computers and humans apart") is a type of challenge-response test, which is used to protect websites from unwanted robots. Typically users are asked to type several letters or digits from a distorted image displayed on screen.

By June 2012, almost 70 million newspaper articles were available online,[26] and a total of over 66 million lines of text had been corrected.[27]

Furrer and Volk (2011) explicitly make reference to Australian Newspapers as inspiration for a similar system for two digitization projects, Text+Berg (Volk et al., 2010) and the resolutions by the Zurich Cantonal Government from 1887 to 1902 (Furrer and Volk, 2011). Their system, called Kokos,[28] is based on a general-purpose open-source wiki,[29] which is extended with a module that allows synchronized viewing of scans and the corresponding editable OCR text. Unlike the correction facility of Australian Newspapers, editing is word-based, not line-based (see Figure 4.9). This makes correction easy if word segmentation is generally correct, but does not allow users to make corrections that span more than a word; the appropriateness of this approach thus depends on the quality of the OCR.

The project "Digitale Rätoromanische Chrestomathie"[30] (Digital Rhaeto-Romanic Chrestomathy[31]) has digitized the *Rätoromanische Chrestomathie*, the largest collection of sagas, fairy tales, incantations, chronicles, and other text in the Rhaeto-Romanic language. The chrestomathy was originally edited by Caspar Decurtins between 1891 and 1919; the edited texts originate from the time of the Reformation until the beginning of the 20th century.

Given the age of the texts, the 400-year time span of their creation, and the variety of idioms (i.e., dialects) in the chrestomathy, OCR is clearly problematic. The project therefore also decided to use collaborative correction to improve the quality of the digitized text. While the projects described above use Web interfaces, Neuefeind et al. (2011) implement an Eclipse-based rich client,[32] which runs on users' local computers and allows them to compare OCR text and scan—both stored on a central server—and make corrections to the text; see Figure 4.10.

A different approach to collaborative OCR correction is taken by the reCAPTCHA[33] system (von Ahn et al., 2008). The reCAPTCHA system offers websites a CAPTCHA-based authentication scheme (see page 44). Websites wishing to use reCAPTCHA for access control subscribe to a free service and are then provided with images of words from the Google Books digitization project that were not recognized by OCR. When a user wants to log in to the site, he or she is shown one of these images and has to decipher it.

In the digitization project, two different OCR programs are used. The outputs of both OCR programs are aligned and then compared to each other and to an English dictionary. Words that are transcribed differently by the OCR programs or that are not found in the dictionary are marked as "suspicious." Von Ahn et al. note that in about 96% of the cases, suspicious words are words that are recognized incorrectly by at least one of the OCR programs, whereas 99.74% of the words *not* marked

---

[26]http://trove.nla.gov.au/system/counts (accessed 2012-06-06)
[27]http://trove.nla.gov.au/system/stats?env=prod#corrections (accessed 2011-06-06)
[28]http://kitt.cl.uzh.ch/kitt/kokos/ (accessed 2012-07-16)
[29]PmWiki, http://www.pmwiki.org/ (accessed 2012-06-06).
[30]http://www.crestomazia.ch/ (accessed 2012-06-06)
[31]A *chrestomathy* is a compilation of passages from reputed authors.
[32]http://github.com/spinfo/drc (accessed 2012-06-06)
[33]http://www.google.com/recaptcha (accessed 2012-07-16)

Figure 4.9: The Kokos system for collaborative OCR correction allows users to click any word in the OCR output (on the left) to correct it; the scan is displayed on the right side.

as suspicious are recognized correctly by both programs. Each suspicious word is then placed in an image along with a so-called control word, i.e., a word for which the correct transcription is already known. To make the task harder for automated programs to solve the challenge, the word images are also distorted. This image is then used as a CAPTCHA challenge, as shown in Figure 4.11. In

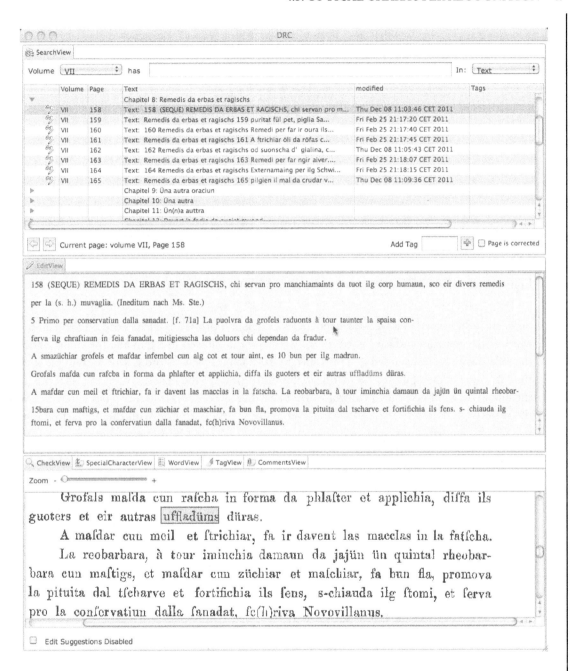

Figure 4.10: Screenshot of the rich client for collaborative correction of the Digital Rhaeto-Romanic Chrestomathy.

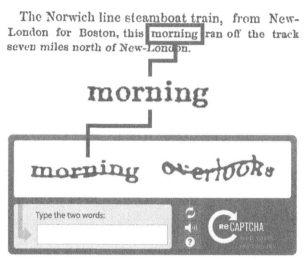

Figure 4.11: reCAPTCHA (from von Ahn et al., 2008).

order to authenticate to a website, users have to type in both the control word and the unknown word. If the control word is entered correctly, the user is allowed to log in and the transcription of the unknown word is recorded as a plausible guess. Each unknown word is sent to multiple users; if the first three human guesses are identical, but different from the readings of both OCR programs, the unknown word becomes a control word for further challenges. If users do not agree on a word, the word is presented to more users and eventually the transcription with the highest number of votes is chosen, with human answers having a weight of 1 and OCR guesses having one of 0.5. A transcription must obtain at least 2.5 votes to be considered a correct reading and to be used in the digitization.

For evaluating the digitization accuracy of reCAPTCHA, von Ahn et al. create a gold standard by having two typists transcribe 50 randomly selected scanned articles from five different years (1860, 1865, 1908, 1935, and 1970) from the New York Times archive (24,080 running word forms in total). When compared to this gold standard, von Ahn et al. report that the reCAPTCHA system achieved a word-level accuracy of 99.1% (216 errors out of 24,080 words), whereas standard OCR on the same set of articles achieved only 83.5% accuracy (3976 errors).

4.4   MANUAL TEXT ENTRY

As we mentioned above, depending on the texts to be digitized, manual text entry is either an alternative to OCR or the only possible approach. In many cases, an approach called *double-keying* is used. Double-keying means that a text is entered by (at least) two typists. The two resulting transcriptions are then compared with each other; where they differ, at least one typist has made a mistake. Double-keying is routinely combined with further error-checking.

Many people associate double-keying with *offshore text entry*, i.e., outsourcing of keyboarding to service providers in countries with lower wages than in Western Europe and North America, in particular to the Philippines, India, or China, which have large text and data entry industries. Strictly speaking, however, it is simply a method for quality control. Who is qualified for keyboarding historical texts depends on the properties of the texts; in general, only material printed in roman type can be outsourced to service providers.

Offshore double-keying can be a cost-effective and highly accurate solution. For texts that could possibly be also processed by OCR, tests should be done to determine the amount and type of post-processing required for the OCR results; the development of correction scripts requires qualified personnel and may be relatively expensive. Offshore double-keying can achieve accuracy better than 99.9%, which reduces the amount of post-processing needed. For example, an accuracy of 99.995% means less than one error per 20,000 characters.

The cost of offshore double-keying depends on the complexity of the text, the amount of text, and the desired quality. The complexity depends on factors such as the presence and number of special characters, which would require training the typists, or whether footnotes and the critical apparatus of an edition are also to be transcribed. To get an impression of the cost, here are some rough numbers. Text entry currently costs about 0.40–0.70 euros per 1,000 characters; extra quality control comes at about 0.15 euros per 1,000 characters.

With respect to markup and formatting, both OCR and double-keying typically require post-processing such as data format conversion, or the addition of semantic markup.

4.5   COMPUTER-ASSISTED TRANSCRIPTION

Material unsuitable for OCR, for example, handwritten documents, printed documents typeset in blackletter typefaces older than 19th century, and anything that requires expert judgment can only sensibly be transcribed by qualified personnel; the same obviously also applies to hieroglyphs or cuneiform writing. In such cases, tools may be used that help transcribers—this is often referred to as *computer-assisted transcription*. Currently, there are no standard tools for computer-aided transcription of historical documents. However, several projects have developed their own tools to support their transcribers. Very little has been published about such tools for internal use, and the software itself is rarely released.

Computer-assisted transcription tools differ in their architecture and their functionality depending on the material to transcribe and the general goals of the digitization. We look only at one class of tools, namely tools designed for line-by-line transcription of manuscripts. One difficulty in this task is that it is easy to accidentally skip lines in the manuscript. To help transcribers, several tools integrate automatic image processing for automatic detection of lines (the detected lines can be modified) and then guide the transcriber by synchronizing the image of the text with the text entry.

One such tool is AGORA (Ramel et al., 2006), which was developed for the French project *Bibliothèques Virtuelles Humanistes*[34] (Virtual Library of Humanists). GIDOC (Terrades et al., 2010)

[34]http://www.bvh.univ-tours.fr/ (accessed 2012-06-06)

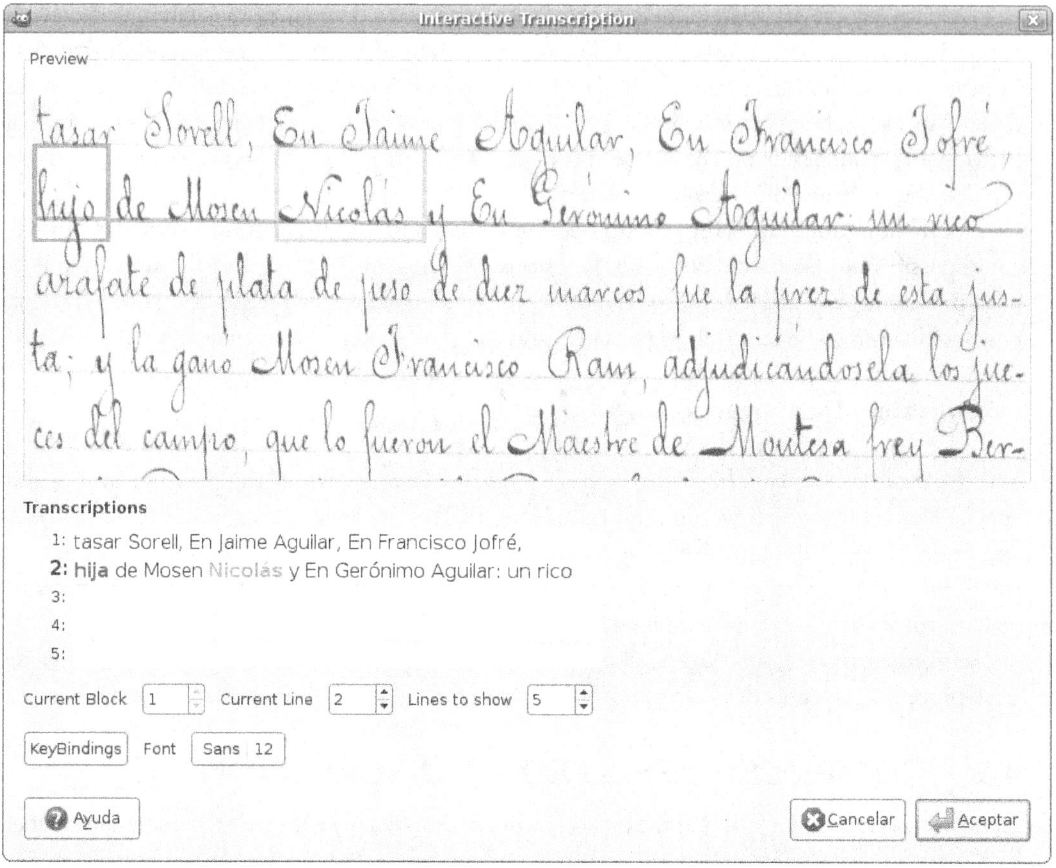

Figure 4.12: GIDOC is an experimental computer-assisted transcription tool for historical manuscripts. It integrates automatic page layout analysis text line detection, and transcription of handwritten text.

is an experimental tool—realized as a plug-in for the open-source GIMP[35] image manipulation program. The system automatically detects text blocks and lines, and learns from the text transcribed so far, so that it can offer possible transcriptions when a similar shape appears again, helping to speed up the transcription process. GIDOC is available as open-source software.[36] Figure 4.12 shows a screenshot of the transcription interface.

T-PEN[37] is a Web-based tool; it also performs automatic line and column segmentation and then provides the transcriber with a text entry box synchronized with the lines in the manuscript image, as shown in Figure 4.13. One can also add annotations (e.g., comments) to each line. T-PEN

[35] http://www.gimp.org/ (accessed 2012-07-16)
[36] https://prhlt.iti.upv.es/page/projects/multimodal/idoc/gidoc (accessed 2012-06-07)
[37] http://t-pen.org/ (accessed 2012-06-07)

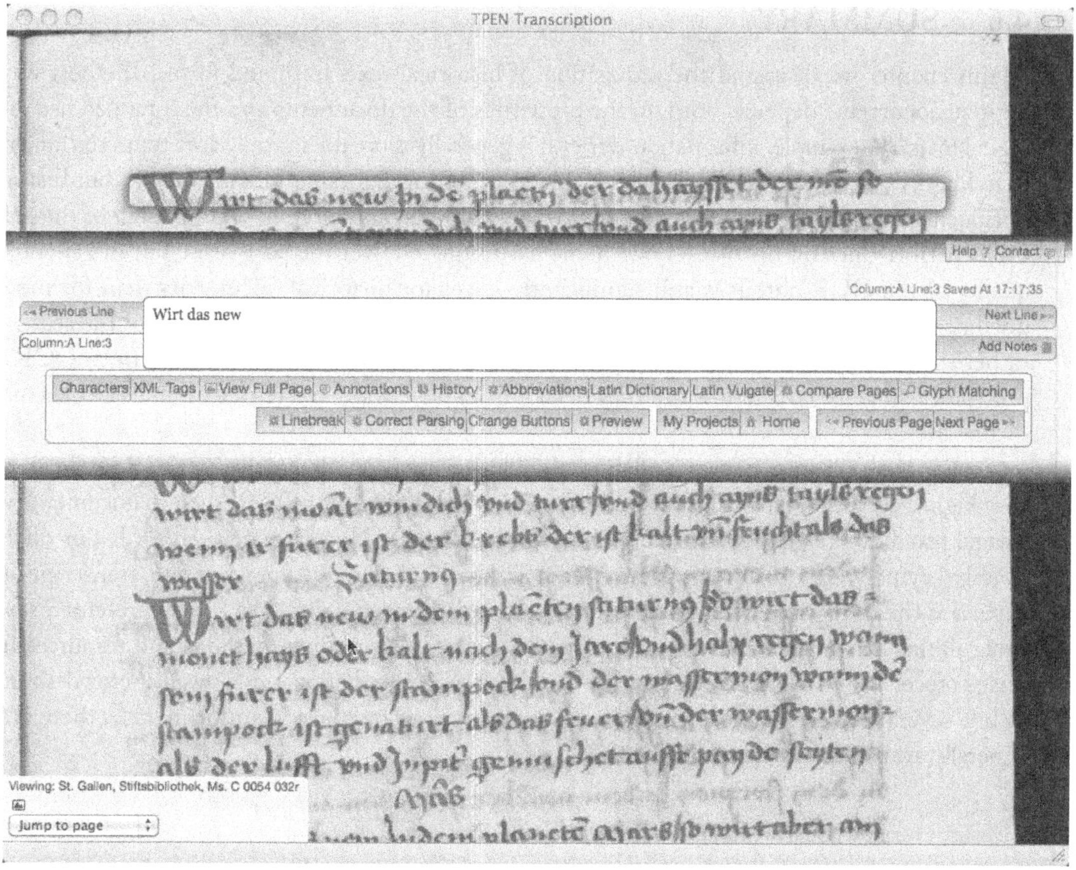

Figure 4.13: T-PEN is a Web-based tool for transcribing historical manuscripts. The transcription text entry box is synchronized with the lines in the page image.

integrates project management facilities for collaboratively working on transcriptions. Transcriptions can be exported in a variety of formats, including TEI (see Section 5.2). The system can be used on the project's server at Saint Louis University; it is planned to be also released as open-source software.

OTTO (Dipper et al., 2010) is a Web-based tool developed in the context of the Reference Corpus Middle High German (see Section 8.6). OTTO is designed for diplomatic transcription of historical texts. The tool aims to speed up text entry by offering shortcuts for characters typically needed for this type of texts, while providing the transcriber with an instant rendering of the transcription for comparison with the original manuscript. OTTO also supports projects with many geographically distributed transcribers. Unlike the systems mentioned above, OTTO does not implement synchronization with manuscript images.

4.6   SUMMARY

In this chapter we discussed the acquisition of historical texts in digital form. The best way to digitize documents depends both on the properties of the documents and the intended use of the digital texts; for example, information retrieval is generally more tolerant towards transcription errors than linguistic analysis. OCR can be a viable solution for digitizing historical texts, but historical documents typically require more diligence when scanning, and more post-processing of the results. OCR performance on historical documents has improved over the past years, but in general, the quality of the OCR output is still significantly lower for historical documents than for modern documents. In many cases, the problem is not—or not only—the image quality of the scans, but rather the lack of NLP resources adapted to the historical language of the text. Both OCR and post-processing of OCR results can thus benefit from NLP tools and resources, in particular special dictionaries.

For large volumes of texts, offshore double-keying is an alternative to OCR, and can offer very high accuracy, in particular for documents that are difficult for OCR, such as documents with several text flows (e.g., footnotes and critical apparatuses). However, neither OCR nor offshore double-keying are generally suitable for older and handwritten documents. Here, transcription by experts is the only way to obtain digital text of a satisfactory quality. We briefly presented several tools aiming to support transcribers; optimally, such tools combine methods and resources from image processing—such as line detection—and NLP—such as dictionaries, as well as crowd-sourcing. While several projects have developed such tools for their own needs, unfortunately, there are no generally available, "off-the-shelf" tools yet.

CHAPTER 5

Text Encoding and Annotation Schemes

Once text has been digitized, it needs to be encoded and annotated for storage and further processing. Of course, this concerns all kinds of text, not just historical text, but due to its special properties (see Section 1.1), historical texts tend to have special requirements. This chapter gives a short overview of two standards that are particularly relevant for the encoding of historical texts: first, *Unicode* for the encoding of characters, then *TEI*, an XML application for the annotation of texts with structural information and metadata.

5.1 UNICODE FOR HISTORICAL TEXT

The following short outline of writing systems is primarily intended to provide readers with some background for the subsequent discussion of Unicode. For a comprehensive study of writing systems see, for example, Daniels and Bright (1996).

Writing is a way of recording language in a medium more permanent than speech. The precondition for writing is the existence of a *script*. A script is a set of conventional symbols that can be used to represent one or more languages in writing. We refer to the elements of a script as *characters*; an alternative term is *grapheme*. We follow the terminology of Sproat (2000) and use the term *writing system* to describe the use of a script for a particular language. A writing system defines language-specific rules and conventions, which assign meanings to the characters of the script. The linguistic unit associated with a character depends on the properties of the script and the writing system, and characters correspond to different linguistic units in alphabetic, syllabic, or logographic writing systems.

Note that a character is an abstract concept and does not have an inherent meaning or form. In fact, one could say that the only inherent property of a character in some script is that it is different from all other characters of this script. The graphical representation of a character is called a *glyph*. There is no general one-to-one correspondence between characters and glyphs. On the one hand, one character may be represented by several different glyphs, for example, the Latin characters *a* and *g* each have two basic glyph variants (the *single-story* forms ɑ and ɡ, and the *double-story* forms a and g), or the Greek character *sigma* has the two positional glyph variants σ and ς. In the Arabic script, all characters have initial, medial, final, and isolated glyphs. In addition, there are thousands of font-specific variations; in handwriting, glyphs must also be considered abstractions, as each individual instance differs from the next. On the other hand, a glyph also does not necessarily correspond to a single character. One example are *ligatures*, i.e., glyphs representing a sequence of several characters, such as the glyph *fi*, which represents the character sequence *f* + *i*. The Latin script nowadays uses only a small number of ligatures, but historical texts make frequent use of ligatures; for example, the symbol & is originally a ligature of *e* + *t* for the Latin word *et* 'and'. Numerous ligatures are used in the Arabic script and the Indic scripts (e.g., Devanagari) ligatures.

In order to process written texts by computer, they must be encoded in a suitable form. The usual approach is to map the set of abstract characters of a script to a set of positive integers, resulting in a *coded character set*, also known as *character encoding*, *coded character repertoire*, *character set definition*, or *code page*. The earliest coded character sets were based on telegraphy codes and used 5 bits. In 1964, ASCII—the American Standard Code for Information Interchange—was published as a standard. ASCII encodes each character in 7 bits, so that 128 different characters can be encoded; 33 codes were reserved for *control characters* (line feed, backspace, etc.), leaving 95 codes for actual characters.

ASCII is sufficient for encoding basic English text, but it is not adequate for encoding text in most other languages using the Latin script, not to speak of languages using other scripts. As computers spread around the world, it became necessary to encode text in languages other than English. This lead to the development of numerous national and corporate character encodings, many of which used 8 bits; a theoretical maximum of 256 characters can be encoded using 8 bit, but most of these encodings aim to be compatible with ASCII and reserve a number of characters, so that in most cases, they can only encode 95–128 characters in addition to ASCII. For encoding larger scripts such as Chinese and Japanese, a variety of double-byte (16 bits) and variable-width multibyte encodings, as well as code-shifting techniques (for switching between various encodings) were devised. Practically all of these encodings were only suitable for one language or a small group of languages, and as many of these encodings were vendor-specific, interoperability was difficult.

To improve this situation, a series of international standard 8-bit character encodings were defined in the 1980s to supplant vendor-specific encodings and national standards, the ISO/IEC 8859 series (usually referred to as ISO 8859). However, as they are limited to 8 bits, these character encodings are still mostly language-specific. ISO 8859 tried to create encodings that cover languages that frequently occur together; for example, ISO 8859-2 can be used to encode mixed German and Polish text—but there is no ISO 8859 encoding that would support mixing French and Polish, and the Cyrillic, Greek, Arabic, Hebrew, and Thai ISO 8859 encodings only contain the Latin characters from ASCII. Furthermore, while some of the ISO 8859 encodings—in particular ISO 8859-1—gained widespread use, many vendor-specific encodings (e.g., IBM Code Page 437 or HP Roman 8) remained in use, and ISO 8859 did nothing to improve the situation for Asian languages.

In order to finally resolve this unsatisfactory situation, in 1987, engineers from Apple and Xerox (Joe Becker, Lee Collins, and Mark Davis) initiated a project called *Unicode* to create a universal character encoding that would cover *all* of the world's languages. Since the first public draft proposal, *Unicode 88* (Becker, 1988), Unicode (The Unicode Standard) and its companion standard ISO/IEC 10646 have revolutionized and radically simplified the encoding—and thus the processing—of multilingual and non-English text. Today, Unicode is regarded as the universal character encoding standard and has made significant progress towards replacing legacy encodings (e.g., ASCII, the ISO 8859 series, KOI-8, or Shift-JIS) for the encoding of new text. Most legacy encodings are now defined in terms of Unicode, i.e., as proper subsets of Unicode. All modern operating systems and programming languages support Unicode.

Unicode is the first character encoding that draws a clear distinction between characters and glyphs; apart from so-called *compatibility characters* (encoded for interoperability with legacy encodings), Unicode aims to encode only characters, not glyphs. By making this distinction, Unicode has a clear definition of the entities it encodes.

Unicode also considers diacritics as characters, which simply have the property to graphically combine in some way with a base character. An accented character such as $\acute{g}$ is thus seen as a combination of the base character g and a *combining character*, here an acute accent. In Unicode, combining characters always follow the base character to which they apply. In principle, any number of combining characters can follow a base character, and all combining characters can be used with any script (see The Unicode Standard, p. 41), but obviously not all combinations can necessarily be displayed in a reasonable way. Due to compatibility considerations, numerous combinations of base characters with diacritics are also available as *precomposed characters*; for example, $\ddot{A}$ is available as a precomposed character for compatibility with ISO 8859-1. Since these characters can thus be encoded in different ways, Unicode also defines equivalence relations such as $B + \ddot{A} \equiv B + A + \ddot{}$ and *normalization forms*, i.e., rules for maximally composing or decomposing characters. The policy of the Unicode Consortium is not to encode any new characters that could be encoded using combining characters.

Unicode makes a further important distinction, namely between *code points*, i.e., the number assigned to a character, and the *encoding scheme*, i.e., the representation of this number by a concrete sequence of bits.[1] Unicode code points are usually written as "U+" followed by the number in hexadecimal, for example, U+0065 for the Latin lowercase letter e.[2] Unicode defines a number of different encoding schemes; the two most important ones are *UTF-8* and *UTF-16*.

UTF-8 is a variable-width encoding; it encodes each Unicode code point using one to four 8-bit bytes. The first 128 characters of Unicode, which correspond to ASCII, are encoded using a single byte and with the same bit sequence as in ASCII; thus, any valid ASCII text is also valid UTF-8-encoded Unicode. This property, and the fact that no null bytes (i.e., bytes in which all bits are 0) can occur, are two important advantages of the UTF-8 encoding scheme, as they ensure compatibility with legacy software. Many standards require support for UTF-8; for example, XML uses UTF-8 as default encoding. Table 5.1 shows the principles of the UTF-8 encoding scheme.

The UTF-16 encoding scheme is the successor of the original 16-bit fixed-width encoding proposed in Unicode 88. In principle, it works like UTF-8, but the code units have a length of 16

---

[1]Our use of the term *encoding scheme* is a slight simplification. In fact, Unicode differentiates between *character encoding forms*—methods of converting a code point to a sequence of one or more fixed-size *code units* (e.g., bytes)—and *character encoding schemes*—methods for mapping code units to a sequence suitable for saving in file system or transmitting over networks, which are typically byte-oriented. For UTF-8, the encoding scheme is trivial.

[2]Unicode also defines standard names for all characters that it encodes; the name corresponding to U+0065 is "LATIN SMALL LETTER E."

Table 5.1: The UTF-8 character encoding scheme translates Unicode code points into bit sequences structured into one to four 8-bit code units. For example, the code point U+00E6 LATIN SMALL LETTER AE is represented in UTF-8 by two code units corresponding to the bit sequence 11000011 10100110 (C3 A6).

Code Point Ranges	UTF-8 Encoding			
	Unit 1	Unit 2	Unit 3	Unit 4
0000–007F	0xxxxxxx			
0080–07FF	110xxxxx	10xxxxxx		
0800–D7FF E000–FFFF	1110xxxx	10xxxxxx	10xxxxxx	
10000–10FFFF	11110xxx	10xxxxxx	10xxxxxx	10xxxxxx

bits. As UTF-16 is not interoperable with ASCII, and because the use of 16-bit units raises byte order issues (there are big-endian and little-endian variants of UTF-16), UTF-16 is more often used for internal text processing by operating systems and programming languages and less often used for encoding text files.

Originally, Unicode was conceived as a 16-bit encoding, assuming that this code space would be sufficient for encoding all characters in modern use; the Unicode 88 draft proposal (Becker, 1988, p. 5) states:

> Unicode gives higher priority to ensuring utility for the future than to preserving past antiquities. Unicode aims in the first instance at the characters published in modern text (e.g. in the union of all newspapers and magazines printed in the world in 1988), whose number is undoubtedly far below $2^{14} = 16,384$. Beyond those modern-use characters, all others may be defined to be obsolete or rare; these are better candidates for private-use registration than for congesting the public list of generally-useful Unicodes.

However, beginning with Unicode 2.0, the standard was extended, adding 16 supplementary *planes* to the original 16-bit code space, which is now called the *basic multilingual plane*, or BMP for short, thus increasing the Unicode code space to over one million code points. This allows for the encoding of historical scripts and rare or obsolete characters, which was started with Unicode 3.0 in 1999. Unicode now defines code points for scripts such as runic, cuneiform, Linear B, and Egyptian hieroglyphs, besides historical characters in Latin, Cyrillic, Greek, and other extant scripts.

Being able to process historical text in the same way as modern text—and using the same basic text processing tools—represents a huge step forward; before, a variety of incompatible systems for encoding historical letters and scripts had to be used, limiting the interchange of texts and the use of off-the-shelf tools. Many of these systems tried to represent relatively large character repertoires using only ASCII characters and various escape mechanisms.

For example, *Beta Code* (Thesaurus Linguae Graecae, 2011) is a widely used system for encoding Ancient Greek (and several other ancient languages), originally developed by David W. Packard in the late 1970s and adopted by the *Thesaurus Linguae Graecae*[3] (Pantelia, 2000) in 1981. The first few words of Herodotus' *Histories*[4],

Ἡροδότου Ἀλικαρνησσέος ἱστορίης ἀπόδεξις ἥδε [...]

are encoded in Beta Code as follows:

```
$*(HRODO/TOU *(ALIKARNHSSE/OS I(STORI/HS A)PO/DECIS H(/DE
```

The dollar sign switches from Latin to Greek; capital letters are indicated by prefixing them with an asterisk.[5] The other non-alphabetic characters represent accents and breathing marks; for lowercase letters, they *follow* the letter on which they are to be placed, for uppercase letters they *precede* the letter on which they are to be placed.[6]

TUSTEP[7] (Ott, 1979, 2000) is a text processing system for the preparation of critical editions, originally developed in the 1970s and widely used in German-speaking Europe. The TUSTEP encoding of the same text would be:

```
#G+%(_Hrod%/otou %(_Alikarnhss%/eow %(istor%/ihw %)ap%/odejiw %(%/hde
```

Here, `#G+` switches to Greek; accents—encoded using escape sequences starting with the percent sign—always *precede* the base letters; however, if an accent is to be placed before a capital letter, an underscore (_) must be inserted between the accent and the letter codes.[8] Note that also the mapping of basic Greek to Latin letters differs from that used by Beta Code; for example, ξ is encoded by j instead of C.

For typesetting the quotation above with LaTeX, yet another notation had to be used:

```
\greektext <Hrod'otou <Alikarnhss'eos <istor'ihs >ap'odexis <'hde
```

In all three encodings—Beta Code, TUSTEP, and LaTeX—sigma is normally encoded by the same character and automatically rendered either as σ or ς depending on its position. In addition, separate codes for medial and final sigma are defined for overriding the automatic decision.

While these notations may be handy for entering Ancient Greek text on a U.S. keyboard, they make text processing—including NLP, of course—tedious. Even basic tools, such as tokenizers or the `sort` and `grep` Unix utilities, will not produce useful results on such texts, and the interchange of texts between projects first requires the conversion from one private encoding into another.

---

[3]http://www.tlg.uci.edu/ (accessed 2012-06-06)

[4]From the 1920 edition by A.D. Godley, as provided by Perseus, http://www.perseus.tufts.edu/hopper/text?doc=Perseus:text:1999.01.0125 (accessed 2012-06-06).

[5]The Perseus project employs a variant of Beta Code, which uses lowercase ASCII characters; Greek capitals are nevertheless marked by prefixing with an asterisk, not by using uppercase characters.

[6]See http://www.tlg.uci.edu/encoding/ (accessed 2012-06-12). However, one also encounters texts in which diacritics follow both uppercase and lowercase letters.

[7]http://www.tustep.uni-tuebingen.de/ (accessed 2012-06-12)

[8]For details see TUSTEP Manual, p. 683–684.

Unicode provides developers and users with a single, comprehensive framework for encoding text. A Unicode-conforming program can provide users with basic text services for all scripts supported by Unicode—whether modern or historical—on the basis of the character properties in the Unicode Character Database, [9] (UCD) which indicate, for example, whether a character is white space, alphabetic, or a punctuation mark. What is more, since modern font technology (TrueType and OpenType) is also based on Unicode, in principle, only a font containing the necessary glyphs is needed for displaying the text.

Despite the progress brought by Unicode, encoding historical texts is often still more challenging than encoding modern texts. When working with modern languages, it is very unlikely to encounter a character not encoded in Unicode; when working with historical languages, however, this is still a common issue. For example, a small selection of combining superscript letters [10] (see Figure 3.5(b) for some examples) needed, for example, for medieval and early modern German, was introduced with Unicode 3.2 in March 2002; a further 20 combining superscript letters [11] were only encoded in version 5.1 in March 2008, but many characters required for medieval texts are still missing from Unicode, for example, a combining superscript w.

Encoding historical text often has to make extensive use of combining characters (such as these superscript letters), as the required combinations of base characters and diacritics are not encoded as precomposed characters. In theory, this is not a problem, as Unicode conformance requires software to support combining characters; however, as modern Western European languages can be encoded using precomposed characters only, some software may have bugs or omissions in their support for combining characters. Unusual combinations of diacritics and base characters also require carefully designed fonts and a suitable rendering engine in order to obtain esthetically acceptable results.

For additional characters and scripts, the Unicode Consortium relies on proposals from users and communities. In order to coordinate the needs of medieval scholars and to advance the encoding of characters found in medieval texts, the Medieval Unicode Font Initiative [12] (MUFI) was founded in July 2001. It reviews proposals from its members and assigns code points in the Private Use Area (PUA) of Unicode for characters missing from the Unicode standard and proposes them to the Unicode Consortium for official encoding. As we noted above, an important principle of Unicode is to encode characters (i.e, abstract units of meaning), not glyphs (specific shapes). However, for many historical texts, in particular for manuscripts, it is not straightforward to determine whether some as yet unknown sign constitutes a character or only a glyph variant. Figure 5.1 shows an example page from the MUFI Character Recommendation.

The Script Encoding Initiative [13] (SEI), established in April 2002, is a project devoted to the preparation of formal proposals for the encoding of scripts and script elements not yet currently

---

[9]http://unicode.org/ucd/ (accessed 2012-06-06)
[10]The code points U+0363 through U+036F: $a, e, i, o, u, c, d, h, m, r, t, v$, and x.
[11]The code points U+1DD3 through U+1DE6.
[12]http://www.mufi.info/ (accessed 2012-06-06)
[13]http://linguistics.berkeley.edu/sei/ (accessed 2012-06-06)

	MUFI character recommendation ※ Part 1: alphabetical order			version 3.0 p. 155 / 165
ꝑ	&pennygerm;	20B0	CurrSymb	GERMAN PENNY SIGN
Э	&scruple;	2108	LettSymb	SCRUPLE
℔	&romaslibr;	F2E0	PUA-12	LATIN AS LIBRALIS SIGN
Ӿ	&romXbar;	10196	AncSymb	LATIN CAPITAL LETTER X WITH BAR
ꭓ	&romscapxbar;	F2E2	PUA-12	LATIN SMALL CAPITAL LETTER X WITH BAR
Ⲩ	&romscapybar;	F2E3	PUA-12	LATIN SMALL CAPITAL LETTER Y WITH BAR
đ	&romscapdslash;	F2E4	PUA-12	LATIN SMALL CAPITAL LETTER D WITH SLASH
ꝺ	&drotbar;	F2E5	PUA-12	LATIN SMALL LETTER D ROTUNDA WITH BAR
ṽ	&ecu;	F2E7	PUA-12	ECU SIGN
ꟻ	&florloop;	F2E8	PUA-12	FLOREN SIGN WITH LOOP
ǥ	&grosch;	F2E9	PUA-12	GROSCHEN SIGN
℔	&libradut;	F2EA	PUA-12	DUTCH LIBRA SIGN
℔	&librafren;	F2EB	PUA-12	FRENCH LIBRA SIGN

※ Characters on shaded background belong to the Private Use Area. Please read the introduction p. 11 carefully before using any of these characters.

Figure 5.1: Example page from the MUFI Character Recommendation, version 3.0, listing Unicode characters for encoding medival texts. Characters on a shaded background are not (yet) part of the Unicode standard and only have code points in the Private Use Area.

supported in Unicode. The goal of the SEI project is to fund the preparation of proposals for historical and minority scripts that will be successfully approved by the Unicode Technical Committee.

To summarize, Unicode has significantly improved the technical infrastructure for processing historical text. Instead of requiring private and ad-hoc solutions, many historical texts can—on the character level—now be stored and processed like modern texts; processing of historical text now also benefits from general improvements to Unicode support. Unicode is therefore the only reasonable character encoding for any new project involving historical texts, and anyone working with digital historical texts should have a good understanding of Unicode, especially when creating software. If required characters are missing, Unicode's Private Use Area (PUA) provides users with a well-defined extension mechanism; in order to ensure the widest possible support—and possibly inclusion into the Unicode standard—the use of the Private Use Area should be coordinated through bodies such as MUFI or SEI.

For further reading on Unicode we refer to the books by Korpela (2006) or Haralambous (2007); while they do not cover the most recent developments, they explain the principles underlying Unicode and provide readers with the background knowledge required for understanding Unicode Technical Reports and other technical specifications.

5.2 TEI FOR HISTORICAL TEXTS

Just like Unicode is the standard for encoding characters today, XML (Bray et al., 2006) is the standard for adding higher-level information—*markup* and *metadata*—to texts. A good introduction to XML from a document-oriented perspective is the section "A Gentle Introduction to XML" in the TEI Guidelines (TEI Consortium, 2007). XML has enjoyed tremendous success since its first publication as a W3C Recommendation in 1998. Nowadays there are few areas of computing where, in some way or another, XML does not play a role. There are probably hundreds of specifications and standards built on XML, and dozens of related technologies, such as XSLT (Kay, 2007), XQuery (Boag et al., 2010), XML Schema, XLink, XPointer, SOAP, etc. The W3C press release on the occasion of the ten-year anniversary of XML quotes Tim Bray, one of the editors of the XML Recommendation, as saying, "[t]here is essentially no computer in the world, desk-top, hand-held, or back-room, that doesn't process XML sometimes."[14]

Not surprisingly, XML also plays an important role in NLP, especially for annotating corpora and texts, for example with information on tokens, sentence boundaries, part-of-speech tags, morphological analyses, chunking, or named entities. XML is also used for the management and exchange of language resources, such as lexicons. For an introduction to the use of XML in NLP see, for example, Wilcock (2009).

It is important to remember that XML is not a markup language, but a meta-language for creating markup languages. In principle, an infinite number of XML-based markup languages can be conceived, and XML is indeed frequently used for private or ad-hoc markup schemes. Even if the annotated texts are never exchanged with others, the use of an XML-based annotation format simplifies processing, as standard methods and tools can be applied. However, the value of XML is realized in particular when it is used for the interchange of text and data. Some examples of XML formats used for interchange in NLP are TIGER-XML (Mengel and Lezius, 2000) for treebanks, TimeML (Pustejovsky et al., 2010) for temporal annotations, and TEI, which will be the main topic of this section. The ISO TC 37/SC 4 subcommittee on language resource management has published several XML-based interchange formats for language resources (including ISO-TimeML, ISO 24617-1:2012) and is working on further formats.

The Text Encoding Initiative (TEI) was established in 1987 in order to develop vendor-independent standards for encoding digital humanities data, in particular text. In 2000, it was incorporated as a non-profit organization, the TEI Consortium. The TEI Consortium is an international organization, sustained by its members, mostly universities, libraries, and research projects. The mission of the TEI Consortium is "to develop and maintain a set of high-quality guidelines

---

[14]http://www.w3.org/2008/xml10/xml10-pressrelease (accessed 2012-06-06)

for the encoding of humanities texts, and to support their use by a wide community of projects, institutions, and individuals."[15]

These guidlines are published as *The Text Encoding Initiative Guidelines for Electronic Text Encoding and Interchange*; they have established themselves as an international standard, widely used by research projects and institutions in the humanities (e.g., libraries and museums) for encoding all kinds of textual material. The major revisions of the Guidelines are P1 (1990), P2 (1992), P3 (1994), P4 (2001), and P5, which was released in 2007.

The TEI Guidelines define a markup language for annotating texts with respect to their structural, visual, and conceptual properties. According to their own description, the primary focus of the Guidelines is on "the encoding of documents in the humanities and social sciences, and in particular on the representation of primary source materials for research and analysis."[16] The TEI Guidelines comprise an XML schema and extensive documentation with hundreds of examples illustrating its application; both parts are published under an open-source license and are available from the TEI Consortium's website.[17] The TEI XML schema is available in different formats (DTD, Relax NG (ISO/IEC 19757-2), and W3C XML Schema (World Wide Web Consortium, 2004)) and is probably one of the largest XML schemata in existence.

Due to its size and the diversity of its uses, the TEI schema is divided into several modules, which can be used alone or in combination. There are modules for text types, such as poetry, drama, dictionaries, or transcribed speech, and modules for the annotation of specific text elements, such as names, dates, persons, and places, manuscript features, certainty, or linguistic analyses. To support overlapping markup—which occurs, for example, when both physical and logical properties are annotated—the TEI Guidelines also define a mechanism for *standoff markup*, i.e., markup that is not embedded in the text—as is usual for XML—but separate from the text. This allows users to apply several independent "layers" of markup to a text, irrespective of potentially overlapping structures.

TEI is much more complex than, say, HTML, but a large portion of this complexity is inherent in the task of annotating historical documents. When starting a new project, the first step is thus to define what aspects of a text are to be annotated; only in a later step should these features be mapped to elements from the TEI vocabulary. As texts vary widely, the size and contents of TEI subsets used by different project also vary widely.

All TEI documents start with a block of metadata, the *TEI header*. The TEI header contains four major parts: the file description, a full bibliographical description of the computer file itself, an encoding description, which describes the relationship between the electronic text and its source or sources, a text profile, containing classificatory and contextual information about the text (e.g., subject matter, persons described, context of its creation), and a revision history. The TEI header allows for a very detailed description of the encoded text and can thus easily be larger than the text itself; however, only the file description (the `<fileDesc>` element) is mandatory. Listing 5.1 shows an example of a minimal TEI header.

---

[15]http://www.tei-c.org/About/mission.xml (accessed 2012-06-06)
[16]http://www.tei-c.org/Guidelines/ (accessed 2012-06-06)
[17]http://www.tei-c.org/ (accessed 2012-06-06)

```
<teiHeader>
 <fileDesc>
  <titleStmt>
   <title>Thomas Paine: Common sense, a machine-readable
     transcript</title>
   <respStmt>
    <resp>compiled by</resp>
    <name>Jon K Adams</name>
   </respStmt>
  </titleStmt>
  <publicationStmt>
   <distributor>Oxford Text Archive</distributor>
  </publicationStmt>
  <sourceDesc>
   <bibl>The complete writings of Thomas Paine, collected and edited
     by Phillip S. Foner (New York, Citadel Press, 1945)</bibl>
  </sourceDesc>
 </fileDesc>
</teiHeader>
```

Listing 5.1: Example of a minimal TEI header (from Section 2.6 of the TEI Guidelines (TEI Consortium, 2007)).

Following the TEI header is the actual content, contained in a `<text>` element. For text collections such as corpora, TEI also includes the `<teiCorpus>` element, which makes it possible to store several texts in a single document, each with its own header. The outermost TEI header then contains metadata applicable to the whole collection of texts.

The TEI core module contains elements that are used in most types of texts, and the elements of the core module are available in all TEI documents. These elements include paragraphs and lists, highlighting and quotations, simple editorial changes, names, numbers, dates, and bibliographic references. Further modules define support for particular text types (e.g., verse, drama, or dictionaries), for special document elements (e.g., tables, formulas, or graphics), or for recording additional metadata (e.g., manuscript descriptions, certainty and precision of annotations, or segmentation and alignment).

As a practical example, Figure 5.2 illustrates the encoding of a primary source using TEI. The source is the so-called *Älteres Landbuch*, a code of laws and customs from the Swiss canton of Appenzell, originally created around 1540, but with many later additions and changes. The excerpt shown here is titled "How the bailiff and the summoner swear"[18] and specifies the content of their oath and their obligations; for example, they had to swear that they would promote prosperity and honor of the land and to defend it from all harm.

---

[18]The translation of the German terms *Landammann* and *Weibel* as *bailiff* and *summoner*, respectively, is historically not fully accurate, but sufficient for our purposes.

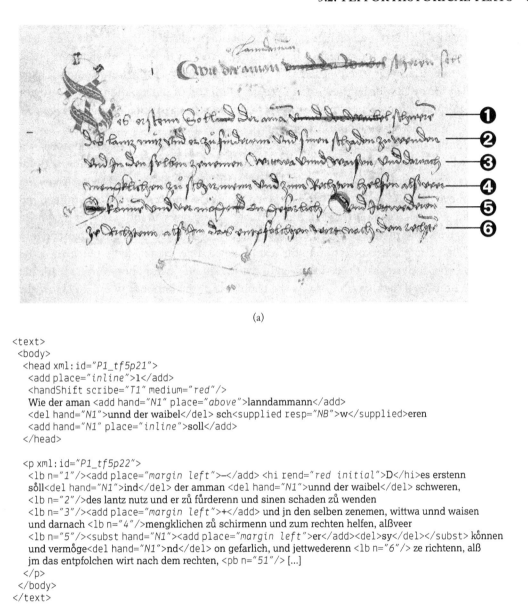

(a)

```
<text>
 <body>
  <head xml:id="P1_tf5p21">
   <add place="inline">1</add>
   <handShift scribe="T1" medium="red"/>
   Wie der aman <add hand="N1" place="above">lanndammann</add>
   <del hand="N1">unnd der waibel</del> sch<supplied resp="NB">w</supplied>eren
   <add hand="N1" place="inline">soll</add>
  </head>

  <p xml:id="P1_tf5p22">
   <lb n="1"/><add place="margin left">–</add> <hi rend="red initial">D</hi>es erstenn
   sőll<del hand="N1">ind</del> der amman <del hand="N1">unnd der waibel</del> schweren,
   <lb n="2"/>des lantz nutz und er zů fůrderenn und sinen schaden zů wenden
   <lb n="3"/><add place="margin left">+</add> und jn den selben zenemen, wittwa unnd waisen
   und darnach <lb n="4"/>mengklichen zů schirmenn und zum rechten helfen, alßveer
   <lb n="5"/><subst hand="N1"><add place="margin left">er</add><del>sy</del></subst> kőnnen
   und vermőge<del hand="N1">nd</del> on gefarlich, und jettwederenn <lb n="6"/> ze richtenn, alß
   jm das entpfolchen wirt nach dem rechten, <pb n="51"/> [...]
  </p>
 </body>
</text>
```

(b)

Figure 5.2: TEI encoding of a manuscript: (a) excerpt from page 50 of the *Älteres Landbuch* (ca. 1540; State Archives of Appenzell Innerrhoden (LAA), Common Archives, C.XI.01); (b) example TEI encoding (excluding the TEI header; adapted from the TEI version of SSRQ_AR/AI 1. The numbers given in the attribute n of the <lb> element refer to the lines of the manuscript.

The TEI encoding shown here is based on the TEI version of SSRQ AR/AI 1. Encoding such a text in TEI is not a mechanical process, but depends in many cases on the paleographical, linguistic, and historical interpretation of the text. Thus, many different encodings are possible. Here, the basic transcription is based on the rules of the Collection of Swiss Law Sources; changes to the text called for by call for by these rules (e.g., the addition of punctuation marks) are not marked. For the purpose of this example, we may say that the text consists of a heading (tagged as `<head>`) followed by a series of paragraphs (tagged as `<p>`), of which only one is shown here.

Both in the heading and in the text there are a number of deletions and additions by a different scribe, who is given the identifier "N1" here; these are tagged using the `<add>` and `<del>` TEI elements. For example, scribe N1 prepended the digit 1 to the heading, wrote *landammann* 'country bailiff' above the word *aman* 'bailiff', crossed out the words *unnd der waibel* 'and the summoner', and added the word *shall* 'soll' at the end. The attribute `place` gives an indication of the position of the addition, here `inline` or `above`. In addition to recording these changes, the transcriber (identified as "NB") has also made a correction to the text by supplying a missing letter (element `<supplied>`); it is clear from the text that the scribe meant to write *schweren* 'swear', not *scheren* 'shear'. In summary, scribe N1 changed the title from "How the bailiff and the summoner swear" to "How the country bailiff shall swear."

In the paragraph following the heading, the original line breaks (more precisely: the beginning of lines) are marked using the `<lb>` element; the number given in the attribute n here refer to the line numbering in Figure 5.2(a). The red initial is tagged using `<hi>`, a general-purpose TEI element for marking "a word or phrase as graphically distinct from the surrounding text" (TEI Consortium, 2007). In the left margin we can see a dash and a cross; these signs were apparently added by a law revision commission around 1567, probably in order to indicate the status of an article, but their exact meaning is unknown (SSRQ AR/AI 1, p. XXXI). We have therefore encoded them as marginal additions on lines 1 and 3, but one could also argue that they concern the article as a whole and that their exact position is thus irrelevant; if one takes this case, one could, for example, encode them as `<add place="margin left">- +</add>`.

Scribe N1 also made changes reflecting his change to the heading, i.e., the statute no longer applies to the bailiff and the summoner, but to the bailiff only. He therefore deleted the reference to the summoner in line 1 and changed verbs from plural to singular (*sollind* 'shall' to *soll* in line 1 and *vermögend* 'are able to' to *vermöge* in line 5). He also changed the personal pronoun from plural *sy* 'they' to singular *er* 'he' in line 5 by crossing out the former and writing the latter in the margin. Since we interpret this as a single intervention (replacing *sy* with *er*), we group the `<add>` and `<del>` elements using a `<subst>` (substitution) element. Finally, the `<pb>` element (page break) marks the beginning of the next page of the original, page 51.

This example illustrates how features found in a given historical text can be encoded in TEI. Here only a small number of TEI elements is needed; however, it also shows that the exact encoding depends on the interpretation of the text and on the goals of the encoding, for example, the desired level of detail. For example, we marked the inital as being different from the text, but we did not

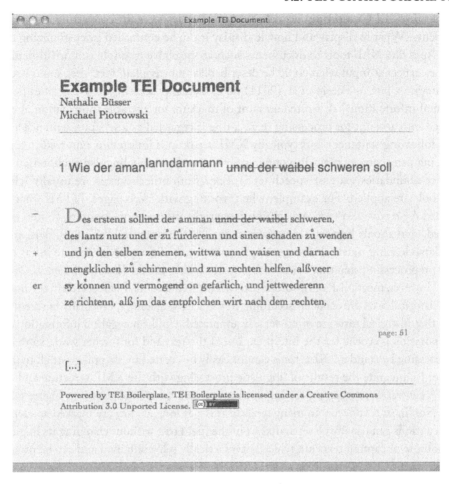

Figure 5.3: Example rendering of the TEI document shown in Figure 5.2(b) using TEI Boilerplate.

encode further details such as its size or style. We also chose not to tag the flourish at the bottom of the page. TEI defines a `<decoDesc>` element for describing decorations such as initials, borders, miniatures, etc. For some of our encoding decisions we relied on historical knowledge not contained in the text itself; this demonstrates that encoding of historical texts frequently requires experts in order to achieve consistent results.

A TEI-encoded text can be processed in numerous ways; the most obvious one is perhaps for display. Figure 5.3 shows one possible rendering of the document given in Figure 5.2(b) (and a minimal header, which is not shown) in a Web browser using TEI Boilerplate,[19] which uses XSLT and CSS (World Wide Web Consortium, 2010) stylesheets for transforming a TEI document for

---

[19]`http://teiboilerplate.org/` (accessed 2012-06-24)

display. The TEI Consortium also ships a set of stylesheets for converting and formatting TEI documents. What to display and how to display it can be controlled by customizing stylesheets.

Applying NLP tools to documents such as the above example is more difficult. Most NLP pipelines expect as input what could be described as "mostly plain text," i.e., input text may contain some markup, but, as Poesio et al. (2011) note, "actual processing (mostly) takes no advantage of structural information." A limited amount of markup, for example information about titles, may be taken into account for processing (e.g., a title is regarded as a separate sentence and not as part of the following sentence), but typically XML markup is ignored or removed in a preprocessing step. Linguistic corpora typically contain only text and possibly linguistic annotation (tokenization, sentence boundaries, part-of-speech, etc.) Texts from other sources are usually "cleaned" before NLP tools are applied. For example, when working with Web pages, HTML markup as well as so-called *boilerplate text* (e.g., navigation, copyright information, headers, footers), are generally removed, so that only linguistic material remains. With respect to Web pages, Bernardini et al. note that "data cleaning must take center stage, unlike in traditional NLP, where it has been seen as a minor preprocessing step that is not really worth talking about" (Bernardini et al., 2006, p. 19).

However, most NLP of historical texts occurs in the context of research in the humanities; thus, many historical texts are encoded according to the TEI Guidelines, especially in recent projects. This means that historical texts are often densely annotated. Unlike navigation information on Web pages, the annotation is crucial for the interpretation of the text and for further work, so that text suitable for processing by standard NLP tools cannot easily be created by stripping out all markup. The goal is rather to integrate the results of linguistic processing with the XML structure and annotation.

A central issue when processing documents such as the one shown in Figure 5.2(b) is nonlinearity. Nonlinear text occurs in many types of texts; as long as they are marked as such, footnotes or figure captions can usually be separated from the main text without changing its linguistic structure, and footnote or caption texts are typically syntactically self-contained and can be processed without the main text.[20]

Annotated historical texts, however, frequently contain nonlinearity in the main text itself. For example, the TEI document in Figure 5.2(b) actually contains (at least) two texts: the original version and the changed version created by the additions and deletions by scribe N1. Another example is the TEI `<choice>` element, which can be used to record phenomena like alternate readings, erroneous and corrected text, or original and normalized spellings. Listing 5.2 shows a short extract from an Early New High German text (from the digital edition of SSRQ_AR/AI 1, simplified), illustrating the use of `<choice>`: The manuscript reads *simer*, which was regularized by the editor "NB" to *sinner* 'his', which is the spelling also used in the last line of the sample.[21]

---

[20]This is not to say that footnote or caption texts are necessarily complete sentences—a footnote consisting only of a URL is not even a natural-language utterance—or that they make sense in isolation, but only that their syntactic structure does not depend on text outside the footnote or caption.

[21]The passage is part of an oath and states what will happen to anyone swearing a false oath. Approximate translation: "… and I shall be denied to see the face of our Lord Jesus Christ and his mother Maria and all his saints now and forever."

```
<p>[...] unnd ich sol ouch beroptt werden der /<pb ed="original"/>
  begirlichenn annschowung desß angesichtz unnsers herenn
  <persName ref="#IDX0574">Jeßu Criste</persName> unnd
  <choice>
    <orig>simer</orig>
    <reg resp="NB">sinner</reg>
  </choice>
  wirdigenn <persName ref="#IDX0779">mutter Maria</persName> unnd
  aller sinner hailgenn jemer unnd ewennklich.</p>
```

Listing 5.2: The TEI <choice> element allows annotators to record variants, here original spelling and correction. Example taken from the TEI-encoded version of SSRQ AR/AI 1.

The TEI Guidelines define and document standard mechanisms such as <choice> and <subst> for handling such phenomena. However, this does not reduce their inherent complexity and the resulting complexity for processing. While removing a footnote from a text will normally leave the main text intact, simply stripping the markup away from the text in Listing 5.2 will obviously yield an incorrect text containing *both* versions:

(1)   * ... Jeßu Criste unnd <u>simer sinner</u> wirdigenn mutter Maria ...

As noted above, what we have here are actually *two* texts:

(2)   a. ... Jeßu Criste unnd <u>simer</u> wirdigenn mutter Maria ...

      b. ... Jeßu Criste unnd <u>sinner</u> wirdigenn mutter Maria ...

Thus, in order to apply NLP tools to such a text, one has to decide *which* version one wants to process; note that there may be many more such cases, possibly involving different levels of certainty, or being otherwise qualified with an editorial status.

These issues usually do not occur with modern texts; if NLP tools handle XML input at all, they tend to treat it as linear text, possibly containing negligible markup. Consequently, there is currently virtually no support for NLP of complex TEI documents. It is possible, of course, to extract certain elements and their textual content using XSLT or XQuery and then run an NLP tool, for example, a part-of-speech (POS) tagger, on it. Similarly, reintegrating the annotation produced by the POS tagger into the original TEI document is not impossible (e.g., by tracking IDs and character positions), but requires a significant amount of work.

5.3   SUMMARY

In this chapter we discussed how historical texts can be represented in the digital medium and described two important standards: Unicode for encoding characters and the TEI Guidelines for encoding higher-level structures, complex annotations, and metadata. Together, these two standards provide a solid foundation for encoding and processing many types of historical texts and represent a significant advance over proprietary and ad-hoc solutions. Most new projects that are concerned with digital historical texts base their work on Unicode and TEI; however, many older resources, such as corpora (see Chapter 8), are still encoded in legacy formats and will often require conversion.

CHAPTER 6

Handling Spelling Variation

If we want to apply natural language processing and information retrieval methods to historical texts, we have to cope with the three issues discussed in Chapter 3:

1. spellings that differ from today's orthography (difference);

2. spellings that are highly variable and often inconsistent (variance); and

3. uncertainty, such as transcription artifacts and digitization errors.

In this chapter we discuss practical approaches for coping with the problems caused by these issues in NLP. We primarily focus on texts in historical varieties of *living* languages, since this is currently the most frequent application of NLP for historical texts. Texts in dead or extinct languages and scripts certainly pose additional challenges.

6.1   SPELLING CANONICALIZATION

How to deal with the issues of difference, variance, and uncertainty in spelling, when NLP normally works with texts in standardized orthography? The assessment of these issues depends on the application. For computational linguistics applications, such as tagging and parsing, the goal is usually to bring the historical language closer to the modern language in order to enable the use of the methods, tools, and resources available for the modern language. Thus, given a historical word form, we are interested in a corresponding modern word form. The modern word form is usually what Jurish (2010a) refers to as *canonical cognate*: an extant equivalent of a historical word that preserves the morphological root and the morphosyntactic features of the historical form. For example, the canonical cognate of the historical word form *folowynge* in Caxton's preface to *Eneydos* (see Figure 3.2) would be *following*. Historical words that have disappeared from the language do not have canonical cognates; for example, the Middle English word *swei* 'sound, noise' does not have a canonical cognate.

The process of mapping historical spellings to modern—canonical—spellings is usually referred to as *normalization* or *canonicalization*. In principle, neither of the terms implies that the canonical word form is necessarily a modern word form. For example, critical editions of Middle High German typically use a normalized spelling (the so-called *Normalmittelhochdeutsch*, introduced in the 19th century by the German philologist Karl Lachmann), which homogenizes the highly variable spelling of the original manuscripts and their copies (Paul, 2007, p. 17). In NLP, however, canonicalization and normalization usually imply a mapping to a modern form. *Spelling modernization* would possibly be a more precise term for this approach.

For information retrieval applications, the goal is typically to enable modern-language queries on collections of historical documents. In other words, given a modern word form in a query, we would like to (also) find the corresponding historical word forms in the documents. There are three potentially applicable basic IR approaches. First, this task can be considered a variant of the general IR technique of *query expansion* (see Manning et al., 2008, Chapter 9): just like a search engine may expand a query with related terms from a thesaurus, such as WordNet (Fellbaum, 1998), a modern query term may be expanded with historical spelling variants. Jurish (2012, p. 3) refers to query expansion in this context as "inverse canonicalization." In an IR system, this approach would typically be applied at query time.

Alternatively, spelling normalization may be implemented as a type of *term conflation*. Stemming is a typical method for term conflation that aims to map different inflected forms (e.g., singular and plural) to a single index term; spelling normalization could thus also be regarded as a type of term conflation that maps different spellings of a word to one canonical spelling. Term conflation is usually done at indexing time.

Finally, the task of finding historical forms using modern-language query terms could also be considered an application of *approximate matching*. Approximate matching is commonly used for making IR systems tolerant towards spelling mistakes and minor spelling variations, as they occur in modern texts (e.g., *color* vs. *colour*), so that one could think of applying the same technique to historical spelling variation. However, historical texts often contain more extensive spelling variation, so that the approximate matching typically will have to be "looser" to achieve the desired recall; queries may then inadvertently match irrelevant terms, resulting in a significant drop in retrieval precision.

As mentioned previously, spelling normalization and query expansion are related and can be considered the inverse of each other. In the first case, we need some function f that maps all elements of a set H of historical word forms to some modern word form w_m, for example:

$$\{\text{wirdet}, \text{wirt}, \text{wirdt}, \text{wird}\} \mapsto \text{wird}$$
$$\{\text{booke}, \text{boke}\} \mapsto \text{book}$$

In the second case, we need some function g that maps a modern word form w_m to a set H of historical word forms, i.e.:

$$\text{wird} \mapsto \{\text{wirdet}, \text{wirt}, \text{wirdt}, \text{wird}\}$$
$$\text{book} \mapsto \{\text{booke}, \text{boke}\}$$

Unfortunately, natural language is often more complex. One problem is that the relation of modern forms to historical forms is not $1 : n$ but rather $n : m$. For example, in English texts from the time of Shakespeare, the spelling *weeke* was used for the modern words *weak*, *week*, and *wick* (Craig and Whipp, 2010, p. 38).

6.2   EDIT DISTANCE

Since exact string matching is rarely possible or useful when working with historical texts, a frequent requirement is to determine whether two strings are *similar*. In the context of modern text, the same requirement arises in the context of spell-checking. For example, when a spell-checker encounters a word form not in its dictionary, it may want to find similar word forms to suggest a correction; in this case, *mann* would likely be considered similar to *man*, although the exact definition of similarity depends on the exact application. For example, when spell-checking text typed on a QWERTY keyboard, *where* and *qhere* would be considered similar, on the grounds that the Q and W keys are adjacent on the keyboard and only one replacement would be necessary to transform one string into the other. Phonetically, however, these two strings would not be considered similar.

Edit distance—also known as *Levenshtein distance*—(Levenshtein, 1966) is the most common method for determining the similarity of two strings. The edit distance $edit(x, y)$ between two strings x and y is the smallest number of editing operations required to transform x into y. The possible editing operations are: (1) *deletion* (delete one character); (2) *insertion* (insert one character); and (3) *substitution* (replace one character with another).

If we denote the edit distance between x and y by $edit(x, y)$, we can state some fundamental properties:

- $edit(x, y) = 0$ iff $x = y$, i.e., the edit distance of two identical strings is 0;

- $edit(x, y) = edit(y, x)$, i.e., the edit distance is symmetric; and

- $edit(x, z) \leq edit(x, y) + edit(y, z)$, i.e., the distance from x to z is at most as large as the sum of the distance from x to y and the distance from y to z. This is the so-called *triangle inequality*. As it holds for edit distance, it means that edit distance is a true metric (or distance function) in the mathematical sense.

For example, the edit distance between *berynge* and *bearing* is 3:

1. *berynge* → *bearynge* (insertion of *a*);

2. *bearynge* → *bearinge* (substitution of *y* with *i*);

3. *bearinge* → *bearing* (deletion of *e*).

One way to compute the edit distance is to use a table. Let $m = |x|$, $n = |y|$, and $m \leq n$. The table E is defined as

$$E[i, j] = edit(x[1 \ldots i], y[1 \ldots j])$$

Table 6.1: Table E for calculating the Levenshtein edit distance between *berynge* and *bearing*.

		b	e	a	r	i	n	g
	0	1	2	3	4	5	6	7
b	1	0	1	2	3	4	5	6
e	2	1	0	1	2	3	4	5
r	3	2	1	1	1	2	3	4
y	4	3	2	2	2	2	3	4
n	5	4	3	3	3	3	2	3
g	6	5	4	4	4	4	3	2
e	7	6	5	5	5	5	4	**3**

with $0 \leq i \leq m$ and $0 \leq j \leq n$. In other words, the table cell at the position $[i,j]$ contains the edit distance between the string x up to position i and the string y up to position j. The table cells of E are computed as follows:

$$E[0,j] = j$$
$$E[i,0] = i$$
$$E[i,j] = \min(E[i-1,j] + 1, E[i,j-1] + 1, E[i-1,j-1] + \delta(x[i], y[j])),$$

where

$$\delta(a, b) = \begin{cases} 0 & \text{if } a = b \\ 1 & \text{otherwise.} \end{cases}$$

This formula considers the operations of deletion, insertion, and substitution (in this order).

Table 6.1 shows E for the above example, where x = berynge and y = bearing. The cell $E[m, n]$ (i.e., $E[7, 7]$) contains the edit distance, namely 3, as we have determined above.

The implementation can be derived from the above formula in a straightforward way; it is a good example of dynamic programming. Note that all entries of the table E are computed, even though in the end we are only interested in $E[m, n]$. One possible optimization is thus to store only the last column (or row) in order to reduce the required memory. There are a number of more complex optimizations (see, e.g., Wu et al., 1990).

Different approaches for computing the edit distance are also possible; for example, it can also be formulated as a graph-theoretical problem and computed using Dijkstra's shortest path algorithm (see Crochemore and Rytter, 2002).

A number of variations of the basic Levenshtein edit distance are possible. For example, for handling spelling errors in typewritten texts, Damerau (1964) adds the *transposition* of two adjacent characters as a fourth edit operation. As Robertson and Willett (1992) point out, transposition errors are a characteristic of fast keyboarding and thus rarely occur in historical texts, which are usually hand-written or hand-typeset (i.e., using a typecase and a composing stick).[1] One may also assign different costs to the editing operations to penalize certain operations.

It is also possible to record the required editing operations. For example, Bollmann et al. (2011b) word-aligned the first edition of the Luther Bible with a modernized edition and then used the recorded edits to learn rules for transforming Early Modern German spellings into today's orthography.

Finding the longest common subsequence (LCS) between two strings is a problem closely related to edit distance and can also be used for approximate matching. A *subsequence* of a string is a sequence of characters that may occur at non-contiguous positions in the string but maintains the order the characters have in the original string. A *substring* can thus be seen as a restricted form of subsequence, in which all characters must be adjacent in the original string. For example, *books* is a subsequence of *bookys*, but not a substring. The LCS is the longest subsequence shared between two strings; for example the LCS of *latyn* and *latin* is *lat*. Note that these two strings have another, shorter, common subsequence, namely *n*.

Efficient algorithms for *all* cases of LCS are the subject of ongoing research. There are numerous approaches implementing it; see Bergroth et al. (2000) for an overview; newer approaches are described by Crochemore et al. (2002), Bergroth et al. (2003), Xiang et al. (2007), or Blum et al. (2009), to cite just a few.

The comparison of two files (e.g., what the Unix `diff` utility (Hunt and McIlroy, 1977) does) is another case of the LCS problem. In the context of historical texts, this application is relevant for comparing double-keyed texts (see Section 4.4).

Approximate string matching—also known as *string matching with errors* and *fuzzy string searching*—can be seen as an application of the edit distance problem: instead of determining the edit distance of two strings, the goal is to find a string y approximately matching the search string x, i.e., within a certain edit distance or allowing for k errors or differences. There are many different approaches to approximate matching; Navarro (2001) gives a good overview.

6.3 APPROACHES FOR HANDLING SPELLING VARIATION IN HISTORICAL TEXTS

All current canonicalization approaches essentially treat the problem of mapping historical forms to modern forms as an error correction problem, similar to spelling correction. Pollock (1982) introduces the distinction between *absolute* and *relative* methods for spelling correction. Absolute methods deduce the correction directly from the misspelling (e.g., by using a list of common misspellings), whereas relative methods use knowledge of correct forms (e.g., a dictionary) and approximate matching to find potential corrections. Whereas modern spell-checkers generally use a relative

---

[1] Transpositions may of course have been introduced during digitization.

approach (i.e., knowledge of correct words), both methods are used for canonicalization of historical texts.

6.3.1 ABSOLUTE APPROACHES TO CANONICALIZATION

A straightforward *absolute* approach to spelling canonicalization is to use special dictionaries that associate observed historical variants with modern word forms; the mapping is precise and can handle cases where the association is non-trivial, such as the mapping *thystorye* $\mapsto$ *the history* in Figure 3.2, or when no canonical cognate exists. The downside is that the construction of such dictionaries is time-consuming and their coverage is necessarily limited.

This approach was implemented in the first versions of the VARD tool (Rayson et al., 2005): it used a large, manually created list of variants (ca. 45,000 entries) with their modern equivalents for finding and replacing spelling variants in Early Modern English texts. Baron and Rayson (2009) report that this approach worked well for reducing the amount of spelling variation found in Early Modern English text; however, they found it "impossible to include all viable spelling variants in a pre-defined list due to the nature of Early Modern English producing an endless variety of potential forms" (Baron and Rayson, 2009, p. 4). As implemented by VARD, once a match was found, the replacement was made unconditionally, which may not be appropriate in all cases.

Besides the fully manual dictionary construction as used for VARD, different semiautomatic approaches are described in the literature. Craig and Whipp (2010) constructed a normalization lexicon for 17th-century English from the spelling variants listed in the *Oxford English Dictionary*; they extended the resulting lexicon by adding further spelling variants collected by matching short passages from Shakespeare plays in the spelling of their first edition with parallel passages in a Shakespeare edition using modernized spelling.

Gotscharek et al. (2011) semiautomatically constructed a lexicon of about 10,000 entries for IR on historical German-language documents, starting from a corpus of historical texts and then using approximate matching techniques to suggest potential modern cognates from a modern lexicon. The suggestions are then manually reviewed and, if necessary, corrected.

Giusti et al. (2007) automatically constructed a Historical Dictionary of Brazilian Portuguese (HDBP) from a corpus containing texts from the 16th to the 19th century. A clustering algorithm generated the lexicon entries, using the most frequent term in the cluster as the canonical form. Brisaboa et al. (2003) semiautomatically extracted a diachronic lexicon for Galician from a corpus using a rule-based stemmer (Brisaboa et al., 2002). The last two approaches differ from those above in that the "modern" form is not necessarily an actual, linguistically motivated word, but may be an artificially constructed stem.

When looking at historical text such as the sample in Figure 3.2, one notes that many of the differences with modern orthography are more or less regular. Examples are the use of *-yng* or *-ynge* for modern *-ing* (*sittyng, berynge, folowying*), the use of *u* for modern *v* inside of words, and the use of *v* for modern *u* at the beginning of words.[2]

---

[2]The modern distinctions between *u* and *v* (and *i* and *j*) were only established later, in English by about 1630.

Mapping rules from historical to modern spellings are an obvious alternative to static dictionaries. This approach has been used by Gotscharek et al. (2009b) to support the semiautomatically constructed dictionaries of actually observed variants (witnessed dictionaries) for historical German; consequently, they refer to the mapping rules as *hypothetical dictionaries*.

The RSNSR project (rule-based search in text databases with nonstandard orthography) (Pilz et al., 2006; Pilz, 2009) exclusively relied on rules to support IR on historical German documents. As a query expansion approach is used, the rules are applied to modern German query terms to generate potential historical spellings, for example, ei $\mapsto$ {ei, ey, ai, ay}. These rules were constructed semiautomatically from unannotated corpora (Ernst-Gerlach and Fuhr, 2010).

Bollmann et al. (2011b) derive mapping rules for Early New High German from a word-aligned parallel corpus containing the 1545 version of the Luther Bible[3] and a modernized version (possibly from 1892) of the same text. They then align sentences (using the Gargantua[4] toolkit (Braune and Fraser, 2010)) and word forms (using Giza++[5] (Och and Ney, 2003)) of both versions, resulting in a corpus of 550,000 aligned pairs of words or phrases.

Bollmann et al. then use a variant of the Levenshtein edit distance algorithm (see Section 6.2), which records the edit operations (deletion, insertion, substitution) required to transform the old form into the new form. They also record the left and right context for each transformation. Two examples given in Bollmann et al. (2011b, p. 37) are:

1. $\epsilon \rightarrow h / j \_ r$

2. $v \rightarrow u / \# \_ n$

That is, *h* is inserted between *j* and *r*, and *v* is replaced by *u* between the left word boundary (#) and *n*. Since previous edits may have changed the left context, the characters in the left context come from the target word, whereas the right context contains the unmodified rest of the original word form.

The regular Levenshtein algorithm only calculates the edit distance, i.e., the minimum number of edit operations required to transform one string into another; however, there may be several ways to do the transformation, each with the same number of edits. For example, *jrem* could be transformed into *ihrem* 'their' either by replacing *j* with *i* and then inserting an *h*, or by prepending an *i* and then substituting *j* with *h*. Bollmann et al. therefore require further operations for selecting rules; they also merge several adjacent rules into rules for longer sequences.

The normalization process is essentially the same in reverse. Rules are applied word by word. Since typically several rules are applicable at every position, a ranking is required to select the "best" rule. The first approach evaluated by Bollmann et al. is to always select the most frequent rule. However, the selection of a rule determines which rules can be selected later on; thus, the selection of the most frequent rule at position p_0 may force the application of a low-frequency (i.e., unlikely) rule

---

[3]The Luther Bible is the German Bible translation by Martin Luther; the New Testament was published in 1522, the complete Bible (Old and New Testaments and Apocrypha) in 1534.

[4]http://sourceforge.net/projects/gargantua (accessed 2012-06-06)

[5]http://code.google.com/p/giza-pp/ (accessed 2012-06-06)

at position p_n and eventually result in an incorrect normalization. A second approach thus assigns a probability score to each generated variant. The probability of a rule is defined as its frequency (as generated from the parallel texts) divided by the sum of all rule frequencies. The probability of a complete word form is then calculated from the probabilities of the rules that generated it. In a final step, the generated word form is checked against a dictionary of modern word forms.

Bollmann et al. report good evaluation results on their test corpus, a portion of the Luther Bible not used for training. Since about 65% of the word forms are identical in the original text and the modernized text, a useful method must achieve at least this level of correctness. Using any of the ranking methods results in match ratios above 83%; adding dictionary lookup raises the accuracy to about 91%.

However, Bollmann et al. (2011a) report that applying these rules to a different text corpus, a collection of different versions of the text *Interrogatio Sancti Anselmi de Passione Domini* from the 14th to the 16th century, results in much lower performance, about 42% matching token after normalization, which is probably a significant improvement over the baseline of 32%, but a rather disappointing result in general. As the baseline is low itself, this shows the difficulty of the task. Since the texts are more diverse in this corpus (written by different authors over a period of 200 years), the major problem is that the rule-based approach cannot handle spelling variation not encountered in the training corpus. This problem could be partly resolved, the authors suggest, by using more sophisticated similarity measures, such as phonetic or graphemic similarity. More generally, however, the problems point to the limitations of spelling canonicalization methods, which we will discuss further in Section 6.5.

6.3.2   RELATIVE APPROACHES TO CANONICALIZATION

Robertson and Willett (1993) divide relative correction methods into three main classes: *reverse-error* methods, phonetic and non-phonetic *coding* methods, and *string similarity* methods.

The reverse-error approach was first proposed by Damerau (1964) for spelling correction of modern text. The basic idea of the original approach is as follows. If a word form is encountered in the text that is not in the dictionary, the word form is systematically tested for insertion of a character, deletion of a character, substitution of a character, or transposition of two adjacent characters; if a dictionary match is obtained by "reversing" one of these errors, this is assumed to be the correct spelling.[6] Damerau only considered misspellings with a single error, on the basis of his finding that this accounts for 80% of actual spelling errors. Note that the error types are the edit operations of the Levenshtein edit distance metric—with the addition of transposition—so testing for errors essentially means determining the edit distance between the text word form and a dictionary entry; a distance of 1 then means that the text word form is a misspelling of the corresponding dictionary entry. While conceptually simple, the method is relatively expensive—as many comparisons have to be made—and is not applicable if multiple errors occur in a word form. As far as we know, the reverse-error approach has not been used for normalizing historical text.

---

[6]This may of course yield several dictionary matches.

Coding approaches are based on the idea of replacing a word form with a code that abstracts from spelling details, so that a misspelling and the correct spelling would be assigned the same code, so that they can be matched. The most widely known coding method is *Soundex*, originally devised for matching American surnames. It is a phonetic coding method based on conflating groups of characters that are pronounced similarly in American English; the code always consists of the initial letter of the name followed by three digits. For example, *Smith*, *Smyth*, *Smythe*, and *Schmidt* all receive the code S530. There exist many variants of Soundex, as well as improved methods (e.g., Phonix (Gadd, 1988), Metaphone) and similar methods for other languages (e.g., the Kölner Phonetik for German). The Double Metaphone algorithm (Philips, 2000) is an improved version of Metaphone by the developer of Metaphone; Metaphone and Double Metaphone are not only used for matching names, but are also widely employed in spell-checkers, for example, Aspell.[7]

Phonetic algorithms have also been used for normalizing and retrieving historical text. Somewhat related to phonetic coding are approaches that use the grapheme-to-phoneme converter (GTP) of a text-to-speech (TTS) system to determine the pronunciation of historical word forms, which can then matched to the pronunciation of modern word forms. A prerequisite for applying both methods is that the phonetic coding algorithm or the GTP is able to produce a coding or a phonetic representation of the historical spelling that matches the coding or representation of the modern spelling. This is possible when the historical spelling uses the same basic letter-sound correspondences as the modern orthography and the two differ primarily in their distribution. For example, in 19th-century German one often finds spellings such as *Brod* for modern *Brot* 'bread', *spaziren* for modern *spazieren* 'to stroll', or *Thor* for modern *Tor* 'gate'. However, the same letter-sound correspondences (<d> for /t/, <ir> for /iːr/, and <th> for /t/) still exist in modern German orthography, for example, in the words *Tod* 'death', *mir* 'me', and *Thron* 'throne'. Thus, a GTP for modern German would map the 19th-century spellings to the same phonetic representations as the modern spellings, i.e., /broːt/, /ʃpatsiːrən/, and /toɐ/; given a modern German dictionary with pronunciation information, the phonetic representation could then be used to retrieve the modern spelling. In an actual system one would clearly also have to account for inflection, derivation, and compounding. One could also use a specialized algorithm for phonetic alignment as described by Kondrak (2003) to match not only identical but similar pronunciations as well.

Rogers and Willett (1991) and Robertson and Willett (1993) evaluate several phonetic coding methods on historical English texts; for information retrieval on a collection of 17th-century letters,[8] Rogers and Willett develop a variant of the Phonix method optimized for historical spellings rather than for modern misspellings. Koolen et al. (2006) use the GTP of the Nextens TTS for Dutch to generate phonetic representations of historical word forms, and Jurish (2008) adapts the German phonetization function of the Festival TTS system for canonicalizing historical German text.

String-similarity methods are based on a metric quantifying the similarity between two strings, for example, between a potential spelling error and a dictionary entry or between a historical word

---

[7]`http://aspell.net/metaphone/` (accessed 2012-06-06)
[8]The *Hartlib Papers*, the collected papers and correspondence of Samuel Hartlib (ca. 1600–1662), a 17th-century polymath.

form and a modern word form. We have already described the most widely known and used string similarity metric in Section 6.2: the *Levenshtein edit distance*. Further well-known methods are the Wagner-Fischer (Wagner and Fischer, 1974) and Needleman-Wunsch algorithms (Needleman and Wunsch, 1970); one example of the use of the Needleman-Wunsch algorithm in the context of NLP for historical text can be found in Kestemont et al. (2010). Edit distance can be generalized and regarded as a metric with set of edit operations with associated costs. For example, the classic Levenshtein distance uses the operation deletion, insertion, substitution; Damerau (1964) added transposition as another operation, whereas LCS only permits insertion and deletion, but not substitution of characters; and the Hamming distance is even more restricted in that it only has substitution and thus only applies to strings of the same length. The notion of edit distance can be further generalized by also assigning a cost depending on the position where an edit operation is applied (as, e.g., the Smith-Waterman algorithm (Smith and Waterman, 1981)) or depending on the characters that are involved in the operation (e.g., replacing d with t could be cheaper than replacing it with, say, g).

A further approach to determining string similarity is to use *n-grams*. *N*-grams are widely used in NLP for a variety of applications; for determining the similarity of two strings, *n*-grams (typically with $n = 2$ or $n = 3$) are generated for both of them, and their similarity is essentially based on the number of *n*-grams they have in common. Another way to put it is to say that both strings are represented by vectors of *n*-grams and to define similarity as, for example, the cosine between these two vectors.[9]

In the context of historical texts, Robertson and Willett (1992) use *n*-grams for retrieval of English texts from the 16th, 17th, and 18th centuries. The same approach was used by O'Rourke et al. (1996) for Medieval French text from the 12th century.

Skip-grams or *s-grams* (Pirkola et al., 2002; Järvelin et al., 2007) are a generalization of *n*-grams, which include character sequences that do not necessarily consist of adjacent characters, but where k intervening characters are skipped.

Skip-grams are being used in NLP to overcome data sparsity (e.g., Guthrie et al., 2006) and to search for syntactic patterns (e.g., Stehouwer and van Zaanen, 2010), and in information retrieval for approximate matching in tasks such as cross-language information retrieval (CLIR) (e.g., Keskustalo et al., 2003) and named entity recognition (e.g., Piskorski et al., 2009). Especially the latter tasks share challenges with tasks in NLP for historical languages; however, as far as we know, skip-grams have not yet been used for spelling normalization or retrieval of historical text.

For an overview of methods for approximate matching, see Navarro (2001); to our knowledge, most of these methods have not yet been applied to historical texts.

6.4 DETECTING AND CORRECTING OCR ERRORS

Most approaches for spelling normalization combine detection and normalization—like spell-checkers today usually combine the detection of possible errors and the presentation of potential

---

[9]If A is the alphabet, the dimensionality of the vector space is $|A|^n$.

corrections. In some applications, however, it makes sense to treat them separately. In the context of OCR errors in historical texts, it may not be possible to reliably determine the correction automatically. Furthermore, errors in OCR-processed text may indicate problems with scanning or with OCR parameters, such as a paper jam or an incorrect language setting.

This section describes two approaches that detect potential errors in texts without the need for linguistic resources. Whereas the normalization techniques described above mainly aim to address the issues of spelling difference and variance, these approaches deal with issues of spelling uncertainty.

6.4.1   TEXT-INDUCED CORPUS CLEAN-UP

Reynaert (2005) describes extensive work on detecting and correcting OCR errors (or typos) in large corpora on the basis of the data contained in the corpus itself, i.e., without external dictionaries, error models, or prior training, as required by most prior approaches, such as that by Kolak et al. (2003), which uses finite state-models. The conceptual approach and the implementation are called *text-induced corpus clean-up* (TICCL). In principle, TICCL can be used to detect any kind of lexical variation, whether it is due to OCR errors, typing errors, historical spelling, or morphological variation. It has been used in the large-scale digitization effort of the National Library of the Netherlands on a variety of modern and historical text collections (Reynaert, 2008).

The original implementation of TICCL sequentially processes the word forms of the target corpus, at each step focusing on one isolated word (the *focus word*), in a fashion similar to a regular spell-checker. An alternative approach, referred to as *character confusion-based approach*, was described by Reynaert (2011). Both approaches are based on an approximate matching method called *anagram hashing*.

Anagram hashing is based on a hashing function that assigns the same hash key to all strings that consist of the same set of characters, regardless of their order. For example, the strings *act* and *cat* (as well as the four other permutations) would all be assigned the same hash key. In the TICCL implementation, the function for calculating the hash key h for a string w is defined as

$$h(w) = \sum_{i=1}^{|w|} c_i^k \, ,$$

where c_i is the code point of the character at position i in the string w, and k is a constant; in the current implementation of TICCL, $k = 5$ (this value was empirically determined to yield the best results). The hash key for *act* and its anagrams would thus be $97^5 + 99^5 + 116^5 = 39,100,657,332$. Unlike typical hash functions, which aim to produce as few collisions as possible, TICCL's hash function is designed to produce the same hash key for input strings that only differ in their order of characters. Anagram hashing can thus be regarded as a type of *locality-sensitive hashing* (Gionis et al., 1999; Paulevé et al., 2010).

In the focus-word approach, the first step is to build an anagram hash containing all the word forms of the target corpus, possibly augmented by a dictionary of known correct word forms. TICCL then examines each token in the corpus and retrieves potential variants (within some predefined edit distance d) of the current focus word from the anagram hash. Due to the nature of the anagram keys, the edit operations of deletion, insertion, and substitution can be realized by adding or subtracting the key values of individual characters; for example:

$$h(\text{act}) - h(\text{c}) = h(\text{at}) \qquad \text{Deletion}$$
$$h(\text{act}) + h(\text{t}) = h(\text{tact}) \qquad \text{Insertion}$$
$$h(\text{act}) - h(\text{t}) + h(\text{t}) = h(\text{car}) \qquad \text{Substitution}$$
$$h(\text{act}) - h(\text{t}) + h(\text{n}) + h(\text{s}) = h(\text{cans}) \qquad \text{Multiple substitutions (also matches } scan\text{)}$$

In this way, word forms similar to a focus word can be found in the vocabulary of the corpus.

The character confusion-based approach starts with the alphabet A of the corpus and calculates the anagram keys for all possible combinations of length d (the desired maximum edit distance) of the characters in A; then, all possible additions, deletions, and substitutions are performed. For $d = 2$ and $|A| = 31$, this results in 123,752 unique values, which represent all possible minimal confusions for these values of A and d. In the next step, the anagram hash for the corpus (constructed as in the focus-word approach) is queried for pairs of keys that differ by the values of the minimal confusions computed before.

Both approaches yield *confusion sets*, i.e., sets of tokens for which the anagram keys differ by some amount. However, since the anagram keys ignore the order of characters, the actual word form surfaces may be very different. Therefore the edit distance between the members of confusion sets is calculated, and all members for which the edit distance exceeds d are discarded. Various other types of filtering are performed on the output (which we will not discuss here) to obtain sets of likely word pairs, which represent potential errors or spelling variants. Additional resources (e.g., dictionaries or other information on correct or canonical forms) may be used to further narrow down the output to only the pairs with the highest probabilities.

Reynaert (2011) evaluate TICCL on a corpus of OCR-processed modern texts, the *Staten-Generaal Digitaal* [10] (the digitized proceedings of the Dutch parliament) for 1989–1995 and a corpus of OCR-processed historical Dutch newspaper articles (*Het Volk*) from 1918. [11] The OCR quality of the newspaper corpus was much lower, and the texts are also in an older orthography. Reynaert constructed gold standards for each corpus by exhaustively gathering all variants for 20 word forms in the *Staten-Generaal Digitaal* corpus and for 17 word forms in the *Het Volk* corpus. For example, 56 variants (mostly OCR errors) were found for the word *belastingen* 'taxes' in the *Staten-Generaal Digitaal* corpus, and 1468 variants (also mostly OCR errors) were found for the word *regeering* 'government' were identified in the *Het Volk* corpus.

The evaluation was done for isolated word forms, with $d = 2$, on the n best ranked correction candidates returned by the system. The results are summarized in table 6.2. The tests were with both the focus word-based approach and the character confusion-based approach; the results were almost

[10] http://statengeneraaldigitaal.nl/ (accessed 2012-07-17)
[11] http://kranten.kb.nl/ (accessed 2012-07-17)

Table 6.2: TICCL (character confusion-based approach) performance results (*n*-best ranking scores) on types (summarized from Reynaert, 2011). SGD: Staten-Generaal Digitaal; R: recall, P: precision, F: F-measure.

Level rank	SGD 1989–1995			Het Volk 1918		
	R	P	F	R	P	F
1	0.923	0.956	0.939	0.937	0.929	0.933
2	0.963	0.949	0.956	0.957	0.928	0.942
3	0.963	0.947	0.955	0.961	0.924	0.942
5/10	0.963	0.947	0.955	0.963	0.923	0.942

identical, but the latter approach proved to be an order of magnitude faster. Here we only show the results reported for the character confusion-based approach.

The performance scores indicate that the system was able to successfully identify and remove a large portion of the spelling variation caused by OCR errors. It is interesting to see that the evaluation results for the historical corpus are comparable to those obtained for the modern corpus, i.e., the system was equally effective on the much more difficult historical corpus. This also shows that the performance of the TICCL approach is indeed largely independent of language and genre.

6.4.2   ANOMALOUS TEXT DETECTION

In large-scale digitization projects the material may vary widely with respect to age, paper and print quality, language, domain, etc., and when large volumes are scanned, mechanical and operator errors will also occur. OCR quality is consequently likely to vary as well. In such a scenario one may not want to try to automatically correct the OCR output but rather identify text regions that are anomalous and thus suspicious. Once identified, one can then inspect these regions and decide how to best treat them, for example by rescanning the corresponding pages with adjusted parameters or by manually correcting the page segmentation (e.g., when images were erroneously recognized as text), or whether manual correction of the text is necessary.

Popat (2009) describes a technique for detecting anomalous text segments, which was developed in the context of the Google Books digitization project. The approach is based on an adaptive mixture of character-level *n*-gram language models; if available, the position of the text on the original page is also taken into account, but the detector is independent of a particular OCR engine. Popat evaluated the performance of the approach on text samples from Google Books in 32 languages against human raters, who were asked whether the text would be appropriate for display in an e-book, and against dictionary-based and heuristics-based approaches (Taghva et al., 2001; Kulp and Kontostathis, 2007). Two dictionary-based methods were implemented; in the first, a text passage is scored down by the fraction of out-of-vocabulary terms it contains; in the second, a passage is scored down by the total edit distance of its constituent terms to dictionary entries (normalized by passage length). The evaluation found that Popat's approach performed well for a wide variety of languages, and its scores appeared to correlate well with the human rankings. The performance of the dictionary-based approaches was generally somewhat lower, but they worked better than expected, even for morphologically rich languages. However, Popat's approach has the additional advantages that one does not have to specify the language of a text, and that it does not require language-specific tokenization, segmentation, or decompounding.

6.5   LIMITS OF SPELLING CANONICALIZATION

The effectiveness of all canonicalization approaches described in this chapter depends on the "distance" between the historical and the modern language variants, i.e., the extent of the differences in spelling and morphology. It thus depends on the language and the particular collection; the results are generally better for more recent texts. For example, the results reported for German by Ernst-Gerlach and Fuhr (2010) show a marked improvement in precision from the 16th to the 17th and then to the 18th century.

Since virtually all studies pertain to specific text collections, it is not surprising to find contradictory results in the literature; for example, while Koolen et al. (2006) (for Dutch) and Jurish (2008) (for German) successfully use grapheme-to-phoneme converters of text-to-speech systems, Pilz et al. (2006, p. 5) state that such a system "will fail when faced with historical, and therefore, untrained variants."

The text collections to which canonicalization has been applied so far also tend to be relatively homogeneous (for historical texts), as they primarily or exclusively contain *printed* texts; for example, Jurish notes that he would like to verify his results "using larger and less homogeneous corpora than the test corpus used here" (Jurish, 2010b, p. 37), referring to the *Deutsches Textarchiv*,[12] which consists of printed German texts from 1780–1900. When looking at a German book from the 18th century, readers today will find a number of differences in spelling, vocabulary, and syntax, and—when looking at books from different publishers—variation in spelling. However, comparing a printed text to a manuscript from the same period reveals that the degree of standardization in printed texts is much higher than in manuscript texts, as we discussed in section 3.2.2. This means that even for text collections containing only texts from a limited period, spelling canonicalization must be considered on a text by text basis.

A general problem for all canonicalization techniques is that a given historical spelling may correspond to several modern words, as discussed in Chapter 3. Craig and Whipp (2010) give the English example of the word *prey* in Shakespeare, which may either correspond to *prey* or to *pray* in modern spelling. If the wrong mapping is chosen, canonicalization may add errors to the text. Jurish (2010b) observes that advanced methods—such as phonetic matching—offer good recall, but, due to this problem, suffer from low precision. To address this problem, he introduces a method for disambiguating word-level canonicalization hypotheses by using sentence context.

---

[12]http://www.deutschestextarchiv.de/ (accessed 2012-06-06)

A further problem aggravating spelling canonicalization—and an issue to be addressed separately—is that it operates on the surface of lexical items but does not consider their semantics. However, even when historical words have extant cognates, they may have undergone considerable meaning shifts.

For example, in a collection of historical German texts, a query for *Frau* 'woman' may be expanded (using one of the approaches described above) to include historical spelling variants such as *frauw, fraw, frŭo, frouw, frāw, froŏw*, or *vrau*. If we assume that matching documents are in the collection, this will indeed return results. However, these documents may not be relevant for the user's information need, as historically *Frau* referred only to noblewomen; the historically equivalent word would be *Weib* (spelled, *wib, wip*, etc.), which later acquired a pejorative meaning.

Another, slightly different case is *Freund*, which today exclusively means 'friend' (in the sense of a companion), but which was a synonym for *Verwandter* 'relative' until the 17th or 18th century. Search results for a query of *Freund* will thus not match the expectations of the user—whereas a query for *Verwandter* will return only a small portion of the relevant results. These problems obviously cannot be solved by surface-level approaches; more semantic knowledge would be required.

6.6   SUMMARY

Back in 1970, Froger concisely summarized the problems encountered when digitizing historical texts (on punched cards at that time): "C'est la question de l'orthographe qui est la plus embarrassante."[13] (Froger, 1970, p. 212).

The highly variable spelling found in many historical texts has remained one of the most troublesome issues for NLP. We have seen in this chapter that there are a variety of approaches for dealing with the issues of spelling, but there is no general solution. The right approach always depends on the properties of the text and on the goals one is trying to reach. The needs of laypersons searching a collection of 19th-century documents clearly differ from those of a historical linguist studying the use of pronouns in 9th-century texts. Until now, NLP research has primarily focused on mapping relatively recent historical spellings to modern orthography. This is useful for applying NLP tools designed for modern languages and for information retrieval targeting non-expert users. Mapping of variant spellings to a historical canonical form (possibly a hypothetical normalized form, as used by historical dictionaries) is still mostly done manually.

The comparison of different approaches for spelling canonicalization indicates that the problem is far from being generally solved. Canonicalization (or its inversion for query expansion) can improve retrieval effectiveness for text collections that are relatively homogeneous and not too old, so that the historical language is relatively close to modern language. However, current approaches for spelling normalization cannot account for lexical and semantic changes; different approaches will be needed to cope with older texts and diachronic text collections. Canonicalization can thus be useful for particular collections, but it is not a general solution for historical texts.

---

[13]"The question of spelling is the most troublesome." (My translation.)

In addition to the references given in this chapter, there are a number of papers comparing different approaches for handling spelling variants in historical German: Kempken et al. (2006) compare different distance measures for historical spelling variants; Hauser et al. (2007) compare various matching strategies for relating modern language keywords with old variants. Gotscharek et al. (2009a) also evaluate different approaches and suggest combining special dictionaries and matching procedures to achieve better results. Most recently, Jurish (2010a) compares three different methods for canonicalization of historical German text, including a new method based on a domain-specific rewrite transducer.

CHAPTER 7

NLP Tools for Historical Languages

This chapter gives an overview of NLP tools for historical languages. The goal is not to give an exhaustive listing of available tools, but rather to illustrate the variety of approaches that may be used for creating NLP tools for historical languages.

In general, historical languages can be considered *less-resourced languages*, i.e., languages for which few or no NLP resources and tools are available. Minority languages, such as Basque, Sami, or Welsh, are typical examples of less-resourced languages, but this designation does not only apply to minority languages: Thai, Hindi, or Bahasa Indonesia have very large communities of speakers but there is nevertheless a lack of NLP resources for these languages. However, statistical, data-driven approaches to NLP clearly are more suitable for larger languages with a high volume of text production; statistical machine translation also requires that a sufficient amount of text is translated from a language or into it (see Joscelyne, 2010). In historical languages, typically no texts are being produced any more and only relatively few texts may be available at all. Modern less-resourced languages and historical languages thus have many issues in common.

Many NLP approaches for historical stages of extant languages (say, Old Czech or Middle English) therefore often try take advantage of the NLP resources and tools available for the living language, typically by first applying some sort of spelling canonicalization, as discussed in Chapter 6.[1]

Krauwer (1998) formulates the requirement for each language to develop a *basic language resource toolkit* (BLARK), defining it as "the minimal set of language resources that is necessary to do any precompetitive research and education at all" (Krauwer, 2003, p. 11). A BLARK is not a fixed set of tools and resources, but its composition is considered to be dependent on a particular language. As potential parts of a BLARK, Krauwer (2003) lists resources and tools such as written and spoken language corpora, monolingual and bilingual dictionaries, terminology collections, grammars, taggers, morphological analyzers, parsers, speech recognizers, text-to-speech systems, and annotation standards and tools. This list illustrates the language-dependent nature of BLARKs. Resources and tools for processing spoken language are clearly irrelevant for historical languages, as are terminological resources. On the other hand, historical languages typically require tools for spelling canonicalization (see Chapter 6).

---

[1]The use of a *pivot language* for bootstrapping resources for less-resourced modern languages (e.g., Tsunakawa et al., 2008; Lardilleux et al., 2010) could be—in some respects—considered a comparable approach.

Currently, most historical (and many living) languages do not have a BLARK. Most NLP for historical languages is carried out in specific projects, and there are few coordinated attempts to create open, reusable tools and resources. However, it is important to note that this situation is not due to a lack of cooperation between researchers, but rather due to inherent properties of historical languages, some of which we discussed in Chapter 1. For example, Early New High German is not a language in the modern sense: Since supraregional standards did not exist, the language (let alone the spelling) of texts from the same period may differ widely.

Latin may be considered as an exception to the rule. While it is still a less-resourced language, the long linguistic tradition, the existence of a "standard" orthography,[2] a canon of texts, etc. are factors that do not pertain from most other historical languages[3], and these have certainly assisted the work on language resources for Latin (see Passarotti, 2010a).

Passarotti (2010a) sketches a "BLARK-like set" for Latin, which could probably be used as a starting point for most historical languages. Under the heading "Data" he lists the following resources as requirements:

- an unannotated corpus of text;
- a syntactically annotated corpus of text (treebank);
- a monolingual lexicon (valency lexicon); and
- a semantically and pragmatically annotated corpus of text.

Under the heading "Modules" he lists the following tools as requirements:

- text preprocessing (tokenization and named entity recognition);
- lemmatization: morphological analysis and morpho-syntactic disambiguation (POS taggers);
- syntactic analysis: parsers and shallow parsing;
- anaphora resolution; and
- semantic and pragmatic analysis.

As the most urgently needed components, Passarotti identifies POS taggers and parsers, a treebank, a valency lexicon, and, as supporting tools, annotation and retrieval tools.

In the following sections we will have a look at various approaches for creating NLP tools for historical languages.

7.1   PART-OF-SPEECH TAGGING

Part-of-speech (POS) taggers annotate the word forms of a text with part-of-speech and lemma information. Since many NLP applications critically depend on these pieces of information, POS

---

[2]This is not to say that all Latin texts were (originally) written in this orthography. However, even for Medieval Latin the spelling variation is much smaller than for the vernacular languages of this time, and the existence of an agreed-upon orthography makes spelling canonicalization much easier, as there exists a point of reference.
[3]With the possible exception of other classical languages, such as Ancient Greek or Quranic Arabic.

taggers are generally considered to belong to the basic infrastructure required for NLP. Most modern POS taggers are statistical taggers, trained on annotated corpora; for a description of the theoretical background see, for example, Manning and Schütze (1999); for a practical introduction see, for example, Wilcock (2009). There are a number of conceivable approaches for creating a tagger for a historical language:

1. One can create a tagger "from scratch" by manually or semiautomatically annotating a corpus of that language and training the tagger on it. For example, the TreeTagger parameter files for Latin[4] were created from manually annotated corpora from the PROIEL project, the Perseus Latin dependency treebank, and *Index Thomisticus Treebank* (see Section 8.8). In a series of experiments Dipper (2010) train the TreeTagger on various subcorpora of the Reference Corpus Middle High German (see Section 8.6).

2. Another conceptually straightforward approach is to extend the coverage of a tagger designed for a modern language to a historical variety by expanding the lexicon with historical forms; this approach is used by Sánchez-Marco et al. (2011) for Spanish.

3. Instead of starting from scratch, one can use a modern tagger on a historical text, manually correct the errors, and then retrain the tagger on the corrected output.

4. In a preprocessing step, one can also first "modernize" the spelling of the historical texts to more closely match the modern spelling and then use a tagger trained for the modern language stage. This approach is used quite often, for example, by Scheible et al. (2011a) for Early Modern German, by Rayson et al. (2007) for Early Modern English, and by Hana et al. (2011) for Old Czech.

5. One can also take the inverse approach and "age" a modern annotated corpus, so that its spelling and possibly other features more closely resemble the historical target language, and then retrain a tagger on the "aged" corpus; Hana et al. (2011) explore this approach for Old Czech.

6. Finally, one can bootstrap a POS tagger for a historical language by aligning historical and modern texts and then project the tags assigned to the modern text to the historical text. For example, Moon and Baldridge (2007) align parallel Biblical texts in modern English and Middle English, project the tags from the modern English version to the Middle English version, and then train a tagger on the Middle English text.

The applicability of each approach clearly depends on the availability of resources—historical corpora, modern corpora, a POS tagger for the modern language, etc.—and the properties of the historical target language, such as its linguistic distance from the modern language—and whether there is a modern variety of the language at all—and the consistency of the spelling. In some cases, a combination of these approaches may also be possible.

---

[4]http://www.ims.uni-stuttgart.de/projekte/corplex/TreeTagger/ (accessed 2012-06-06)

If the spelling of the historical language is inconsistent and highly variable, this also hinders POS tagging; we discuss approaches for coping with spelling variation in Chapter 6. In the rest of this section, we will discuss some of the approaches listed above in some more detail and give examples from the literature.

A brief note on the evaluation measures reported in this chapter. For most systems described below we only report *accuracy*. Accuracy, i.e., the proportion of correct results (true positives and true negatives), is an intuitive measure, but it has a number of disadvantages compared to *precision*, *recall*, and the *F measure* (the weighted harmonic mean of precision and recall). First, accuracy is not very sensitive to the (typically relatively small) numbers of true positives, false positives, and false negatives, which means that by not selecting (or labeling, etc.) anything, a system can achieve very high accuracy. Precision and recall, however, do take the numbers of true positives, false positives, and false negatives into account. Second, accuracy is only sensitive to the number of errors, whereas the *F* measure is higher for results with more true positives, which is often desirable. Third, using precision and recall allows one to weigh false negatives and false positives differently rather than lumping them together as "errors" (for more details, see Manning and Schütze, 1999, pp. 267–271). However, many of the publications cited below only report accuracy rates, so we could only quote precision and recall for some, but not all, systems. Furthermore, we are discussing systems for very different languages evaluated on very different corpora, and with historical languages, the notion of "correctness" is much less clearly defined than for modern languages. Thus, unlike the situation in a shared task, the performance figures reported for the different systems described below should not be assumed to be directly comparable.

7.1.1   CREATING A POS TAGGER FROM SCRATCH

Creating a POS tagger "from scratch" is probably the most straightforward approach. First, it is the approach one would use for creating a POS tagger for a modern language when there are no pre-existing resources available, and second, it is essentially clear what needs to be done. This does not necessarily mean that it is easy, though.

First, a suitable and sufficiently large training corpus is required. If the corpus has already been tagged, it can be used (more or less) directly to train a tagger—but this is rather the exception than the rule for historical languages. As a rule of thumb, a tagged corpus of at least 30,000 word forms is required for training a POS tagger.

If a tagged corpus is not available, it has to be constructed, which means that texts need to be acquired, a tagset has to be defined, and the texts must then be tagged. An incremental approach can be used for training a POS tagger. At first, only a relatively small amount of text is tagged manually for the initial training of the tagger. The tagger is then run on a larger amount of text, and the assigned tags are corrected manually. These tagged texts are then added to the training corpus, and the tagger is retrained on this larger corpus. This process can be repeated until the performance level of the tagger is satisfactory.

The approach described above is *supervised*, as it starts from manually annotated data. In principle, unsupervised training methods (e.g., the iterative Baum-Welch algorithm) could be used to infer POS groups from an *untagged* corpus. Since generally few resources are available for historical languages, and since manual creation of resources is a labor-intensive task, unsupervised taggers look like the perfect solution for historical languages. Furthermore, as Biemann (2009) points out, unsupervised methods are better at handling noisy input and potential differences between the domains of the training corpus and the input text. However, unsupervised tagging requires large corpora, which are usually not available for historical languages. For example, Biemann (2009) uses corpora with millions of sentences; on the Web site of his unsupos tagger[5] he notes:

> Should be at least 2 Million tokens (100k sentences) to get something going, 50 million tokens (3M sentences) to get reasonable results and 500 million tokens (30M sentences) to obtain really nice performance. More is better.

This requirement precludes the use of unsupervised POS tagging for most historical languages.

Three historical languages for which supervised POS taggers have been built "from scratch" are Latin, Old French, and Classical Chinese. Much effort has been put into creating language resources "from scratch" for Latin—perhaps because there exists no contemporary variant from which resources could be adapted. Passarotti (2010b) explicitly states the goal of creating a BLARK for Latin. As mentioned in Section 8.8, two large Latin treebanks have been created: the *Latin Dependency Treebank* for Classical Latin and the *Index Thomisticus Treebank* for Medieval Latin.

Bamman and Crane (2008) trained TreeTagger on version 1.4 of the *Latin Dependency Treebank* (Bamman and Crane, 2011) (30,457 running word forms, see Section 8.8). They report an accuracy of 83% in correctly disambiguating the full morphological analysis (part of speech, person, number, tense, mood, voice, gender, case, and degree) and 95% accuracy for part of speech only.

Passarotti (2010a) trains HunPos (Halácsy et al., 2007) on a 61,024-token subset of the *Index Thomisticus Treebank* and achieved an accuracy of 89.90% for the full morphological analysis and 96.75% for part of speech only.

Stein (2007) trains TreeTagger (Schmid, 1994) on the Amsterdam Corpus of Old French (see Section 8.5), which had been been manually annotated with numeric tags from a 225-item tagset. In addition to the corpus, Stein makes use of several other resources, in particular lists of lemmas and inflectional and spelling variants extracted from several dictionaries of Old French. The various resources were brought into a common format and merged into an electronic lexicon of Old French forms (containing 235,000 entries) and the tagset reduced to 50 tags.

The lexicon and a 2.7 million word form subset of the corpus were then used for training TreeTagger. The resulting parameter file is freely available.[6] The rest of the corpus (0.5 million word forms) were used for the evaluation of the tagger. Stein (2007) reports an accuracy of 92.7% for the assignment of the part of speech.

---

[5]http://wortschatz.uni-leipzig.de/~cbiemann/software/unsupos.html (accessed 2012-06-06)
[6]http://www.uni-stuttgart.de/lingrom/stein/downloads/stein-oldfrench.par.zip (accessed 2012-06-06)

The BFM project (*Base de Français Médiéval*, see Section 8.5) also created a TreeTagger parameter file for Medieval French (11th–15th century). The parameter file is based on six manually tagged and verified texts of the BFM. The parameter file is released under a Creative Commons license.[7] No performance data has been published yet.

Much less work has been done for Classical Chinese than for either Latin or Old French. However, Huang et al. (2002b) created a statistical POS tagger for Classical Chinese. For training and testing the tagger, a small corpus of classical works was built, containing about 6,000 running characters or 1,200 sentences. In Classical Chinese, one character corresponds to one word, so that—unlike for modern Chinese—no word segmentation is necessary. A subset of 5,500 words was used as training set and the remaining 500 words as test set. Huang et al. report a tagging accuracy of 94.9% for bigram and 97.6% for trigram models, using a tagset of 21 tags.

When starting from scratch, the choice of tagger may also be an issue to consider, in particular, if the tagger has not yet been used for a language with characteristics similar to the historical language in question. Poudat and Longrée (2009) evaluate the performance of three POS taggers—MBT (Daelemans et al., 1996), TnT (Brants, 2000b) and TreeTagger (Schmid, 1994)—for morphosyntactic annotation of Classical Latin texts. The authors had access to a large, manually annotated corpus of Classical Latin, the LASLA database (see Section 8.8), so they had access to training data and a gold standard for evaluation. Apart from the evaluation of the general performance of the taggers, Poudat and Longrée were particularly interested in their sensitivity to stylistic, diachronic, genre, or discursive variation. The evaluation is also interesting because the LASLA database uses a very large tagset consisting of 3,732 tags, as the tags encode detailed morphological information.

For example, the word form *urbem* is associated with the lemma *VRBS* 'city' and may have the tag 13C, indicating that it is a noun (1) of the 3rd declension (3) in accusative singular (C). The verb form *habuere* is associated with the lemma *HABEO* 'to have' and the tag 52L14, indicating a verb (5) of the 2nd conjugation in the active voice (2), 3rd person plural (L), indicative (1) perfect (4).

This tagset is much larger than most tagsets used in modern-language NLP, but large tagsets are quite common for historical languages; for example, Rögnvaldsson and Helgadóttir (2008) use a 700-element tagset for Old Norse. This has two consequences. First, some taggers would not support tagsets of this size; Poudat and Longrée thus had to exclude TreeTagger from further evaluation, because it only supports tagsets with up to 200 tags (Poudat and Longrée, 2009, p. 138). Second, the accuracy of POS tagging is necessarily lower when using a larger tagset; Poudat and Longrée note that achieving an accuracy around 97% is unlikely with a tagset of this size. They find that the performance of TnT is systematically slightly better than that of MBT, achieving an accuracy of up to 88.08%, whereas the best result for MBT is 84.59%. These scores correspond to those reported by Bamman and Crane (2008) (see above). Poudat and Longrée (2009) note, however, that the taggers generally behave similarly with respect to the type and amount of training data, even though they found that for one test case (poem 66 of Catullus) more training data *reduced* the performance of TnT, possibly indicating a higher sensitivity to stylistic, diachronic, or genre variation.

---

[7]http://bfm.ens-lyon.fr/article.php3?id_article=324 (accessed 2012-06-06)

Skjrholt (2011) trains the TnT tagger on a subset of the Latin part of the *PROIEL* corpus (see Section 8.8), comprising the *Vulgata* and Caesar's *De bello gallico* and totaling 139,620 running word forms. He then evaluates the tagger's performance on Cicero's *Epistulae ad Atticum* (61,193 running word forms). In the evaluation, the tagger achieved an accuracy of 76.9%, which compares favorably with the results reported by Poudat and Longrée (2009) for a similar setup (77.2%), in particular as Poudat and Longrée had 352,820 running word forms of training data.

Dipper (2010) performs a series of experiments with TreeTagger on a corpus of Middle High German texts (1050–1350), using a variant of the STTS tagset (Schiller et al., 1999)—with 54 tags, this tagset is much smaller than the LASLA tagset.[8] STTS can be considered the standard tagset for modern German. The corpus contains 51 texts with 211,000 running word forms, representing different periods and dialects (Middle German and Upper German). The texts of the corpus are available in diplomatic and normalized transcriptions; the normalized transcription uses the normalized spelling that is also used by dictionaries of Middle High German. The texts were semiautomatically annotated with POS tags and lemmas.

Dipper creates different taggers by training TreeTagger on various subsets of the corpus (the Middle German portion, the Upper German portion, and the complete corpus) and on different types of transcriptions. The taggers were then evaluated both on the type of texts they were trained on as well as on other types of texts.

The results can be summarized as follows. As expected, the accuracy was highest when working with the normalized transcription; also, taggers matching the type of text and taggers trained on the complete corpus performed better than taggers trained on a different type of texts. What is more surprising is that tagging performance was generally higher for texts from the Upper German dialect area, even though the size of the Upper German subcorpus is only 75% of the size of the Middle German subcorpus; Dipper notes that this may be due to the fact that the Middle German subcorpus is more diverse and has a higher type/token ratio. The highest accuracy, 92.91%, was achieved for normalized Upper German text by a tagger trained on this type of data. The lowest accuracy, 65.48%, was obtained when a tagger trained on Upper German was applied to Middle German texts in diplomatic transcription. In general, the accuracy is comparable to the numbers reported by Poudat and Longrée (2009) for Latin (i.e., 80–90%).

7.1.2   USING A MODERN-LANGUAGE POS TAGGER

When working with a historical variant of an extant language, a frequent approach is to start off with an existing tagger for the modern variant.

Rayson et al. (2007) evaluate the performance of the CLAWS tagger for modern English (Garside and Smith, 1997) on a test set of Early Modern English texts consisting of comedies by Shakespeare and tracts and pamphlets from the *Lampeter Corpus* (see Section 8.4). From each text, a 1,000-word sample was taken; each sample was tagged by CLAWS once in its original form, once after automatic modernization using VARD (see Chapter 6, and once after manual modernization.

---

[8]The corpus is originally annotated with a larger tagset, which was mapped to STTS for the experiments.

Table 7.1: Effect of spelling normalization on tagging accuracy for the GerManC-GS corpus, as reported by Scheible et al. (2011a). 12,744 word forms of the 57,845 total word forms were affected by normalization; the numbers and percentages refer to this portion of word forms.

Tagging Behavior	Count	Percentage
Only tagged correctly when normalized	5,981	47%
Tagged correctly regardless of normalization	4,119	32%
Tagged incorrectly regardless of normalization	2,339	18%
Only tagged correctly when not normalized	305	3%
Total	12,744	100%

In addition, a gold standard was produced by manual correction of the CLAWS output for the unmodified texts.

CLAWS achieves 96% to 97% accuracy on modern British English texts; on the unmodified Shakespeare texts, average accuracy dropped to 81.94%. Automatic spelling modernization raised accuracy to about 85%, manual modernization resulted in about 89% accuracy. The Lampeter texts are more recent and thus closer to modern language and spelling, resulting in 88.46% average accuracy for unmodified texts, 89% for the automatically modernized texts, and 91% for manually modernized texts.

This experiment shows the level of accuracy to expect when using a tagger for modern English on Early Modern English texts as well as the extent to which modernization of spelling can improve the accuracy. For the historical texts considered by Rayson et al. (2007), one may conclude that an unmodified modern-language tagger with some preprocessing is sufficient; however, these results do not necessarily transfer to other languages.

Scheible et al. (2011a) evaluate a similar approach for Early Modern German texts (from the period 1650–1800) from the *GerManC* corpus (see Section 8.6). The authors use a manually annotated gold-standard subcorpus (GerManC-GS) containing 57,845 running word forms; GerManC-GS is annotated with POS tags, lemmas, and normalized word forms. Scheible et al. run TreeTagger with the standard parameter file for modern German both on the original, unnormalized texts and on the normalized texts. Schmid (1995) reports an accuracy of about 97% on modern German; at 69.6%, the accuracy for the original historical texts is thus relatively low. Running the tagger on the normalized texts improved accuracy by about 10 percentage points to 79.7%.

Particularly interesting is the analysis of the effects of spelling variation on tagger accuracy. Scheible et al. find that spelling normalization has a positive effect for 47% of the normalized word forms, i.e., the word form in the original spelling would have been tagged incorrectly. For 50%, of the normalized word forms, normalization has no effect on tagging accuracy, i.e., they are tagged correctly or incorrectly regardless of normalization. Table 7.1 lists the detailed results.

Rögnvaldsson and Helgadóttir (2008) evaluate the performance of TnT on Old Norse sagas. They had previously trained TnT on a corpus of modern Icelandic texts (590,297 running word forms), using a tagset of almost 700 tags and achieving an accuracy of 90.4%. For tagging the corpus of sagas (from the 13ᵗʰ and 14ᵗʰ century, totaling 1,651,398 running word forms), they decided to start with the tagger for modern Icelandic since modern Icelandic is still relatively similar to Old Norse in many respects. Spelling was not an issue since the historical text came from editions that normalize the spelling to modern Icelandic conventions.

Indeed, the application of the modern tagger to the sagas results in an accuracy of 88.0%. Rögnvaldsson and Helgadóttir then manually correct the tagger output for some 95,000 running word forms and retrain the tagger on this sample. This tagger achieves an accuracy of 91.7%, which is even better than the 90.4% the modern tagger achieved on modern text, despite the much smaller training corpus. In a third experiment, TnT is trained on the union of the modern and the historical training corpora. This tagging model results in an even higher accuracy of 92.7%.

These results are surprising, as we have seen that the accuracy of POS tagging is usually lower for historical languages than for modern languages. There are a number of reasons that explain these results. First of all, the initial results showed that Old Norse is indeed very close to modern Icelandic when it comes to POS tagging. Second, Rögnvaldsson and Helgadóttir report that many errors found in the first run were highly systematic; consequently, correcting these errors boosted the performance in the second run. Third, a major factor for the lower accuracy compared to modern Icelandic in the first run was the presence of unknown words, which made up 14.6%. With the smaller Old Norse training corpus this number dropped to 9.6%; this shows that the vocabulary in the historical corpus is much smaller than in the modern corpus. These factors are probably specific to this particular linguistic situation and cannot be generalized.

Sánchez-Marco et al. (2011) work on Old Spanish, i.e., Spanish from the 12ᵗʰ to the 16ᵗʰ century. In order to annotate a large diachronic corpus[9] (over 20 million running word forms) with part-of-speech and morphological information, they take the following approach (see also Sánchez-Marco et al., 2010).

First, they create a gold standard corpus by tagging a 30,000-token subset of the corpus using the FreeLing tagger[10] (Padró et al., 2010) for modern Spanish and manually correcting the output. Second, they expand the lexicon used by the tagger by adding spelling variants from the corpus; the spelling variants are found using a set of rules. Third, they adapt other tagger modules. The FreeLing POS tagger uses affixation rules for recognizing derivations (e.g., adverbs formed by appending *-mente*) or clitics attached to verbs. These rules are expanded with Old Spanish affixes and clitics. The FreeLing tokenizer was also enhanced in order to correctly handle the peculiarities of the historical texts.

---

[9]Compiled from electronic texts published by the Hispanic Seminary of Medieval Studies (`http://www.hispanicsociety.org/hispanic/HSMS.htm` (accessed 2012-06-06))

[10]`http://nlp.lsi.upc.edu/freeling/` (accessed 2012-06-06)

Finally, Sánchez-Marco et al. retrain the adapted tagger on the gold standard corpus. In the evaluation of the resulting tagger, the authors report an accuracy of 94.5% for the word class, 89.9% for the full tag including detailed morphosyntactic information, 92.6% for the lemma.

Moon and Baldridge (2007) explore a different approach for creating a tagger for Middle English: alignment of a modern and a historical text and projection of the POS tags from the modern text to the historical text. For their approach they use the modern New English Translation (NET) Bible and Wycliffe's Bible from the late 14th century.

In a first step, Moon and Baldridge traine the C&C POS tagger (Curran and Clark, 2003) on the Wall Street Journal texts from the Penn Treebank and use this tagger to tag the NET Bible. They then aligne the NET and Wycliffe Bibles using (1) the Dice coefficient (Kay and Röscheisen, 1993) and (2) Giza++ (Och and Ney, 2003), and project the POS tags from the NET Bible to the Wycliffe Bible. Not every word form in the target text can necessarily aligned to a word form in the source text, so not all word forms in the target text receive a tag. Moon and Baldridge therefore train a bigram tagger on the (incomplete) alignment results and use it to fill in the gaps by retagging the entire target text before training the C&C POS tagger on the Wycliffe Bible. This bootstrap corpus contains 920,000 running word forms.

For testing, Moon and Baldridge use subsections M3 and M34 of the *Penn-Helsinki Parsed Corpus of Middle English* (PPCME), which contains texts of a similar age, including portions of Wycliffe Bible. The C&C POS tagger trained on the bootstrap corpus yields an accuracy of 61.3% on the test corpus (using the Penn Treebank tagset); this is a significant improvement over the baseline, the C&C POS tagger trained on the Wall Street Journal, which results in an accuracy of only 56.2%. On the PPCME version of the Wycliffe Bible, the tagger achieved an accuracy of 79.5%.

To determine the upper bounds, Moon and Baldridge train the C&C POS tagger on the manually tagged PPCME version of the Wycliffe Bible and apply it to the test set; this gives an accuracy of 71.0%. They also train the C&C POS tagger on a different selection of texts from the PPCME (327,000 running word forms), which are closer in genre to the test set than the Bible; this gives an accuracy of 93.7%, illustrating the effect of genre and domain.

To estimate the cost of manually tagging the target text compared to the bootstrapping approach, Moon and Baldridge train the C&C POS tagger on randomly selected sets of sentences from the PPCME (disjoint from the test corpus). They find that 50 labeled sentences were sufficient to obtain an accuracy exceeding that of the bootstrapped tagger on the test corpus; however, 400 sentences are required to achieve the accuracy of the bootstrapped tagger on the PPCME version of the Wycliffe Bible. This clearly shows that the best approach is dependent on how well the domains of the source and target texts match. They also find that about 600 tagged sentences from the PPCME Wycliffe Bible are required to achieve the performance of the bootstrapped tagger on the PPCME Wycliffe Bible. Moon and Baldridge conclude that, when the target domain differs strongly from the available aligned texts, manual annotation of a small number of randomly selected example sentences from the target text is a reasonable approach. On the other hand, it is hard to predict whether the approach will be successful, whereas the bootstrapping approach may quickly produce a usable tagger that can then be further improved and also used for preannotating text for manual tagging.

However, based on this experiment alone it is hard to judge how well the alignment-and-projection approach translates to other historical corpora; for example, in the setup used by Moon and Baldridge, the approach may have benefited from the fact that the variant of Middle English found in the Wycliffe Bible is already relatively close to Modern English. The experiment also clearly showed that the performance of a tagger for historical language depends on the similarity of the training and target domains.

Most approaches that use a modern tagger on historical language attempt to modernize the historical text to make it resemble the modern language more closely. Hana et al. (2011) additionally use the inverse approach. In order to create a tagger for Old Czech (13th–16th century), they not only modernize the Old Czech text (740,000 running word forms from the Old-Czech Text Bank (STB)[11]), but also apply a number of transformations to the annotated corpus of modern Czech (700,000 running word forms from the Prague Dependency Treebank (Hajič et al., 2001)), which was used for training the tagger.

The "aging" procedure for the modern Czech corpus includes dropping the animacy distinction, which Old Czech did not have, and changing various forms (e.g., the modern infinitive ends in -t, whereas in Old Czech it ended in -ti. Hana et al. then train the TnT tagger on this corpus.

In the next step, they modernize the corpus of Old Czech by transforming the spelling using a number of rules. Like other languages from this period, Old Czech did not have a standard orthography; however, in the corpus of Old Czech the spelling was regularized using the conventions of modern Czech. Hana et al. thus do not have to cope with spelling variation. This modernized historical corpus is then tagged using the tagger trained on the aged modern corpus.

Finally, the modernized word forms in the tagged modernized historical corpus are replaced with the original word forms, resulting in a tagged corpus of Old Czech. Training the tagger on this corpus produces a tagger for Old Czech. The accuracy of this tagger is evaluated on a manually annotated subset (1,000 word forms) of the Old Czech corpus. Overall accuracy is 70.6%; one has to note, though, that the Prague Dependency Treebank tagset has over 4,200 tags, capturing detailed morphological information. When taking only the POS into account, the accuracy is 91.5%.

In a further experiment, Hana et al. create a tagger using the transition probabilities from the aged modern Czech corpus and a simple morphological analyzer based on various Old Czech and modern Czech word lists. As this tagger performs better on verbs, but worse for other word classes, it is combined with the tagger described above, in a setup where one tagger predicted only verbs and the other all other word classes. The combined taggers give a better overall performance (74.1% accuracy), but the accuracy on nouns drops.

Overall, this approach successfully produces a usable tagger for Old Czech. As other researchers, Hana et al. note the problem of genre mismatch: the Old Czech corpus comprises a variety of genres, including poetry, cookbooks, and religious texts, whereas the modern corpus contains mostly

---

[11]http://vokabular.ujc.cas.cz/ (accessed 2012-06-06)

newspaper texts, which differs both lexically and syntactically from other genres—for example, imperatives and second-person pronouns are very rare in newspaper text.

7.2   LEMMATIZATION AND MORPHOLOGICAL ANALYSIS

Lemmatization is the process of determining the lemma—also known as the *base form*—of an inflected word form found in a text. For example, the English word forms *go*, *went*, and *gone* all belong to the lemma *to go*. However, a particular word form may potentially be a form of more than one lemma; for example, depending on the context, the lemma belonging to the English word form *can* may be either *can* (noun), *to can*, or *can* (modal verb), or the Latin word form *caelo* may be a form of the masculine noun *caelus* 'heaven', the neuter noun *caelum* 'heaven', or of the verb *caelare* 'to carve'. It is thus necessary to know the part of speech to find the correct lemma. Lemmatization is thus a closely related procedure, and indeed some POS taggers also attempt to annotate word forms not only with POS tags but also with lemmas. Morphologically rich languages often require a separate, more specialized component for lemmatization.

As we have seen in the preceding section, creating high-accuracy taggers for historical languages tends to be difficult; thus there are only few reports on lemmatization. In this section, we will outline work on lemmatizers for four historical languages: Old French, Middle French, Old Swedish, and Middle Dutch.

One of the goals of the *Nouveau Corpus d'Amsterdam* project (Kunstmann and Stein, 2007) (see Section 8.5) was to add lemma information to the *Corpus d'Amsterdam*, which had been manually annotated with POS tags, but not with lemmas. Stein (2002) uses a number of previously created lexical resources extracted from printed dictionaries and other annotated texts. The lexical resources include, among others, the list of all 37,000 lemmas of the Old French dictionary Tobler-Lommatzsch: *Altfranzösisches Wörterbuch*[12] and lemmatized indices for a number of Old French texts (e.g., *Le Conte du Graal*[13]), which associate the word forms from the texts with the lemmas from Tobler-Lommatzsch; it is thus possible to merge these resources and create a lexicon of Old French word forms, eventually containing 211,000 morphologically tagged forms (using a set of 50 tags). Stein then trains TreeTagger on a portion of the corpus (2.6 million running word forms) using this lexicon. In a preliminary evaluation (on a different portion of the corpus, comprising 415,000 running word forms), the resulting tagger is able to determine a lemma for 272,310 of the 415,000 (66%) word forms of the test corpus. The TreeTagger parameter file is freely available (see Section 8.5).

Whereas Kunstmann and Stein uses an off-the-shelf NLP tool, Souvay and Pierrel (2009), in the context of the work on the *Dictionnaire du moyen français* (Dictionary of Middle French, DMF), aim to create a lemmatizer specially designed for the specific requirements of Middle French as language without standardized orthography.[14]

---

[12]http://www.uni-stuttgart.de/lingrom/stein/tl/ (accessed 2012-06-30)
[13]http://www.uottawa.ca/academic/arts/lfa/activites/textes/perceval/cgrpres.htm (accessed 2012-06-30)
[14]Middle French is the stage of the development of the French language from ca. 1330–1500.

Table 7.2: Examples of LGeRM normalization rules for Middle French (from Souvay and Pierrel, 2009).

Precondition	word-initial, followed by a vowel
Transformation	SÇ ↦ S
Postcondition	none
Example	presçavoir ↦ presavoir
Precondition	word-final
Transformation	ALES ↦ AL
Postcondition	noun or adjective
Example	abbaciales ↦ abbacial

The system developed by Souvay and Pierrel, LGeRM (lemmes, graphies et règles morphologiques, i.e., lemmas, spellings, and morphological rules), is primarily designed as an aid for finding entries in the DMF, therefore it only works on a single word form without context. Thus, it is not a lemmatizer in the sense given above, but it is nevertheless an interesting system, as it illustrates an alternative, rule-based approach. LGeRM relies on the list of lemmas contained in the DMF, the list of their recorded spelling variants, and a set of morphological and spelling rules. The rules generally consist of a *precondition* (e.g., word-initial, word-final), a *transformation*, and a *postcondition* (e.g., "must result in a verbal form"). Table 7.2 shows examples of two rules.

The system contains about 4,000 rules for verbs, 200 for nouns and adjectives, 100 for fused word forms, and 400 general rules, totaling about 4,700 rules. Unlike a regular lemmatizer, LGeRM does not try to find the (normalized) lemma of an input word form directly, but it rather tries to find, in the database of known spellings, a form as close as possible to the input form, and then outputs a number of hypotheses. In the tests performed by Souvay and Pierrel, LGeRM returns a single, correct lemma for 60% of the input word forms; in 39% of the cases, it suggests several lemmas, including the correct one.

In their work on Old Swedish (13th–15th century), the primary objective of Borin and Forsberg (2008) is also to help students of Old Swedish to look up historical word forms in dictionaries, which obviously requires the lemma. Borin and Forsberg model the morphology of Old Swedish using Functional Morphology (Forsberg and Ranta, 2004). A particular challenge is that the language underwent significant changes during the second half of the Old Swedish period. One example given by Borin and Forsberg is the nominal case system, which changed from a system of four cases (nominative, genitive, dative, accusative) to a system with only one basic form and a genitive clitic, similar to that of English. As the target texts originate from this transitional period, Borin and Forsberg aim to model all attested inflectional variation.

Borin and Forsberg manually translate the descriptions of the 75 inflectional paradigms of Old Swedish as found in grammar books into Functional Morphology rules. In the Functional Morphology framework, a paradigm is modeled by a function, which takes one or more word forms and a set of morphosyntactic categories as input and returns a set of correspondingly inflected word forms as output. A lexicon consisting of 3,000 headwords with information on their inflectional paradigms was manually created on the basis of printed dictionaries of Old Swedish.

Like other languages from the period, Old Swedish did not have a standard orthography, so that Borin and Forsberg also encounter spelling and dialectal variation. The authors decide to handle all variation occurring in inflectional endings—regardless of whether it is due to language change, dialectal variation, or spelling—in the morphology component, and all variation occurring in stems as a spelling correction problem. This approach seems clean at first sight, but has one major weakness, which is also acknowledged by the authors: it does not provide a way to handle ablaut and umlaut phenomena, i.e., changes in the stem due to morphological processes.

We will now have a look at the fourth approach, the work of Kestemont et al. (2010) for the Middle Dutch *Corpus Gysseling* (13th–14th century; see Section 8.3). Kestemont et al. tackle the problem of spelling variation in medieval language using memory-based machine learning. They consider lemmatization as a variant of POS tagging: given a word form in some context, this word form is to be assigned a "tag," which happens to be the lemma. As the *Corpus Gysseling* is annotated with modern Dutch lemmas, these "tags" could be learned from the corpus. For their experiments, Kestemont et al. use the MBT[15] part-of-speech tagger (Daelemans et al., 1996) and train it on word form–lemma pairs from the *Corpus Gysseling*. As in the more conventional POS tagging task, unknown word forms (i.e., word forms not encountered during training) pose the main problem.

To account for spelling variation, the standard Levenshtein edit distance (see Section 6.2) is used to select for each unknown word form the set of training word forms at a minimal edit distance. However, since the correct lemma is not necessarily the most frequent one, majority voting would often select an incorrect lemma, resulting in very low accuracy for unknown word forms (34%). Kestemont et al. therefore devised a new voting procedure that attempts to take the "soundness" of a potential lemma into account, by reranking the candidate lemmas using a "soundness score." This score is based on pairwise character translation vectors. This voting procedure results in an improvement of 11% over the baseline, i.e., 45% overall accuracy. While this is clearly a significant improvement, it is still below the theoretical maximum; for about 60% of the unknown word forms, the correct lemma is found to be among the candidate lemmas. The approach is nevertheless interesting, since it is language-independent, as it does not rely on language-specific translation rules.

7.3   SYNTACTIC PARSING

As part-of-speech tagging and morphological analysis are already more difficult for historical texts than for modern texts, it is not surprising that there is relatively little work on syntactic parsing of historical texts. If high-quality syntactic annotation is required, projects therefore often use manual annotation. For example, for the creation of the *Syntactic Reference Corpus of Medieval French* (SRCMF), it was decided to use manual annotation supported by automatic chunking (Stein, 2008, p. 167) and a specialized annotation tool, NotaBene (Mazziotta, 2010).

---

[15]http://ilk.uvt.nl/mbt/ (accessed 2012-06-30)

There are, nevertheless, attempts to parse historical texts automatically. For example, Huang et al. (2002a) developed a probabilistic context-free grammar (PCFG) parser for a subset of Classical Chinese; for preprocessing, a POS tagger was also built (Huang et al., 2002b). Compared to modern Chinese, Classical Chinese is both easier and more difficult to parse. First of all, morphology and syntax of Classical Chinese differ significantly from modern Chinese. Since Chinese is written without spaces between words, it is always necessary for NLP to first segment the texts into words (see Wong et al., 2009). On the one hand, this is easier for Classical Chinese, because most words consist of a single character, whereas in modern Chinese many words consist of two or more characters. On the other hand, Classical Chinese is more difficult to parse because the ambiguity with respect to the part of speech is even higher for Classical Chinese than for modern Chinese; Huang et al. state that "more than half of the words have two or more possible lexical categories and dynamic shifts of lexical categories are the most common grammatical phenomena in Classical Chinese" (Huang et al., 2002a, p. 2).

Huang et al. (2002a) use a treebank containing 1,000 manually annotated sentences for training and testing; the test set consists of 100 sentences, the rest is used as the training set. An accuracy of 82.3% is reached in the evaluation of the experimental parser. It should be noted, though, that the test sentences were selected not to contain proper names—in order to avoid problems with lexical coverage.

More recently, Schneider (2012) evaluated the performance of the Pro3Gres parser on *ARCHER* (see Section 8.4). Pro3Gres (Schneider, 2008) is a hybrid Dependency Grammar parser for modern English, combining hand-written grammar rules with statistical disambiguation (learned from the Penn Treebank). This parser architecture is interesting for historical texts, because the grammar rules can be adapted to genres, varieties, or historical stages of English for which no or only little training material is available. The parser uses a part-of-speech tagger and a chunker as preprocessors; syntactic parsing proper is only performed between heads of chunks. Pro3Gres can be used with different POS taggers and chunkers (Schneider, 2011), including TreeTagger and LingPipe;[16] the current standard pipeline uses LT-TTT2[17], which integrates POS tagging and chunking.

For the evaluation of Pro3Gres on *ARCHER*, the spelling of the historical text is first normalized using VARD2 (Baron and Rayson, 2008), as a preliminary evaluation on 100 sentences (from the 17th century) had shown that the performance of the (unmodified) parser is clearly better on normalized text.

Schneider evaluates both the unadapted parser and the effect of certain modifications. Not surprisingly, the performance of the unadapted parser increases from about 70% on 17th-century texts to about 80% on texts from the early 20th century. Improving the parser by adapting it to the specific properties of the historical language varieties turns out to be difficult. Schneider finds that adaptations for specific words are easy, such as the use of *but* as adverb—as in: "He is such an

---

[16]http://alias-i.com/lingpipe/ (accessed 2012-06-30)
[17]http://www.ltg.ed.ac.uk/software/lt-ttt2/ (accessed 2012-06-30)

Itinerant, to speak that I have but little of his company," but they only have little impact on general parsing performance. The removal of grammatical constraints often has negative side-effects. For example, in the standard grammar, fronted prepositional phrases are only allowed at the beginning of sentences; relaxing this constraint in order to allow for constructions such as "[…] and went well to bed, where she took as good rest and sleep, as ever before, but in the morning, when she awakened, and attempted to turn herself in her bed, was not able […]" results in serious overgeneration and thus a decrease in precision; allowing only temporal and manner PPs to the left partly recovers precision, but at the cost of recall.

An interesting observation made by Schneider (2012) is that most *types* of errors made by the Pro3Gres parser are the same for historical and modern English, but the problematic phenomena that lead to these errors occur more frequently in historical texts.

7.4   SUMMARY

In this chapter we gave an overview of NLP tools constructed or adapted for historical languages. The diversity of approaches taken by researchers and the results they report illustrate that NLP tools for historical languages are usually specific to a particular collection of texts written in a certain language variety.

NLP for historical texts often occurs in the context of diachronic studies and thus on diachronic corpora; as these corpora are linguistically heterogeneous by definition, one cannot expect a single tool to yield optimal performance on all parts of the corpus. However, the individual parts of a diachronic corpus may be too small for training statistical tools, especially as even texts from the same period typically exhibit much spelling variation, exacerbating the problem of data sparseness—a problem most tools discussed in this chapter have to cope with.

In general, NLP performs worse on historical than on modern texts. However, when comparing performance figures—such as tagger accuracy—one has to keep in mind that the figures reported for modern texts are typically for homogeneous text collections from the same domain on which the tool was trained, typically newspaper texts; the performance on texts from other domains is in most cases lower. One should also keep in mind that gold standards for historical texts are typically less reliable than those for modern texts, for example, because annotators are not native speakers. For example, Brants (2000a) reports 98.6% inter-annotator agreement for manual tagging of a modern German newspaper corpus, whereas Scheible et al. (2011b) achieve only 91.6% inter-annotator agreement on a corpus of Early Modern German texts, using the same tagset.

CHAPTER 8

Historical Corpora

This chapter attempts to give an overview of historical corpora, with a focus on corpora freely available for research. Corpora play a double role: on the one hand, they allow linguists to examine linguistic phenomena and develop linguistic theories; on the other hand, they support the development of NLP tools by providing training and test data. Linguistic research can in turn benefit from theses NLP tools and applications; for example, part-of-speech taggers or lemmatizers allow scholars to query corpora not only for concrete surface forms, but for more abstract entities, in this case words and syntactic roles. Such tools are discussed in Chapter 7.

Rissanen (2008) notes that "the introduction of corpora has had a revolutionary effect on language studies in the last few decades" and that this is "particularly true of historical linguistics, which has to rely on written sources only," since scholars cannot rely on native speakers or on introspection when they study historical languages (Rissanen, 2008, p. 53).

Historical linguistics, however, has effectively always been corpus-based, for the reasons Rissanen mentions. Philologists and theologians have long constructed corpora of classical authors, counted word frequencies, and compiled concordances. In fact, the first machine-readable corpus project ever undertaken was a historical corpus: the *Index Thomisticus*, containing the collected writings of Thomas Aquinas[1] was started by Roberto Busa in 1949 (Winter, 1999), i.e., even before the industrial production of digital computers (see Section 8.8).

Today, historical corpora and text collections exist for various languages, for example, Arabic, Chinese, Dutch, English, French, Galician, German, Ancient Greek, Icelandic, Japanese, Latin, Old Norse, Polish, and Portuguese. In the rest of this chapter, we will present a selection of historical corpora for these languages. Of course, we cannot list all corpora in existence; further corpora are also being constructed; we rather want to give an overview of resources currently available and provide readers with starting points.

8.1 ARABIC

The most important historical variety of Arabic is probably *Quranic Arabic*, i.e., the language used in the Quran (also spelled *Koran* or *Qur'an*), the sacred book of Islam. The Quran consists of 114 chapters (suras), containing 6,236 verses (ayats); its total size is 77,429 word forms. The language dates to the 7th century CE.

---

[1]Thomas Aquinas (1225–1274) was an Italian Dominican friar, theologician, and philosopher. He is regarded as one of the most influential figures of scholasticism.

```
LOCATION          FORM    TAG     FEATURES
(1:1:1:1)         bi      P       PREFIX|bi+
(1:1:1:2)         somi    N       STEM|POS:N|LEM:{som|ROOT:smw|M|GEN
(1:1:2:1)         {ll~ahi PN      STEM|POS:PN|LEM:{ll~ah|ROOT:Alh|GEN
(1:1:3:1)         {l      DET     PREFIX|Al+
(1:1:3:2)         r~aHoma'ni ADJ     STEM|POS:ADJ|LEM:r~aHoma'n|ROOT:rHm|MS|GEN
(1:1:4:1)         {l      DET     PREFIX|Al+
(1:1:4:2)         r~aHiymi ADJ     STEM|POS:ADJ|LEM:r~aHiym|ROOT:rHm|MS|GEN
(1:2:1:1)         {lo     DET     PREFIX|Al+
(1:2:1:2)         Hamodu  N       STEM|POS:N|LEM:Hamod|ROOT:Hmd|M|NOM
(1:2:2:1)         li      P       PREFIX|l:P+
(1:2:2:2)         l~ahi   PN      STEM|POS:PN|LEM:{ll~ah|ROOT:Alh|GEN
(1:2:3:1)         rab~i   N       STEM|POS:N|LEM:rab~|ROOT:rbb|M|GEN
(1:2:4:1)         {lo     DET     PREFIX|Al+
(1:2:4:2)         Ea'lamiyna N       STEM|POS:N|LEM:Ea'lamiyn|ROOT:Elm|MP|GEN
(1:3:1:1)         {l      DET     PREFIX|Al+
(1:3:1:2)         r~aHoma'ni ADJ     STEM|POS:ADJ|LEM:r~aHoma'n|ROOT:rHm|MS|GEN
(1:3:2:1)         {l      DET     PREFIX|Al+
(1:3:2:2)         r~aHiymi ADJ     STEM|POS:ADJ|LEM:r~aHiym|ROOT:rHm|MS|GEN
(1:4:1:1)         ma'liki N       STEM|POS:N|ACT|PCPL|LEM:ma'lik|ROOT:mlk|M|GEN
(1:4:2:1)         yawomi  N       STEM|POS:N|LEM:yawom|ROOT:ywm|M|GEN
```

Listing 8.1: Excerpt from the Quranic Arabic Corpus, version 0.4.

Researchers at the University of Leeds have built the Quranic Arabic Corpus.[2] The corpus is annotated on the levels of morphology, syntax, and semantics.

As of version 0.4 (released on May 1, 2011) the treebank (i.e., the syntactically annotated part) covers 40% of the Quran by word count (30,895 out of 77,429 words). The treebank provides syntactic annotation in the form of a dependency grammar for chapters 1–8 and 59–114 (Dukes and Buckwalter, 2010). Figure 8.1 shows the Web interface to the corpus and an example of a syntactic annotation. An interesting aspect is that online collaboration is used to correct the automatic annotation (Dukes et al., 2011) (see also Section 4.1). The morphologically annotated corpus is available under the GNU General Public License; Listing 8.1 shows an excerpt from the corpus, as it can be downloaded.

The *Perseus Digital Library* (see Section 8.8) also has a collection of Classical Arabic texts and dictionaries, freely available for download in TEI-compliant XML (TEI P4).

8.2 CHINESE

The Chinese language has a long written tradition; the Chinese script is thought to constitute a fully developed writing system since the late Shang dynasty (14th–11th century BCE), and there exist numerous inscriptions from this era (Norman, 1988, p. 58).

---

[2]http://corpus.quran.com/ (accessed 2012-06-06)

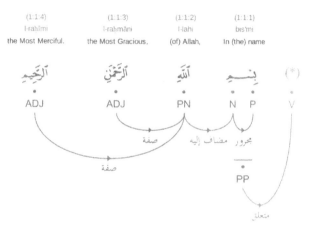

Figure 8.1: Web interface to the Quranic Arabic Corpus (screenshot taken 2011-10-23).

There are, however, relatively few historical corpora available. Hu and McLaughlin (2007) note that most collections of digitized historical Chinese texts[3] are not linguistic corpora in the modern sense. Two exceptions are the *Academia Sinica Tagged Corpus of Early Mandarin Chinese*[4] and the *Sheffield Corpus of Chinese*.[5] Web interfaces allow for online browsing of both corpora, but the corpora are not available for download.

The former corpus was developed by the Institute of Linguistics of the Academia Sinica. It is based on 10 literary works from the Tang to the Qing dynasty (ca. 700–1650), comprising 2,751,646 words. All texts in the corpus were segmented into words and annotated with part-of-speech tagging.

The *Sheffield Corpus of Chinese* is a diachronic corpus developed at the University of Sheffield, consisting of a wide range of fully marked-up Chinese historical texts and a Web-based search and analysis tool. The texts are organized according to text types, genres, and time period. The corpus covers Archaic Chinese (1200 BCE–220 CE), Medieval Chinese (220–1368), and Modern Chinese (1368–1911). The total size of the corpus is 432,670 words; the Archaic Chinese subcorpus comprises 109,670 words, the Middle Chinese subcorpus 147,500 words, and the Modern Chinese subcorpus 175,500 words.

Lee (2012) recently constructed a corpus of Classical Chinese, containing the complete works (521 poems) of the 8th-century poets Wang Wei and Meng Haoran, ca. 32,000 characters in total. As Chinese is written without spaces between words, word segmentation is the first step for any NLP of Chinese texts (see Chapter 7). However, there is no standard for Chinese word segmentation, so that one corpus may treat a sequence of two characters $X_1 X_2$ as one word (with one POS tag), whereas another may consider it two words (possibly with two different POS tags). In order to address this problem, Lee uses a system of nested part-of-speech tags, which makes it possible to apply different criteria for word segmentation. The basic idea of this approach to use two levels, "strings without internal structures" at the lower level, which can then be combined to form "strings with internal structures" at the higher level. The corpus was manually annotated for part of speech using a tagset similar to the tagset used by the *Penn Chinese Treebank* for modern Chinese. The corpus is planned to be made publicly available; interested parties are asked to contact the corpus compiler for details.

On the basis of this corpus, Lee and Kong (2012) also develop a dependency treebank of Classical Chinese poems. The set of dependency relations is based on the Stanford relations for modern Chinese. Lee and Kong use the treebank to study parallelism in Classical Chinese poetry.

8.3 DUTCH

The Institute for Dutch Lexicology[6] makes a number of historical Dutch text collections and corpora available via its TST-Centrale[7] website. The *Corpus of Old Dutch* (Corpus Oudnederlands) contains

---

[3]See the list of digital resources maintained by the Heidelberg University Institute of Chinese Studies at `http://www.zo.uni-heidelberg.de/sinologie/digital_resources/list_az_en.html` (accessed 2012-06-06).

[4]`http://dbo.sinica.edu.tw/Early_Mandarin/` (accessed 2012-06-06)

[5]`http://www.hrionline.ac.uk/scc/` (accessed 2012-06-06)

[6]`http://www.inl.nl/` (accessed 2012-06-06)

[7]`http://www.inl.nl/tst-centrale/` (accessed 2012-06-06)

```
<L 44:1> <C 810_DAT> dat <C 450_ZIJN> sijn <C 0_ADEM> adem
<C 203_GAAN> gaet <C 501_ALDOOR> al+dure <L 44:2> <C 500_OOK> oec
<C 440+203_MEN+VINDEN> vintmen <C 441_SOMMIG> somege
<C 1_SCHRIFTUUR> scrifture <L 44:3> <C 421_DIE> die <C 700_VAN> van
<C 415_DEZE> des<A >er</A> <C 4_BEEST> beesten <C 203_WETEN> weet
<L 44:4> <C 406+800+421_ZIJ+EN+DIE> entiese <C 19_BISON> bisontes
<C 213_HETEN> heet <L 44:5> <C 9_BONASUS> Bonacus <C 210_ZIJN> es
<C 489_EEN> .i.  <C 0_DIER> dier <L 44:6> <C 420_DAT> dat
<C 203_HEBBEN> heuet <C 0+470_HOOFD+HET> thouet <C 700+474_NA+DE> naden
<C 0_STIER> stier <L 44:7> <C 470_HET> dat <C 0_LIJF> lijf
<C 471+800_DE+EN> entie <C 14_MAAN> mane<A >n</A> <C 501_MEDE> mede
<L 44:8> <C 500_RECHT> recht <C 475+700_DE+NA> nader <C 11_PAARD> parde
<C 1_ZEDE> zede
```

Listing 8.2: Excerpt from the *Corpus Gysseling* (Middle Dutch).

all extant sources of Old Dutch from about 475 until 1200, comprising about 43,000 word forms, annotated with lemmas, morphological information, and part of speech. The corpus can be searched using a Web interface[8].

The *Corpus Gysseling* is the collection of 13th century Dutch texts used as source material for the *Vroegmiddelnederlands Woordenboek* (Dictionary of Early Middle Dutch)[9], enriched with word category information and lemmas. For research purposes, the corpus is freely available for download from TST-Centrale. Listing 8.2 shows an excerpt from the corpus and illustrates the corpus encoding format. Kestemont et al. (2010) use the Corpus Gysseling for research into automatic lemmatization of Middle Dutch.

The TST-Centrale offers further historical texts in electronic form, for example, historical Dutch Bibles such as the Delft Bible from 1477 or the Leuven Bible from 1548.

The *Corpus van Reenen-Mulder* (CRM) was created in the 1980s at the Vrije Universiteit Amsterdam on the initiative of Piet van Reenen and Maaike Mulder (van Reenen and Mulder, 2000). It consists of about 3,000 charters from the 14th century, written in Middle Dutch. The charters are dated, geographically localized, lemmatized and morphologically tagged. The CRM was annotated semiautomatically; the annotation was revised and corrected several times; the latest tagging was done using the Adelheid[10] tagger/lemmatizer. The plain-text transcriptions are freely available for downloading[11]; the POS-tagged version is available upon request from the corpus compilers. A portion of the CRM, consisting of 441 charters from southern Flanders and western Brabant and 157 other texts from other regions of Flanders, are publicly available as the *Corpus van veertiende-eeuwse*

---

[8]http://tst.inl.nl/producten/cONW (accessed 2012-06-06)
[9]This and other historical Dutch dictionaries are available online at http://gtb.inl.nl/ (accessed 2011-10-24)
[10]http://adelheid.ruhosting.nl/ (accessed 2012-07-03)
[11]http://www.diachronie.nl/corpora/ (accessed 2012-07-04)

niet–literaire teksten (Corpus of 14th-century non-literary texts, C14NL). [12] The C14NL corpus is marked up according to TEI P4; the set of 157 texts includes part-of-speech and lemma information.

8.4   ENGLISH

Motivated by corpus work for contemporary English, work on corpora for historical varieties of English started quite early, so that today a relatively large number of historical corpora are in existence.

The first comprehensive historical corpus of the English language was the *Helsinki Corpus of English Texts* (Kytö, 1996), which, at the same time, represents pioneer work in the field of historical corpus linguistics as a whole. The *Helsinki Corpus* was compiled between 1984 and 1991 under the direction of Matti Rissanen at the University of Helsinki, Finland. It is a diachronic corpus covering Old, Middle and Early Modern English from ca. 730 to 1710; it consists of about 450 text samples from a variety of genres, totaling about 1.5 million running word forms. The corpus is primarily intended for studying diachronic change. The *Helsinki Corpus* was originally encoded in the COCOA format, a markup scheme that originated with the mainframe concordancing program of the same name. [13] Listings 8.3 and 8.4 show an excerpt from the *Helsinki Corpus* and illustrate the COCOA format (the excerpt is taken from (Kytö, 1996)). Listing 8.3 contains the header for an individual work, namely *Polychronicon*. The header contains the information that this is a prose work of historical writing and non-imaginative narration (encoded in <Q>, <T>, and <V>), which was translated (<G>) from Latin (<F>) into southern English dialect (encoded in <D>) by John Trevisa (<A>), who was between 40–60 years old (<Y>) and his social rank was "professional" (<H>). The original and the manuscript date from the third sub-period of Middle English (1350–1420) (tags <O> and <M>). Following this information (enclosed in [^ ... ^]) is the bibliographical reference for the source text and the volume, and the page and line references for the extracts contained in the corpus.

Listing 8.4 shows the actual text of the first sample. Since the corpus is encoded in ASCII, a number of special character combinations are used for encoding historical characters (e.g., +t for *þ* (thorn) and +g for ʒ (yogh)), typographical features (e.g., = for superscript), changes in language (\(...\)), and emendations (editorial corrections, [{...{]).

Since the format was designed for punched cards, the maximum line length is 80 characters; in order to leave space for further coding, only 65 characters are used; longer lines in the source text are split over several lines, with a hash mark (#) as a line continuation marker.

The conversion of the *Helsinki Corpus* from COCOA format to TEI was recently completed, so that it will be able to process the corpus using modern standard tools. The *Helsinki Corpus* may be purchased from the Oxford Text Archive [14] or from ICAME. [15]

---

[12] http://ctb.kantl.be/corpus/C14NL.htm (accessed 2012-07-03)

[13] The acronym COCOA stands for "word COunt and COncordance on Atlas"; Atlas was a 1960s-era British supercomputer. See also http://www.chilton-computing.org.uk/acl/applications/cocoa/p001.htm (accessed 2012-07-03).

[14] http://ota.oucs.ox.ac.uk/headers/1477.xml (accessed 2012-07-03)

[15] http://icame.uib.no/ (accessed 2012-07-03)

```
<B CMPOLYCH>
<Q ME3 NN HIST TREVISA>
<N POLYCHRONICON>
<A TREVISA JOHN>
<C ME3>
<O 1350-1420>
<M 1350-1420>
<K CONTEMP>
<D SL>
<V PROSE>
<T HISTORY>
<G TRANSL>
<F LATIN>
<W WRITTEN>
<X MALE>
<Y 40-60>
<H PROF>
<U X>
<E X>
<J X>
<I X>
<Z NARR NON-IMAG>
<S SAMPLE X>


[^TREVISA, JOHN.
POLYCHRONICON RANULPHI HIGDEN,
MONACHI CESTRENSIS, VOLS. VI, VIII.
ENGLISH TRANSLATIONS OF JOHN TREVISA AND OF
AN UNKNOWN WRITER OF THE FIFTEENTH CENTURY.
ROLLS SERIES, 41.
ED. J. R. LUMBY.
LONDON, 1876, 1882.
VI, PP. 209.14 - 231.7 (SAMPLE 1)
VIII, PP. 83.1 - 111.19 (SAMPLE 2)
VIII, PP. 347.1 - 352.13 (SAMPLE 3)^]
```

Listing 8.3: Excerpt from the *Helsinki Corpus* (part 1).

Portions of the *Helsinki Corpus* have been syntactically annotated and are available as separate corpora. The *Brooklyn-Geneva-Amsterdam-Helsinki Parsed Corpus of Old English* is a selection of texts from the Old English part of the *Helsinki Corpus*, syntactically and morphologically annotated, and each word is glossed. The *Brooklyn Corpus* contains 106,210 running word forms. The *Penn-Helsinki Parsed Corpus of Middle English*, second edition (PPCME2) is a syntactically annotated corpus of prose text samples from the period from 1150 until 1500. It can be bought on CD-ROM from

```
<S SAMPLE 1>
<P VI,209>
[} (\CAPITULUM VICESIMUM QUARTUM.\) }]

Leo +te emperour lete be +te enemyes of +te empere, and
werrede a+genst figures and ymages of holy seyntes. Pope
<P VI,211>
Gregory and Germanius of Constantynnoble wi+tstood hym
nameliche, as +te olde usage and custome wolde +tat is allowed
and apreeved by holy cherche, and seide +tat it is wor+ty and
medeful to do hem +te affecioun of worschippe. For we #
worschippe+t
in hem but God, [{and{] in worschippe of God and of
holy seyntes, +tat man have+t in mynde efte by suche ymages,
God allone schal be princepalliche worschipped, [{and after
hym creatures schal be i-worschipped{] in worschippe of hym.
Beda, (\libro 5=o=, capitulo 24=o=.\) +Tat +gere deide #
Withredus kyng
of Caunterbury, and Thobias bisshop of Rouchestre, +tat cou+te
Latyn and Grew as wel as his owne longage. (\Paulus,
libro 7=o=.\) +Tat +gere Sarasyns com to Constantynnoble and #
byseged
it +tre +gere, and took +tennes moche good and catel.
```

Listing 8.4: Excerpt from the *Helsinki Corpus* (part 2).

the University of Pennsylvania. [16] Finally, the *Penn-Helsinki Parsed Corpus of Early Modern English* (PPCEME) is a syntactically annotated corpus of prose text samples from 1500 until 1710. Its size is about 1.8 million running word forms. Like PPCME2, it is distributed by the University of Pennsylvania.

We have already mentioned *ARCHER* in sections 3.2.2 and 7.3. *ARCHER* [17] (A Representative Corpus of Historical English Registers) is a multigenre corpus of British and American English covering the period 1650–1999. The first version was constructed by Douglas Biber and Edward Finegan in the 1990s, further development is done by a consortium of participants at fourteen universities in seven countries. The current version is known as *ARCHER 3.1*, released in 2006. Work on version 3.2 is ongoing at the time of this writing. [18] Projected to contain about 3.2 million running word forms, version 3.2 will be almost twice the size of the previous version (1.8 million running word forms). It will also contain morphosyntactic annotation according to the CLAWS C8 tagset. [19] *ARCHER* is only available to consortium member institutions, where it may only be accessed on-site.

---

[16]http://www.ling.upenn.edu/hist-corpora/ (accessed 2012-06-06)
[17]http://www.llc.manchester.ac.uk/research/projects/archer/ (accessed 2012-06-06)
[18]http://www.llc.manchester.ac.uk/research/projects/archer/ (accessed 2012-07-01)
[19]http://ucrel.lancs.ac.uk/claws8tags.pdf (accessed 2012-06-06)

The *Dictionary of Old English Corpus* (DOE Corpus) contains a complete record of all surviving Old English texts except for some variant manuscripts of individual texts. The corpus contains over three million words of Old English and fewer than a million words of Latin. It was compiled as part of the Dictionary of Old English project at the University of Toronto. The corpus uses TEI P5-conformant XML encoding. The corpus can be accessed online on a subscription basis or bought on CD-ROM from the University of Toronto.[20]

The *York-Toronto-Helsinki Parsed Corpus of Old English Prose* (YCOE)[21] is a syntactically annotated subset (1.5 million running word forms) of the DOE Corpus. The YCEO is designed as a "sister corpus" to the *Penn-Helsinki Parsed Corpus of Middle English* (PPCME2, see below) and uses the same form of annotation. It can be obtained from the Oxford Text Archive[22] free of charge for non-commercial use.

The *Lampeter Corpus of Early Modern English Tracts* (Siemund and Claridge, 1997) is a collection of texts on various subject matters published between 1640 and 1740. For each decade of the century covered by the corpus, two texts were selected from each of the six domains religion, politics, economy and trade, science, law, and "miscellaneous," i.e., 120 texts in total, amounting to about 1.1 million running word forms. The corpus contains complete texts, generally only first editions, including front and back matters such as dedications, prefaces, postscripts, etc.; the texts vary in length from about 3,000 to 20,000 running word forms. The *Lampeter Corpus* is encoded according to the TEI Guidelines and freely available under a Creative Commons license from the Oxford Text Archive.[23]

The *Corpus of Historical American English* (COHA)[24] contains 400 million words of text of American English from 1810 to 2009; it is thus an example of a diachronic corpus covering a relatively recent period of time. COHA is accessible via a Web interface.

The *Zürich Corpus of English Newspapers* (ZEN)[25] is an example of a domain-specific historical corpus: the ZEN corpus covers early English newspapers published between 1661 and 1791. The corpus consists of 349 complete newspaper issues containing 1.6 million running word forms. The ZEN corpus is encoded according to the TEI P4 guidelines (for an overview, see Lehmann et al., 2006) and can be licensed from the University of Zurich.

Middle English Medical Texts (MEMT) (Taavitsainen et al., 2005) and *Early Modern English Medical Texts* (EMEMT) (Taavitsainen and Pahta, 2010) are further examples of domain-specific historical corpora. MEMT consists primarily of editions of medical treatises from about 1375 to 1500 (86 texts with about 500,000 running word forms), whereas EMEMT covers the period from 1500 to 1700 (450 texts with about 2 million running word forms). Both corpora are distributed on CD-ROMs that come with the cited books.

---

[20]http://www.doe.utoronto.ca/ (accessed 2012-06-06)

[21]http://www-users.york.ac.uk/~lang22/YCOE/YcoeHome.htm (accessed 2012-07-03)

[22]http://www.ota.ox.ac.uk/desc/2462 (accessed 2012-07-03)

[23]http://ota.ox.ac.uk/desc/3193 (acccsed 2012-07-01)

[24]http://corpus.byu.edu/coha/ (accessed 2012-06-06)

[25]http://www.es.uzh.ch/Subsites/Projects/zencorpus.html (accessed 2012-06-06)

The Corpus Resource Database (CoRD)[26], maintained by the Research Unit for Variation, Contacts and Change in English at the University of Helsinki, collects information on English-language corpora; the Web interface also allows users to search the database by criteria such as period or availability.

8.5 FRENCH

There are a number of historical French corpora available. The *Base de Français Médiéval* (BFM)[27] (Guillot et al., 2007) is composed of 26 full texts written between the 9th and the end of the 15th century and contains about 1.5 million running word forms. The BFM is a diachronic and diatopic corpus, i.e., the texts come from different geographic regions. It covers different genres and includes prose as well as poetry. The corpus is annotated using TEI P5 (Heiden et al., 2010); see Listing 8.5 for an example.[28]

Six texts of the BFM were manually tagged by two experts; these texts were then used to train a morphosyntactic model of Medieval French for use with TreeTagger. The model is freely available under a Creative Commons license from the BFM website.[29] The corpus is accessible online for research purposes after signing a license agreement.

A complementary corpus—based on the same principles—covering Old French from the 9th to the end of the 12th century is currently under construction; it is called *Corpus représentatif des premiers textes français* (CoRPTeF).[30]

Another corpus of Medieval French is the *Nouveau Corpus d'Amsterdam* (NCA)[31] (see Stein, 2008). The original *Corpus d'Amsterdam* had been compiled in the early 1980s as the basis for the *Atlas des formes linguistiques des textes littéraires de l'ancien français* (Dees, 1987) and contains about 300 text samples with a total of about 3 million running word forms. The corpus was manually annotated with numeric tags from a 225-item tagset. The NCA is a revised, lemmatized, and XML-formatted version of the corpus. Version 1.0 of the NCA was released in 2006; version 3.0 was released in 2011. The original corpus had been manually annotated with part of speech and morphological information; this information was used for training TreeTagger.

The corpus, the lexical resources used for the annotation (such as the TreeTagger parameter file), and the documentation are available free of charge for non-commercial, non-profit research purposes, but it is necessary to register and sign a license agreement.[32]

The *Syntactic Reference Corpus of Medieval French* (SRCMF)[33] (Stein, 2008) is a project to improve BFM and NCA, the two largest corpora of Medieval French, by adding a common syntactic annotation layer covering both corpora. The syntactic layer will be added manually (using the

---

[26]http://helsinki.fi/varieng/CoRD/ (accessed 2012-06-06)

[27]http://bfm.ens-lyon.fr/ (accessed 2012-06-06)

[28]The data is freely available at http://textometrie.risc.cnrs.fr/txm/ (accessed 2011-10-24).

[29]http://bfm.ens-lyon.fr/article.php3?id_article=324 (accessed 2012-06-06)

[30]http://corptef.ens-lyon.fr/ (accessed 2012-06-06)

[31]http://www.uni-stuttgart.de/lingrom/stein/corpus/ (accessed 2012-06-06)

[32]http://www.uni-stuttgart.de/lingrom/stein/corpus/ (accessed 2012-06-06)

[33]http://www.uni-stuttgart.de/lingrom/forschung/projekte/srcmf.html (accessed 2012-06-06)

```
<p n="1">
<lb n="1"/>
<s n="1" xml:id="s_fro_1">
<supplied resp="#cmn" source="#ms_Z" reason="arraché">
<w type="PRE" xml:id="w_fro_000001">A</w>
<w type="DETdef" xml:id="w_fro_000002">la</w>
<w type="NOMcom" xml:id="w_fro_000003">veille</w>
<w type="PRE" rend="aggl" xml:id="w_fro_000004">de</w>
<w type="DETdef" rend="aggl" xml:id="w_fro_000005">la</w>
<w type="NOMpro" xml:id="w_fro_000006">Pentecoste</w>
<lb n="2"/>
<w type="CONsub" xml:id="w_fro_000007">quant</w>
<w type="DETdef" xml:id="w_fro_000008">li</w>
<w type="NOMcom" xml:id="w_fro_000009">compaignon</w>
    <lb n="3"/>
<w type="PRE" xml:id="w_fro_000010">de</w>
<w type="DETdef" rend="aggl" xml:id="w_fro_000011">la</w>
<w type="NOMcom" xml:id="w_fro_000012">table</w>
<w type="ADJqua" xml:id="w_fro_000013">reonde</w>
<lb n="4"/>
<w type="VERcjg" xml:id="w_fro_000014">furent</w>
<w type="VERppe" xml:id="w_fro_000015">venu</w>
```

Listing 8.5: La Queste del saint Graal (The Quest for the Holy Grail) in Old French, prepared in the BFM project, illustrating the TEI markup used for the BFM and CoRPTeF corpora.]Excerpt from a TEI version of *La Queste del saint Graal* (The Quest for the Holy Grail) in Old French, prepared in the BFM project, illustrating the TEI markup used for the BFM and CoRPTeF corpora.

NotaBene annotation tool developed for this project (Mazziotta, 2010), see also Section 7.3) and independently from existing annotation layers. When finished, this resource will be of high interest for NLP for Medieval French.

The *Textes de Français Ancien* corpus [34] (Martineau, 2004) contains about 1 million word forms of historical French from texts from the 12th to the 15th century. The corpus can be searched through a Web interface but is not available for download.

The *Modéliser le changement : les voies du français* (MCVF) (Modeling Change: The Paths of French) corpus [35] (Martineau et al., 2007; Martineau, 2008) contains about 2.5 million word forms and aims to cover the development of French from the Middle Ages until the 18th century. The corpus is encoded in TEI P5. An explicit goal of the project was to create a morphosyntactically annotated corpus that is comparable to historical parsed corpora available for other languages, in particular the *Brooklyn-Geneva-Amsterdam-Helsinki Parsed Corpus of Old English*, *Penn-Helsinki Parsed Corpus of Middle English*, *Penn-Helsinki Parsed Corpus of Early Modern English* (see Section 8.4), and the *Tycho*

[34]http://artfl-project.uchicago.edu/content/tfa (accessed 2012-06-06)
[35]http://www.voies.uottawa.ca/ (accessed 2012-06-06)

Brahe Parsed Corpus of Historical Portuguese (see Section 8.9)(Martineau, 2004, p. 137). The MCVF corpus can be queried online, but is not available for download.

Guillot et al. (2008) provide an overview (in French) of the corpora described in this section and of a few other corpora of Old and Middle French texts from the perspective of French historical linguistics.

8.6 GERMAN

Compared to English, corpora of historical German are just starting to become available now. The *Bonner Frühneuhochdeutschkorpus* (Bonn Corpus of Early New High German)[36] was built between 1972 and 1985, but counting only about 16,000 running word forms, it is very small. However, it was later transformed into an XML format (Diel et al., 2002) and is publicly available.

The *Historisches Textkorpus* (Historical Text Corpus)[37] of the Institute for the German Language (IDS) is a large historical corpus of German, containing approximately 45 million running word forms from 1700 until about 1918. However, due to legal issues, the corpus is not available for download and only a subset may be searched via the IDS COSMAS II online retrieval tool.

More recently, coordinated efforts have been made to create a set of comparable syntactically annotated reference corpora for each historical stage of (High) German. These are:

- *Referenzkorpus Altdeutsch* (Reference Corpus Old German)[38], covering the period from 750 to 1050 (Old High and Low German); when completed, the corpus will contain about 650,000 running word forms;

- *Referenzkorpus Mittelhochdeutsch* (Reference Corpus Middle High German)[39], covering the period from 1050 to 1350 (Middle High German); and

- *Referenzkorpus Frühneuhochdeutsch* (Reference Corpus Early New High German), covering the period from 1350 to 1650 (Early New High German).

These corpora are currently under construction. They will all be managed using the ANNIS system[40] (Zeldes et al., 2009), but the exact terms of availability have not yet been announced.

GerManC (Bennett et al., 2010), a corpus covering the subsequent period from 1650 to 1800 has recently been completed.[41] *GerManC* aims to be a representative corpus and to provide a basis for comparative studies of the development of the grammar and vocabulary of English and German during the period covered. The design of *GerManC* therefore closely follows that of *ARCHER* for English (see Section 8.4): *GerManC* consists of text samples of about 2000 words each from eight different genres (drama, newspapers, sermons, and personal letters), and the same number of texts

[36]http://www.korpora.org/Fnhd/ (accessed 2012-06-06)
[37]http://ids-mannheim.de/lexik/HistorischesKorpus/ (accessed 2012-06-06)
[38]http://clients.designato.de/humboldt/ddd/ (accessed 2012-06-06)
[39]http://www.linguistics.rub.de/~dipper/project_ddd.html (accessed 2012-06-06)
[40]http://www.sfb632.uni-potsdam.de/d1/annis/ (accessed 2012-06-06)
[41]http://www.llc.manchester.ac.uk/research/projects/germanc/ (accessed 2012-06-06)

from each genre was selected for each fifty-year period. The complete corpus thus consists of 360 samples, totaling about 800,000 words. *GerManC* is annotated using TEI P5 and freely available (also in several other formats besides TEI) from the Oxford Text Archive.[42]

With the *Deutsches Textarchiv* (DTA),[43] the Berlin-Brandenburg Academy of Sciences and Humanities aims to digitize first editions of German-language books from the period of 1650 until 1900. During the first, recently completed phase, about 650 books from 1780 to 1900 were digitized; by 2014, books from 1650 to 1780 are to be added to the corpus. The texts are lemmatized and encoded according to TEI P5 and can be queried online. The full XML-encoded texts—but only without lemmatization—are freely available (under a Creative Commons license).

The TextGrid project[44] makes available the *Digitale Bibliothek*, a collection of texts from about 1500 to the early 20th century (but not necessarily first editions). A part of the collection is marked up using TEI. All texts are freely available under a Creative Commons license.

8.7   NORDIC LANGUAGES

The Medieval Nordic Text Archive (Menota)[45] is a good example of the work on digital historical texts and associated resources going on in Scandinavia. Menota is a cooperation between a number of research institutions (currently 18) from Denmark, Norway, Sweden, and Iceland. Menota has defined common guidelines—based on TEI—for encoding medieval texts (Haugen, 2008) and is active in the Medieval Unicode Font Initiative (MUFI) (see Chapter 5).

The text archive itself currently contains 17 medieval Nordic texts, about 923,000 running word forms in total; some of the texts are fully lemmatized. The HTML versions of the texts are freely accessible; the XML source is not generally available.

The *Icelandic Parsed Historical Corpus* (IcePaHC)[46] is a diachronic treebank for Icelandic from the 12th to the 21th century, with text samples of about 100,000 word forms for each century; total size is about 1 million word forms (Rögnvaldsson et al., 2011). The corpus is annotated with lemma, part of speech, and phrase structure; the annotation was manually checked and corrected, where needed. The spelling of historical texts is modernized. IcePaHC aims to be compatible with the corpora of historical English developed at the University of Pennsylvania (see Section 8.4). Unlike many other parsed corpora, IcePaHC is licensed under the GNU Lesser General Public License (LGPL) and is thus freely available.

For Old Swedish, Språkbanken (the Swedish Language Bank)[47] at the University of Gothenburg and Fornsvensk textbank (the Old Swedish Text Bank)[48] at Lund University have sizable collections of Old Swedish texts. Språkbanken has also digitized the standard reference dictionaries

---

[42]http://www.ota.ox.ac.uk/desc/2544 (accessed 2012-05-10)
[43]http://www.deutschestextarchiv.de/ (accessed 2012-06-06)
[44]http://www.textgrid.de/ (accessed 2012-06-06)
[45]http://menota.org/ (accessed 2012-06-06)
[46]http://www.linguist.is/icelandic_treebank/ (accessed 2012-06-06)
[47]http://spraakbanken.gu.se (accessed 2012-06-06)
[48]http://www.nordlund.lu.se/Fornsvenska/Fsv%20Folder/ (accessed 2012-06-06)

of Old Swedish and makes them available for looking up words via a Web interface.[49] The full text of the dictionaries is available for research purposes by special agreement (Borin and Forsberg, 2008).

8.8   LATIN AND ANCIENT GREEK

The LASLA database (Denooz, 1978) is a manually lemmatized and morphosyntactically annotated corpus of Classical Latin and Greek, containing currently almost 2 million running word forms of Latin text—prose and verse texts from authors such as Caesar, Cicero, Ovid, or Virgil—and about 1.2 million running word forms of Greek, including texts by authors such as Aristotle, Euripides, or Plato. Work on this resource started in 1961 at the University of Liège in Belgium. The Latin texts of the LASLA database—called *Opera Latina* (Denooz, 2004)—are freely accessible (after registration) via a Web application for interactive exploration;[50] the results of a query can also be downloaded.

The *Perseus Digital Library*[51] is probably the largest repository of freely available digital texts in Classical Latin and Ancient Greek.

The Perseus project has also developed the Ancient Greek and Latin dependency treebanks[52] (Bamman and Crane, 2011). As of version 1.5, the *Latin Dependency Treebank* contains texts from eight authors, totaling 53,143 running word forms. The *Ancient Greek Dependency Treebank* (currently in version 1.2) is made up from Homer's *Iliad* and *Odyssey*, Sophocles' *Ajax*, and the complete works of Hesiod and Aeschylus for a total of 309,096 running word forms. The syntactic annotation of the treebanks was accomplished in a collaborative effort involving over 200 contributors. Both treebanks are freely available for download under a Creative Commons license.

The *Index Thomisticus Treebank*[53] (McGillivray et al., 2009; Passarotti, 2010a) is a syntactically annotated subset of the *Index Thomisticus* created by Father Roberto Busa (mentioned in the introduction of this chapter), currently comprising about 6,600 syntactically annotated sentences (ca. 130,000 running word forms; the complete *Index Thomisticus* contains about 10.6 million running word forms). Like the Ancient Greek and Latin dependency treebanks and the PROIEL treebank, it uses the *Prague Dependency Treebank*[54] (for Czech) as a model. The *Index Thomisticus Treebank* can be browsed online, but it is not available for download.

The PROIEL project[55] (Pragmatic Resources in Old Indo-European Languages) studies the language in the Greek text of the New Testament and as its translations into Latin, Gothic, Armenian and Old Church Slavonic. For this purpose, the project is building a parallel corpus of New Testament translations (Haug and Jhndal, 2008). The corpus (including the XML files) is publicly available under a Creative Commons license.

---

[49]http://spraakbanken.gu.se/fsvldb/ (accessed 2012-06-06)
[50]http://www.cipl.ulg.ac.be/Lasla/descriptionop.html (accessed 2012-06-06)
[51]http://www.perseus.tufts.edu/hopper/ (accessed 2012-06-06)
[52]http://nlp.perseus.tufts.edu/syntax/treebank/ (accessed 2012-06-06)
[53]http://itreebank.marginalia.it/ (accessed 2012-06-06)
[54]http://ufal.mff.cuni.cz/pdt2.0/ (accessed 2012-06-06)
[55]http://www.hf.uio.no/ifikk/proiel/ (accessed 2012-06-06)

```
<p><seg type="formulaicText" n="harengue">Acuzo a Receção da sua de 10
do Corrente que me<lb/> deixa na ciença dos <gap reason="illegible"
extent="6 words"/><lb/> com que se vê ataquado o seu espritto, o
que<lb/> sinto Como se eu proprio persebeçe, <abbr>pr</abbr> que<lb/>
nengem mais do que eu estima o seu suçego e thra<lb/>nquilidade</seg>
da maneira que Le vô ComuniCar<lb/>
```

Listing 8.6: Short extract from the CARDS/FLY corpus, illustrating the type of annotation used.

The TITUS project[56] (Thesaurus Indogermanischer Text- und Sprachmaterialien, 'Thesaurus of Indo-European Text and Language Material') makes available texts from languages that are relevant for Indo-European studies, including Latin and Ancient Greek texts. Most of the texts are freely available from the TITUS server for scholarly purposes.

There is also a Latin WordNet (Minozzi, 2009), built according to the principles of MultiWord-Net (Pianta et al., 2002) and browsable through the MultiWordNet Web interface.[57] MultiWordNet is a multilingual lexical database which is closely aligned with Princeton WordNet 1.6 for English.

8.9   PORTUGUESE

A number of corpora of historical Portuguese are available. The largest corpus is probably the *Corpus do Português*,[58] containing 45 million running word forms from the 14th until the 20th century. The corpus can be queried using a Web interface, but is not available for download.

The *Tycho Brahe Parsed Corpus of Historical Portuguese*[59] (Paixão de Sousa and Trippel, 2006) consists of texts written by authors born between 1380 to 1845. At the time of this writing, it contains about 2.5 million running word forms in 53 texts; 32 of these contain part-of-speech information, 15 texts are annotated syntactically. After registration, the corpus is freely available for download.

The *Corpus Informatizado do Português Medieval* (CIPM)[60] comprises texts from the 9th until the 16th century; the earliest texts (until the 12th century) are in Proto-Portuguese, the later ones in Old Portuguese. The total size is about 2 million running word forms. A part of the corpus contains morphosyntactic annotation. It is freely available after registration.

The *CARDS/FLY* corpora[61] are specialized corpora of historical private letters from the periods 1500–1900 (CARDS) and 1900–1974 (FLY) (Marquilhas, 2012). Each of the corpora contains about 2,000 letters. The corpus uses a TEI-conformant XML annotation and is freely available for download. The letters are annotated with pragmatic information (Hendrickx et al., 2010), see Listing 8.6.

---

[56]http://titus.uni-frankfurt.de/ (accessed 2012-06-29)
[57]http://multiwordnet.fbk.eu/ (accessed 2012-06-06)
[58]http://www.corpusdoportugues.org/ (accessed 2012-06-06)
[59]http://www.tycho.iel.unicamp.br/ (accessed 2012-06-06)
[60]http://cipm.fcsh.unl.pt (accessed 2012-06-06)
[61]http://alfclul.clul.ul.pt/cards-fly/index.php?page=mainen (accessed 2012-06-06)

For the *Historical Dictionary of Brazilian Portuguese* a large corpus of texts from the 16th to the 18th century was created, the *HDBP corpus* [62] (see Vale et al., 2008; Candido Jr. and Aluísio, 2009). The corpus contains 2,458 texts or about 7.5 million running word forms. It is annotated with basic TEI markup. The corpus itself is not publicly available, but a number of tools used in building and managing the corpus are, among them Procorph (Candido Jr. and Aluísio, 2008), a system for dictionary management, Siaconf, a system for automatic spelling variant extraction based on transformation rules, and Renahb, an online system for retrieval of abbreviated named entities. Also available for download are resources derived from the corpus, such as a list of spellings automatically extracted from the HDBP corpus by Siaconf or a glossary with (abbreviated) names of river, location, and person names. [63]

The article by Santos (2011) contains an overview of Portuguese corpora and language tools, including an overview of historical corpora.

8.10 SUMMARY

In this chapter we gave an overview of corpora for various historical languages. This chapter illustrates a number of different approaches to historical corpora, different technical realizations (e.g., newer corpora tend to use XML formats based on TEI—see Section 5.2—whereas older corpora typically use project-specific encoding conventions), and different licensing models, where one can see a trend towards more open licenses (e.g., Creative Commons). At first it may be surprising that some historical corpora are encumbered by publishers' copyrights, as the texts are usually older than even the idea of copyright. However, many corpora are based on critical editions, which may be protected by copyright. If a corpus is not publicly available, it is always a good idea to contact the creators of the corpus, as it may be possible to obtain a license for research purposes even if it is not explicitly stated on a project's website.

---

[62]http://www.nilc.icmc.usp.br/nilc/projects/hpc/ (accessed 2012-06-06)
[63]URL for all tools and resources: http://www.nilc.icmc.usp.br/nilc/projects/hpc/ (accessed 2012-06-29).

CHAPTER 9

Conclusion

In this book we tried to give an overview of the state of the art in natural language processing for historical texts. We discussed the acquisition and digitization of historical texts, issues of text encoding and annotation, existing historical corpora and tools, approaches for handling spelling variation—a pervasive problem when processing historical texts—as well as the relationship of NLP for historical languages to the emerging field of digital humanities.

Throughout this book we made reference to numerous projects and publications in this area, which we hope are useful for the reader interested in specific details. The references also illustrate the wide variety of projects and approaches for processing historical texts. In fact, one may state that there are very few, if any, "canonical" techniques; the field of NLP for historical texts is still very much in a state of flux. This differs from other subareas of NLP and computational linguistics, where there are established sets of methods and techniques. These areas are also very dynamic and progress quickly, but there is a common understanding of the essentials students in this area have to know. Machine translation could be named as an example: the IBM models, parallel texts, and alignment are some of the core concepts in this area, and tools such as Giza++ and Moses (Och and Ney, 2003) are part of any introduction to machine translation (for more information specifically on alignment, see Tiedemann, 2011).

We do not yet have a similar situation in the area of NLP for historical texts. There is, for example, no universal baseline approach for spelling normalization. The methods and tools used are highly project-specific; quite often the methods chosen reflect the particular background of the NLP researchers (e.g., in machine learning or finite state techniques). This book reflects this situation in that it does not aim to teach a certain set of core techniques but rather tries to give an overview of projects and the methods used therein, so that readers can compare approaches and judge for themselves which of them may be appropriate for their own work.

We repeatedly pointed out in this book that computer processing of historical language has a long history, but NLP—in the narrow sense—for historical texts is nevertheless a relatively new area of research. It is, however, starting to establish itself. One indicator for the sustainability of a scientific community are conferences and workshops. The workshop series "Language Technology for Cultural Heritage, Social Sciences, and Humanities"[1] (LaTeCH) has now been running continuously since 2007; it is not restricted to the processing of historical text, but this area clearly plays a major role. A selection of papers from the LaTeCH workshop series (in revised and extended form) was recently published as a book (Sporleder et al., 2011). Similar workshops are now starting to appear,

---

[1] http://ilk.uvt.nl/LaTeCH2012/ (accessed 2012-07-01)

and at EACL 2012 in Avignon, the establishment of an ACL special interest group on language technologies for the humanities (SIGHUM) was formally proposed, indicating not only sustained, but growing interest in this field. Given the increasing amount of digitized historical texts available, this is certainly a good thing.

What are the future challenges for the field of NLP for historical texts? We see three major challenges: one theoretical, one practical, and one organizational. The theoretical challenge has already been mentioned in Chapter 2. NLP needs to achieve a better theoretical understanding of language variation and develop appropriate models for handling it; historical spelling variation is just one—very obvious—instance of variation in language.

The practical challenge is to develop tools that are able to process marked-up texts—in particular TEI-encoded texts—effectively and efficiently (see Section 5.2). Again, this need is not restricted to the processing of historical texts, but it is particularly pressing for historical texts, since they often critically depend on markup.

The organizational challenge is to bring together NLP and the digital humanities. As suggested in Chapter 2, we believe that closer cooperation would be a huge benefit for both sides, and from a technical perspective, it would be logical. However, there are still organizational barriers between the two fields; to overcome these barriers and to realize the full potential of NLP for historical languages is perhaps the biggest challenge the field is facing.

Bibliography

Antonacopoulos, Apostolos and Andy C. Downton (2007). Special issue on the analysis of historical documents. *International Journal on Document Analysis and Recognition*, 9(2):75–77. doi: 10.1007/s10032-007-0045-1. (cited on p. 27)

Arica, Nafiz and Fatos T. Yarman-Vural (2001). An overview of character recognition focused on off-line handwriting. *IEEE Transactions on Systems, Man and Cybernetics, Part C (Applications and Reviews)*, 31(2):216–233. doi: 10.1109/5326.941845. (cited on p. 27)

Bamman, David and Gregory Crane (2008). Building a dynamic lexicon from a digital library. In *Proceedings of the 8th ACM/IEEE-CS joint conference on Digital libraries (JCDL '08)*, pages 11–20. New York, NY, USA: ACM. doi: 10.1145/1378889.1378892. (cited on pp. 89 and 90)

Bamman, David and Gregory Crane (2011). The Ancient Greek and Latin dependency treebanks. In Caroline Sporleder, Antal van den Bosch, and Kalliopi Zervanou, eds., *Language Technology for Cultural Heritage*, Theory and Applications of Natural Language Processing, chap. 5, pages 79–98. Berlin/Heidelberg: Springer. doi: 10.1007/978-3-642-20227-8_5. (cited on pp. 89 and 114)

Baron, Alistair and Paul Rayson (2008). VARD 2: A tool for dealing with spelling variation in historical corpora. In *Proceedings of the Postgraduate Conference in Corpus Linguistics*. Birmingham, UK: Aston University. (cited on p. 99)

Baron, Alistair and Paul Rayson (2009). Automatic standardization of texts containing spelling variation, how much training data do you need? In *Proceedings of Corpus Linguistics 2009*. URL http://ucrel.lancs.ac.uk/publications/cl2009/314_FullPaper.pdf. (cited on p. 74)

Baron, Alistair, Paul Rayson, and Dawn Archer (2009). Word frequency and key word statistics in corpus linguistics. *Anglistik*, 20(1):41–67. (cited on pp. 14, 15, 16, and 17)

Barthélemy, François (2007). Cunéiforme et SMS: analyse graphémique de systèmes d'écriture hétérogènes. In *Acte du 26ᵉ Colloque international Lexique Grammaire*. URL http://infolingu.univ-mlv.fr/Colloques/Bonifacio/proceedings/barthelemy.pdf. (cited on p. 9)

Bautier, Robert-Henri (1977). Les demandes des historiens à l'informatique. La forme diplomatique et le contenu juridique des actes. In Lucie Fossier, André Vauchez, and Cinzio Violante, eds., *Informatique et histoire médiévale. Actes du colloque de Rome (20–22 mai 1975)*, vol. 31 of *Publications de l'École française de Rome*, pages 179–186. Rome, Italy: École Française de Rome. URL `http://www.persee.fr/web/ouvrages/home/prescript/article/efr_0000-0000_1977_act_31_1_2252`. (cited on p. 8)

Becker, Joseph D. (1988). Unicode 88. Tech. rep., Xerox Corp., Palo Alto, CA, USA. URL `http://www.unicode.org/history/unicode88.pdf`. (cited on pp. 54 and 56)

Bennett, Paul, Martin Durrell, Silke Scheible, and Richard J. Whitt (2010). Annotating a historical corpus of German: A case study. In *Proceedings of the LREC 2010 Workshop on Language Resource and Language Technology: Standards—state of the art, emerging needs, and future developments*, pages 64–68. Paris: ELRA. (cited on pp. 33 and 112)

Bergroth, Lasse, Harri Hakonen, and Timo Raita (2000). A survey of longest common subsequence algorithms. In *Proceedings of the Seventh International Symposium on String Processing and Information Retrieval (SPIRE 2000)*, pages 39–48. New York, NY, USA: IEEE. doi: 10.1109/SPIRE.2000.878178. (cited on p. 73)

Bergroth, Lasse, Harri Hakonen, and Juri Väisänen (2003). New refinement techniques for longest common subsequence algorithms. In Mario A. Nascimento, Edleno S. Moura, and Arlindo L. Oliveira, eds., *String Processing and Information Retrieval (SPIRE 2003)*, vol. 2857 of *Lecture Notes in Computer Science*, chap. 22, pages 287–303. Berlin/Heidelberg: Springer. doi: 10.1007/978-3-540-39984-1_22. (cited on p. 73)

Bernardini, Silvia, Marco Baroni, and Stefan Evert (2006). A WaCky introduction. In Marco Baroni and Silvia Bernardini, eds., *Wacky! Working papers on the Web as Corpus*, pages 9–40. Bologna: GEDIT. URL `http://wackybook.sslmit.unibo.it/pdfs/bernardini.pdf`. (cited on p. 66)

Bertholdo, Flávio, Eduardo Valle, and Arnaldo de A. Araújo (2009). Layout-aware limiarization for readability enhancement of degraded historical documents. In *Proceedings of the 9th ACM symposium on Document engineering*, DocEng '09, pages 131–134. New York, NY, USA: ACM. doi: 10.1145/1600193.1600223. (cited on p. 30)

Biemann, Chris (2009). Unsupervised part-of-speech tagging in the large. *Research on Language & Computation*, 7(2–4):101–135. doi: 10.1007/s11168-010-9067-9. (cited on p. 89)

Blum, Christian, Maria J. Blesa, and Manuel L. Ibáñez (2009). Beam search for the longest common subsequence problem. *Computers & Operations Research*, 36(12):3178–3186. doi: 10.1016/j.cor.2009.02.005. (cited on p. 73)

Boag, Scott, Don Chamberlin, Mary F. Fernández, Daniela Florescu, Jonathan Robie, and Jérôme Siméon (2010). XQuery 1.0: An XML Query Language. W3C Recommendation, World Wide Web Consortium. URL `http://www.w3.org/TR/xquery/`. (cited on p. 60)

Bollmann, Marcel, Florian Petran, and Stefanie Dipper (2011a). Applying Rule-Based normalization to different types of historical Texts—An evaluation. In *Proceedings of the 5th Language & Technology Conference*. (cited on p. 76)

Bollmann, Marcel, Florian Petran, and Stefanie Dipper (2011b). Rule-Based normalization of historical texts. In *Proceedings of the RANLP 2011 Workshop on Language Technologies for Digital Humanities and Cultural Heritage*, pages 34–42. Hissar, Bulgaria. URL http://aclweb.org/anthology/W11-4106. (cited on pp. 73, 75, and 76)

Borin, Lars and Markus Forsberg (2008). Something old, something new: A computational morphological description of Old Swedish. In Kiril Ribarov and Caroline Sporleder, eds., *Proceedings of the LREC 2008 Workshop on Language Technology for Cultural Heritage Data (LaTeCH 2008)*, pages 9–16. (cited on pp. 97, 98, and 114)

Boschetti, Federico (2010). *A Corpus-based Approach to Philological Issues*. Ph.D. thesis, University of Trento, Trento, Italy. URL http://eprints-phd.biblio.unitn.it/185/. (cited on p. 7)

Boschetti, Federico, Matteo Romanello, Alison Babeu, David Bamman, and Gregory Crane (2009). Improving OCR accuracy for classical critical editions. In *ECDL'09: Proceedings of the 13th European conference on Research and advanced technology for digital libraries*, pages 156–167. Berlin/Heidelberg: Springer. (cited on pp. 34, 35, 36, 37, 38, 39, and 40)

Brants, Thorsten (2000a). Inter-annotator agreement for a German newspaper corpus. In *Second International Conference on Language Resources and Evaluation (LREC-2000)*. Paris: European Language Resources Association (ELRA). URL http://www.lrec-conf.org/proceedings/lrec2000/pdf/333.pdf. (cited on p. 100)

Brants, Thorsten (2000b). TnT – a statistical part-of-speech tagger. In *Proceedings of the Sixth Applied Natural Language Processing Conference (ANLP-2000)*. URL http://aclweb.org/anthology/A00-1031. (cited on p. 90)

Braune, Fabienne and Alexander Fraser (2010). Improved unsupervised sentence alignment for symmetrical and asymmetrical parallel corpora. In *Proceedings of the 23rd International Conference on Computational Linguistics (Coling 2010): Posters*, pages 81–89. Stroudsburg, PA, USA: Association for Computational Linguistics. URL http://aclweb.org/anthology/C10-2010. (cited on p. 75)

Bray, Tim, Jean Paoli, C. M. Sperberg-McQueen, Eve Maler, and François Yergeau (2006). Extensible Markup Language (XML) 1.0. W3C Recommendation, World Wide Web Consortium. URL http://www.w3.org/TR/xml. (cited on p. 60)

Breuel, Thomas (2009a). Recent progress on the OCRopus OCR system. In *Proceedings of the International Workshop on Multilingual OCR (MOCR '09)*. New York, NY, USA: ACM. doi: 10.1145/1577802.1577805. (cited on p. 40)

Breuel, Thomas M. (2009b). Applying the OCRopus OCR system to scholarly Sanskrit literature. In Gérard Huet, Amba Kulkarni, and Peter Scharf, eds., *Sanskrit Computational Linguistics*, pages 391–402. Berlin/Heidelberg: Springer. doi: 10.1007/978-3-642-00155-0_21. (cited on p. 40)

Brisaboa, Nieves, Carlos Callón, Juan-Ramón López, Ángeles Places, and Goretti Sanmartín (2002). Stemming Galician texts. In Alberto Laender and Arlindo Oliveira, eds., *String Processing and Information Retrieval. 9th International Symposium, SPIRE 2002 Lisbon, Portugal, September 11 13, 2002 Proceedings*, vol. 2476 of *Lecture Notes in Computer Science*, chap. 9, pages 201–206. Berlin/Heidelberg: Springer. doi: 10.1007/3-540-45735-6_9. (cited on p. 74)

Brisaboa, Nieves, Juan-Ramón López, Miguel Penabad, and Ángeles Places (2003). Diachronic stemmed corpus and dictionary of Galician language. In Alexander Gelbukh, ed., *Computational Linguistics and Intelligent Text Processing. 4th International Conference, CICLing 2003*, vol. 2588 of *Lecture Notes in Computer Science*, pages 39–65. Berlin/Heidelberg: Springer. doi: 10.1007/3-540-36456-0_43. (cited on p. 74)

Callison-Burch, Chris and Mark Dredze, eds. (2010). *Proceedings of the NAACL HLT 2010 Workshop on Creating Speech and Language Data with Amazon's Mechanical Turk*. Association for Computational Linguistics. URL http://aclweb.org/anthology/W10-07. (cited on p. 43)

Candido Jr., Arnaldo and Sandra Maria Aluísio (2008). Procorph: um sistema de apoio à criação de dicionários históricos. In *Companion Proceedings of the XIV Brazilian Symposium on Multimedia and the Web (WebMedia '08)*, pages 347–352. New York, NY, USA: ACM. doi: 10.1145/1809980.1810064. (cited on p. 116)

Candido Jr., Arnaldo and Sandra Maria Aluísio (2009). Building a corpus-based historical Portuguese dictionary: Challenges and opportunities. *Traitement Automatique des Langues*, 50(2):73–102. URL http://atala.org/IMG/pdf/TAL-2009-50-2-03-Candido.pdf. (cited on p. 116)

Concepcion, Vicente P. and Donald P. D'Amato (1993). Synchronous tracking of outputs from multiple OCR systems. In *Proceedings of SPIE*, vol. 1906, pages 218–228. The International Society for Optical Engineering. doi: 10.1117/12.143623. (cited on p. 34)

Craig, Hugh and R. Whipp (2010). Old spellings, new methods: automated procedures for indeterminate linguistic data. *Literary and Linguistic Computing*, 25(1):37–52. doi: 10.1093/llc/fqp033. (cited on pp. 71, 74, and 82)

Crane, Gregory (1991). Generating and parsing classical Greek. *Literary and Linguistic Computing*, 6(4):243–245. (cited on p. 36)

Crochemore, Maxime, Costas S. Ilipoulos, and Yoan J. Pinzon (2002). Speeding-up Hirschberg and Hunt-Szymanski LCS algorithms. *Fundamenta Informaticae*, 56:89–103. (cited on p. 73)

Crochemore, Maxime and Wojciech Rytter (2002). *Jewels of Stringology: Text Algorithms*. Hackensack, NJ, USA: World Scientific. (cited on p. 72)

Curran, James R. and Stephen Clark (2003). Investigating GIS and smoothing for maximum entropy taggers. In *Proceedings of the 10ᵗʰ conference of the European chapter of the Association for Computational Linguistics (EACL 2003)*, vol. 1, pages 91–98. Stroudsburg, PA, USA: Association for Computational Linguistics. doi: 10.3115/1067807.1067821. (cited on p. 94)

Daelemans, Walter, Jakub Zavrel, Peter Berck, and Steven Gillis (1996). MBT: A memory-based part of speech tagger-generator. In Eva Ejerhed and Ido Dagan, eds., *Proceedings of the Fourth Workshop on Very Large Corpora*, pages 14–27. URL `http://aclweb.org/anthology/W96-0102`. (cited on pp. 90 and 98)

Damerau, Fred J. (1964). A technique for computer detection and correction of spelling errors. *Communications of the ACM*, 7(3):171–176. doi: 10.1145/363958.363994. (cited on pp. 72, 76, and 78)

Daniels, Peter T. and William Bright, eds. (1996). *The World's Writing Systems*. New York, NY, USA: Oxford University Press. (cited on p. 53)

Dees, Anthonij (1987). *Atlas des formes linguistiques des textes littéraires de l'ancien français*, vol. 212 of *Beihefte zur Zeitschrift für romanische Philologie*. Berlin, Germany: De Gruyter. URL `http://www.degruyter.de/cont/fb/sk/detailEn.cfm?id=IS-9783484522121-1`. (cited on p. 110)

Denooz, Joseph (1978). L'ordinateur et le latin, Techniques et méthodes. *Revue de l'organisation internationale pour l'étude des langues anciennes par ordinateur*, 4:1–36. URL `http://promethee.philo.ulg.ac.be/LASLApdf/lordinateuretlelatin.pdf`. (cited on p. 114)

Denooz, Joseph (2004). Opera latina : une base de données sur internet. *Euphrosyne*, 32:79–88. URN hdl:2268/357. (cited on p. 114)

Denooz, Joseph and Serge Rosmorduc (2009). Preface to the special issue on "NLP and Ancient Languages". *Traitement Automatique des Langues*, 50(2):13–16. (cited on p. 1)

Diel, Marcel, Bernhard Fisseni, Winfried Lenders, and Hans-Christian Schmitz (2002). XML-Kodierung des BonnerFrühneuhochdeutschkorpus. Ikp-arbeitsbericht, Universität Bonn, Bonn, Germany. URL `http://www.korpora.org/Fnhd/ikpab-nf02.pdf`. (cited on p. 112)

Dipper, Stefanie (2010). POS-tagging of historical language data: First experiments. In Manfred Pinkal, Ines Rehbein, Sabine Schulte im Walde, and Angelika Storrer, eds., *Semantic Approaches in Natural Language Processing: Proceedings of the Conference on Natural Language Processing 2010 (KONVENS)*, pages 117–121. Saarbrücken, Germany: Universaar. URN urn:nbn:de:bsz:291-universaar-124. (cited on pp. 87 and 91)

Dipper, Stefanie, Lara Kresse, Martin Schnurrenberger, and Seong E. Cho (2010). OTTO: A transcription and management tool for historical texts. In *Proceedings of the Fourth Linguistic Annotation Workshop*, pages 182–185. Uppsala, Sweden: Association for Computational Linguistics. URL http://aclweb.org/anthology/W10-1828. (cited on p. 51)

Driscoll, Matthew J. (2006). Levels of transcription. In Lou Burnard, Katherine O'Brien O'Keeffe, and John Unsworth, eds., *Electronic Textual Editing*, pages 254–261. New York, NY, USA: Modern Language Association of America. URL http://www.tei-c.org/Activities/ETE/Preview/driscoll.xml. (cited on pp. 19 and 21)

Dukes, Kais, Eric Atwell, and Nizar Habash (2011). Supervised collaboration for syntactic annotation of Quranic Arabic. *Language Resources and Evaluation Journal*. doi: 10.1007/s10579-011-9167-7. (cited on p. 102)

Dukes, Kais and Tim Buckwalter (2010). A dependency treebank of the Quran using traditional Arabic grammar. In *The 7th International Conference on Informatics and Systems (INFOS 2010)*, pages 1–7. New York, NY, USA: IEEE. URL http://ieeexplore.ieee.org/xpls/abs_all.jsp?arnumber=5461810. (cited on p. 102)

Ernst-Gerlach, Andrea and Norbert Fuhr (2010). Advanced training set construction for retrieval in historic documents. In Pu-Jen Cheng, Min-Yen Kan, Wai Lam, and Preslav Nakov, eds., *Information Retrieval Technology: 6th Asia Information Retrieval Societies Conference, AIRS 2010 Taipei, Taiwan, December 1-3, 2010 Proceedings*, vol. 6458 of *Lecture Notes in Computer Science*, pages 131–140. Berlin/Heidelberg: Springer. doi: 10.1007/978-3-642-17187-1_12. (cited on pp. 75 and 82)

Eumeridou, Eugenia, Blaise Nkwenti-Azeh, and John McNaught (2004). An analysis of verb subcategorization frames in three special language corpora with a view towards automatic term recognition. *Computers and the Humanities*, 38(1):37–60. doi: 10.1023/B:CHUM.0000009278.73498.f4. (cited on p. 2)

Fellbaum, Christiane, ed. (1998). *WordNet: An Electronic Lexical Database*. MIT Press. (cited on pp. 11 and 70)

Fischer, Andreas, Markus Wuthrich, Marcus Liwicki, Volkmar Frinken, Horst Bunke, Gabriel Viehhauser, and Michael Stolz (2009). Automatic transcription of handwritten medieval documents. In *2009 15th International Conference on Virtual Systems and Multimedia*, pages 137–142. IEEE. doi: 10.1109/VSMM.2009.26. (cited on p. 28)

Fischer, Franz, Christiane Fritze, and Georg Vogeler, eds. (2011). *Kodikologie und Paläographie im digitalen Zeitalter 2 – Codicology and Palaeography in the Digital Age 2*, vol. 3 of *Schriften des Instituts für Dokumentologie und Editorik*. Norderstedt, Germany: BoD. URL http://kups.ub.uni-koeln.de/4337/. (cited on p. 21)

Forsberg, Markus and Aarne Ranta (2004). Functional morphology. *ACM SIGPLAN Notices*, 39(9): 213–223. doi: 10.1145/1016848.1016879. (cited on p. 97)

Foster, Jennifer (2010). "cba to check the spelling": Investigating parser performance on discussion forum posts. In *Human Language Technologies: The 2010 Annual Conference of the North American Chapter of the Association for Computational Linguistics*, pages 381–384. Association for Computational Linguistics. URL http://aclweb.org/anthology/N10-1060. (cited on p. 9)

Foster, Jennifer, Özlem Çetinoglu, Joachim Wagner, Joseph L. Roux, Stephen Hogan, Joakim Nivre, Deirdre Hogan, and Josef van Genabith (2011). #hardtoparse: POS tagging and parsing the Twitterverse. In *Analyzing Microtext: Papers from the 2011 AAAI Workshop*, vol. WS-11-05 of *AAAI Workshops*, pages 20–25. Palo Alto, CA, USA: AAAI. URL http://www.aaai.org/ocs/index.php/WS/AAAIW11/paper/view/3912. (cited on p. 9)

Froger, Jacques (1970). La critique des textes et l'ordinateur. *Vigiliae Christianae*, 24(3):210–217. URL http://www.jstor.org/stable/1583073. (cited on pp. 9 and 83)

Furrer, Lenz and Martin Volk (2011). Reducing OCR errors in Gothic-script documents. In *Proceedings of the RANLP 2011 workshop on Language Technologies for Digital Humanities and Cultural Heritage*, pages 97–103. (cited on pp. 41 and 45)

Gadd, T. N. (1988). 'Fisching fore werds': phonetic retrieval of written text in information systems. *Program: electronic library and information systems*, 22(3):222–237. doi: 10.1108/eb046999. (cited on p. 77)

Garside, Roger and Nicholas Smith (1997). A hybrid grammatical tagger: CLAWS4. In Roger Garside, Geoffrey Leech, and Tony McEnery, eds., *Corpus Annotation: Linguistic Information from Computer Text Corpora*, pages 102–121. London, UK: Longman. URL http://ucrel.lancs.ac.uk/papers/HybridTaggerGS97.pdf. (cited on p. 91)

Gionis, Aristides, Piotr Indyk, and Rajeev Motwani (1999). Similarity search in high dimensions via hashing. In *Proceedings of the 25th International Conference on Very Large Data Bases (VLDB '99)*, pages 518–529. San Francisco, CA, USA: Morgan Kaufmann. (cited on p. 79)

Giusti, Rafael, Arnaldo Candido Jr., Marcelo Muniz, Lívia Cucatto, and Sandra Aluísio (2007). Automatic detection of spelling variation in historical corpus: An application to build a Brazilian Portuguese spelling variants dictionary. In Matthew Davies, Paul Rayson, Susan Hunston, and Pernilla Danielsson, eds., *Proceedings of the Corpus Linguistics Conference CL2007*. University of Birmingham. URL http://ucrel.lancs.ac.uk/publications/CL2007/paper/238_Paper.pdf. (cited on p. 74)

Gotscharek, Annette, Andreas Neumann, Ulrich Reffle, Christoph Ringlstetter, and Klaus U. Schulz (2009a). Enabling information retrieval on historical document collections: the role of matching procedures and special lexica. In *Proceedings of the Third Workshop on Analytics for Noisy Unstructured Text Data (AND 2009)*, pages 69–76. New York, NY, USA: ACM. doi: 10.1145/1568296.1568309. (cited on p. 84)

Gotscharek, Annette, Ulrich Reffle, Christoph Ringlstetter, and Klaus U. Schulz (2009b). On lexical resources for digitization of historical documents. In *DocEng '09: Proceedings of the 9th ACM symposium on Document engineering*, pages 193–200. New York, NY, USA: ACM. doi: 10.1145/1600193.1600236. (cited on pp. 33, 41, 42, and 75)

Gotscharek, Annette, Ulrich Reffle, Christoph Ringlstetter, Klaus U. Schulz, and Andreas Neumann (2011). Towards information retrieval on historical document collections: the role of matching procedures and special lexica. *International Journal on Document Analysis and Recognition*, 14(2): 159–171. doi: 10.1007/s10032-010-0132-6. (cited on p. 74)

Gouws, Stephan, Donald Metzler, Congxing Cai, and Eduard Hovy (2011). Contextual bearing on linguistic variation in social media. In *Proceedings of the Workshop on Language in Social Media (LSM 2011)*, pages 20–29. Stroudsburg, PA, USA: Association for Computational Linguistics. URL http://aclweb.org/anthology/W11-2210.pdf. (cited on p. 9)

Gray, Alasdair (2000). *The Book of Prefaces*. New York/London: Bloomsbury. (cited on pp. 14 and 15)

Greg, Walter W. (1950). The rationale of Copy-Text. *Studies in Bibliography*, 3:19–36. URL http://www.jstor.org/stable/40381874. (cited on p. 19)

Guenthner, Franz (1996). Electronic lexica and corpora research at CIS. *International Journal of Corpus Linguistics*, 1(2):287–301. doi: 10.1075/ijcl.1.2.07gue. (cited on p. 42)

Guillot, Céline, Serge Heiden, Alexei Lavrentiev, and Christiane Marchello-Nizia (2008). Constitution et exploitation des corpus d'ancien et de moyen français. *Corpus*, 7. URL http://corpus.revues.org/index1495.html (accessed 2011-11-08). (cited on p. 112)

Guillot, Céline, Alexei Lavrentiev, and Christiane Marchello-Nizia (2007). La Base de Français Médiéval (BFM): états et perspectives. In Pierre Kunstmann and Achim Stein, eds., *Le Nouveau Corpus d'Amsterdam. Actes de l'atelier de Lauterbad, 23–26 février 2006*, vol. 34 of *Zeitschrift für französische Sprache und Literatur – Beihefte. Neue Folge (ZFSL-B)*, pages 143–152. Stuttgart, Germany: Steiner. (cited on p. 110)

Guthrie, David, Ben Allison, Wei Liu, Louise Guthrie, and Yorick Wilks (2006). A closer look at skip-gram modelling. In *Proceedings of the 5th International Conference on Language Resources and Evaluation (LREC 2006)*, pages 1222–1225. Paris: European Language Resources Association (ELRA). URL http://www.lrec-conf.org/proceedings/lrec2006/pdf/357_pdf.pdf. (cited on p. 78)

Hajič, Jan, Barbora Vidová-Hladká, and Petr Pajas (2001). The Prague Dependency Treebank: Annotation structure and support. In *Proceedings of the IRCS Workshop on Linguistic Databases*, pages 105–114. Philadelphia, PA, USA: University of Pennsylvania. URL `http://ufal.mff.cuni.cz/pdt2.0/publications/HajicHladkaPajas2001.pdf`. (cited on p. 95)

Halácsy, Péter, András Kornai, and Csaba Oravecz (2007). HunPos: an open source trigram tagger. In *Proceedings of the ACL 2007 Demo and Poster Sessions*, pages 209–212. Stroudsburg, PA, USA: Association for Computational Linguistics. URL `http://aclweb.org/anthology/P07-2053.pdf`. (cited on p. 89)

Han, Bo and Timothy Baldwin (2011). Lexical normalisation of short text messages: Makn Sens a #twitter. In *Proceedings of the 49th Annual Meeting of the Association for Computational Linguistics: Human Language Technologies*, pages 368–378. Stroudsburg, PA, USA: Association for Computational Linguistics. URL `http://aclweb.org/anthology/P11-1038`. (cited on p. 9)

Hana, Jirka, Anna Feldman, and Katsiaryna Aharodnik (2011). A low-budget tagger for Old Czech. In *Proceedings of the 5th ACL-HLT Workshop on Language Technology for Cultural Heritage, Social Sciences, and Humanities*, pages 10–18. Portland, OR, USA: Association for Computational Linguistics. URL `http://aclweb.org/anthology/W11-1502`. (cited on pp. 87 and 95)

Handley, John C. (1998). Improving OCR accuracy through combination: a survey. In *SMC'98 Conference Proceedings. 1998 IEEE International Conference on Systems, Man, and Cybernetics*, pages 4330–4333. New York, NY, USA: IEEE. doi: 10.1109/ICSMC.1998.727527. (cited on p. 34)

Handley, John C. and Thomas B. Hickey (1991). Merging optical character recognition outputs for improved accuracy. In *Proceedings of RIAO'91*, pages 160–175. (cited on p. 34)

Haralambous, Yannis (2007). *Fonts & Encodings*. Sebastopol, CA, USA: O'Reilly. (cited on p. 60)

Haug, Dag and Marius L. Jhndal (2008). Creating a parallel treebank of the old Indo-European Bible translations. In Ribarov and Sporleder (2008). URL `http://www.lrec-conf.org/proceedings/lrec2008/workshops/W22_Proceedings.pdf`. (cited on p. 114)

Haugen, Odd E., ed. (2008). *The Menota handbook 2.0: Guidelines for the electronic encoding of Medieval Nordic primary sources*. Bergen, Norway: Medieval Nordic Text Archive. URL `http://www.menota.org/HB2_index.xml` (accessed 2012-06-27). (cited on p. 113)

Hauser, Andreas, Markus Heller, Elisabeth Leiss, Klaus U. Schulz, and Christiane Wanzeck (2007). Information access to historical documents from the Early New High German period. In Craig Knoblock, Daniel Lopresti, Shourya Roy, and L. Venkata Subramaniam, eds., *Proceedings of IJCAI-2007 Workshop on Analytics for Noisy Unstructured Text Data (AND 2007)*, pages 147–154. URL `http://research.ihost.com/and2007/cd/Proceedings_files/p147.pdf`. (cited on p. 84)

Heiden, Serge, Céline Guillot, Alexei Lavrentiev, and Lauranne Bertrand (2010). *Manuel d'encodage XML-TEI des textes de la Base de Français Médiéval.* UMR ICAR/ENS-LSH, Lyon, France, 4 ed. URL `http://bfm.ens-lyon.fr/IMG/pdf/Manuel_Encodage_TEI.pdf` (accessed 2011-10-24). (cited on p. 110)

Hendrickx, Iris, Michel Généreux, and Rita Marquilhas (2010). Automatic pragmatic text segmentation of historical letters. In Sporleder and Zervanou (2010). URL `http://ilk.uvt.nl/LaTeCH2010/LPF/ws16.pdf.` (cited on pp. 7 and 115)

Hirst, Graeme and Alexander Budanitsky (2005). Correcting real-word spelling errors by restoring lexical cohesion. *Natural Language Engineering*, 11(01):87–111. doi: 10.1017/S1351324904003560. (cited on p. 16)

Holley, Rose (2009a). How good can it get? Analysing and improving OCR accuracy in large scale historic newspaper digitisation programs. *D-Lib Magazine*, 15(3/4). doi: 10.1045/march2009-holley. (cited on pp. 30, 33, and 43)

Holley, Rose (2009b). Many hands make light work: Public collaborative OCR text correction in Australian Historic Newspapers. Tech. rep., National Library of Australia. URL `http://www.nla.gov.au/ndp/project_details/documents/ANDP_ManyHands.pdf.` (cited on p. 44)

Holley, Rose (2010). Crowdsourcing: How and why should libraries do it? *D-Lib Magazine*, 16 (3/4). doi: 10.1045/march2010-holley. (cited on p. 44)

Holley, Rose (2011). Trove: The first year. January 2010 – January 2011. Tech. rep., National Library of Australia, Canberra, Australia. URN hdl:10760/15510. (cited on p. 44)

Howard, Jennifer (2012). Google begins to scale back its scanning of books from university libraries. *The Chronicle of Higher Education*. URL `http://chronicle.com/article/Google-Begins-to-Scale-Back/131109/` (accessed 2012-06-04). (cited on p. 26)

Hu, Xiaoling and Jamie McLaughlin (2007). *The Sheffield Corpus of Chinese (SCC).* University of Sheffield, Sheffield, UK, first ed. URL `http://www.hrionline.ac.uk/scc/db/scc/manual.html` (accessed 2011-10-24). (cited on p. 104)

Huang, Liang, Yinan Peng, Huan Wang, and Zhenyu Wu (2002a). PCFG parsing for restricted Classical Chinese texts. In *Proceedings of the first SIGHAN workshop on Chinese language processing (SIGHAN '02)*, pages 1–6. Stroudsburg, PA, USA: Association for Computational Linguistics. doi: 10.3115/1118824.1118830. (cited on p. 99)

Huang, Liang, Yinan Peng, Huan Wang, and Zhenyu Wu (2002b). Statistical part-of-speech tagging for Classical Chinese. In Petr Sojka, Ivan Kopecek, and Karel Pala, eds., *Text, Speech and Dialogue. 5th International Conference (TSD 2002)*, vol. 2448 of *Lecture Notes in Computer Science*, pages 296–311. Berlin/Heidelberg: Springer. doi: 10.1007/3-540-46154-X_15. (cited on pp. 90 and 99)

Hunt, J.W. and M.D. McIlroy (1977). An algorithm for differential file comparison. CSTR 41, Bell Laboratories, Murray Hill, NJ. (cited on p. 73)

ISO (International Organization for Standardization) (2003). ISO/IEC 19757-2:2003. Information technology — Document Schema Definition Language (DSDL) — Part 2: Regular-grammar-based validation — RELAX NG. (cited on p. 61)

ISO (International Organization for Standardization) (2006). ISO/IEC 14492:2001. Information technology — Lossy/lossless coding of bi-level images. (cited on p. 31)

Järvelin, Anni, Antti Järvelin, and Kalervo Järvelin (2007). s-grams: Defining generalized n-grams for information retrieval. *Information Processing & Management*, 43(4):1005–1019. doi: 10.1016/j.ipm.2006.09.016. (cited on p. 78)

Joscelyne, Andrew (2010). Minority report: helping less-resourced languages to share data. URL http://www.translationautomation.com/perspectives/minority-report-helping-less-resourced-languages-to-share-data.html (accessed 2011-11-08). (cited on p. 85)

Jurish, Bryan (2008). Finding canonical forms for historical German text. In Angelika Storrer, Alexander Geyken, Alexander Siebert, and Kay-Michael Würzner, eds., *Text Resources and Lexical Knowledge*, vol. 8 of *Text, Translation, Computational Processing*, pages 27–37. Berlin/New York: Mouton de Gruyter. doi: 10.1515/9783110211818.1.27. (cited on pp. 77 and 82)

Jurish, Bryan (2010a). Comparing canonicalizations of historical German text. In Jeffrey Heinz, Lynne Cahill, and Richard Wicentowski, eds., *Proceedings of the 11th Meeting of the ACL Special Interest Group on Computational Morphology and Phonology*, pages 72–77. Association for Computational Linguistics. URL http://aclweb.org/anthology/W10-2209. (cited on pp. 69 and 84)

Jurish, Bryan (2010b). More than words: Using token context to improve canonicalization of historical German. *Journal for Language Technology and Computational Linguistics*, 25(1):23–39. (cited on p. 82)

Jurish, Bryan (2012). *Finite-state canonicalization techniques for historical German*. Ph.D. thesis, Universität Potsdam, Potsdam, Germany. URL http://opus.kobv.de/ubp/volltexte/2012/5578/. (cited on p. 70)

Kaufmann, Max and Jugal Kalita (2010). Syntactic normalization of Twitter messages. In *Proceedings of the 8th International Conference on Natural Language Processing (ICON 2010)*. Chennai, India: Macmillan India. URL http://ltrc.iiit.ac.in/icon_archives/ICON2010/10Dec2010/Paper4-File33-Paper189.pdf. (cited on p. 9)

Kay, Martin and Martin Röscheisen (1993). Text-translation alignment. *Computational Linguistics*, 19(1):121–142. (cited on p. 94)

Kay, Michael (2007). XSL Transformations (XSLT) Version 2.0. W3C Recommendation, World Wide Web Consortium. URL `http://www.w3.org/TR/xslt20/`. (cited on p. 60)

Kempken, Sebastian, Wolfram Luther, and Thomas Pilz (2006). Comparison of distance measures for historical spelling variants. In Max Bramer, ed., *Artificial Intelligence in Theory and Practice*, vol. 217 of *IFIP International Federation for Information Processing*, pages 295–304. Boston: Springer. doi: 10.1007/978-0-387-34747-9_31. (cited on p. 84)

Keskustalo, Heikki, Ari Pirkola, Kari Visala, Erkka Leppänen, and Kalervo Järvelin (2003). Non-adjacent digrams improve matching of Cross-Lingual spelling variants. In Mario A. Nascimento, Edleno S. Moura, and Arlindo L. Oliveira, eds., *String Processing and Information Retrieval*, vol. 2857 of *Lecture Notes in Computer Science*, chap. 19, pages 252–265. Berlin/Heidelberg: Springer. doi: 10.1007/978-3-540-39984-1_19. (cited on p. 78)

Kestemont, Mike, Walter Daelemans, and Guy De Pauw (2010). Weigh your words—memory-based lemmatization for Middle Dutch. *Literary and Linguistic Computing*, 25(3):287–301. doi: 10.1093/llc/fqq011. (cited on pp. 78, 98, and 105)

Kolak, Okan, William Byrne, and Philip Resnik (2003). A generative probabilistic OCR model for NLP applications. In *Proceedings of the 2003 Conference of the North American Chapter of the Association for Computational Linguistics on Human Language Technology - Volume 1*, NAACL '03, pages 55–62. Stroudsburg, PA, USA: Association for Computational Linguistics. doi: 10.3115/1073445.1073463. (cited on p. 79)

Kondrak, Grzegorz (2003). Phonetic alignment and similarity. *Computers and the Humanities*, 37(3): 273–291. doi: 10.1023/A:1025071200644. (cited on p. 77)

Koolen, Marijn, Frans Adriaans, Jaap Kamps, and Maarten de Rijke (2006). A cross-language approach to historic document retrieval. In Mounia Lalmas, Andy MacFarlane, Stefan Rüger, Anastasios Tombros, Theodora Tsikrika, and Alexei Yavlinsky, eds., *Advances in Information Retrieval*, vol. 3936 of *Lecture Notes in Computer Science*, pages 407–419. Berlin/Heidelberg: Springer. doi: 10.1007/11735106_36. (cited on pp. 77 and 82)

Korpela, Jukka K. (2006). *Unicode Explained*. Sebastopol, CA, USA: O'Reilly. (cited on p. 60)

Krauwer, Steven (1998). ELSNET and ELRA: A common past and a common future. *ELRA Newsletter*, 3(2). URL `http://elda.org/article48.html`. (cited on p. 85)

Krauwer, Steven (2003). The Basic Language Resource Kit (BLARK) as the first milestone for the language resources roadmap. In *Proceedings of the 2003 International Workshop Speech and Computer (SPECOM 2003)*, pages 8–15. Moscow State Linguistic University. URL `http://www.elsnet.org/dox/krauwer-specom2003.pdf`. (cited on p. 85)

Kulp, Scott and April Kontostathis (2007). On retrieving legal files: Shortening documents and weeding out garbage. In Ellen M. Voorhees and Lori P. Buckland, eds., *Proceedings of The Sixteenth Text REtrieval Conference (TREC 2007)*, no. 500-274 in Special Publication. Gaithersburg, MD, USA: National Institute of Standards and Technology (NIST). URL `http://trec.nist.gov/pubs/trec16/papers/ursinus.legal.final.pdf`. (cited on p. 81)

Kunstmann, Pierre and Achim Stein (2007). Le Nouveau Corpus d'Amsterdam. In *Le Nouveau Corpus d'Amsterdam. Actes de l'atelier de Lauterbad, 23–26 février 2006*, Zeitschrift für französische Sprache und Literatur – Beihefte. Neue Folge (ZFSL-B), pages 9–27. Stuttgart, Germany: Steiner. (cited on p. 96)

Kytö, Merja (1996). *Manual to the diachronic part of the Helsinki Corpus of English texts. Coding conventions and lists of source texts.* University of Helsinki, Helsinki, Finland, 3rd ed. URL `http://icame.uib.no/hc/`. (cited on p. 106)

Lardilleux, Adrien, Julien Gosme, and Yves Lepage (2010). Bilingual lexicon induction: Effortless evaluation of word alignment tools and production of resources for improbable language pairs. In Nicoletta Calzolari, Khalid Choukri, Bente Maegaard, Joseph Mariani, Jan Odijk, Stelios Piperidis, Michael Rosner, and Daniel Tapias, eds., *Proceedings of the Seventh International Conference on Language Resources and Evaluation (LREC'10)*, pages 252–256. European Language Resources Association (ELRA). URL `http://www.lrec-conf.org/proceedings/lrec2010/pdf/293_Paper.pdf`. (cited on p. 85)

Lee, John (2012). A Classical Chinese corpus with nested part-of-speech tags. In Kalliopi Zervanou and Antal van den Bosch, eds., *Proceedings of the 6th Workshop on Language Technology for Cultural Heritage, Social Sciences, and Humanities (LaTeCH 2012)*, pages 75–84. Stroudsburg, PA, USA: Association for Computational Linguistics. URL `http://aclweb.org/anthology/W12-1011`. (cited on p. 104)

Lee, John and Yin H. Kong (2012). A dependency treebank of Classical Chinese poems. In *Proceedings of the 2012 Conference of the North American Chapter of the Association for Computational Linguistics: Human Language Technologies*, pages 191–199. Stroudsburg, PA, USA: Association for Computational Linguistics. URL `http://aclweb.org/anthology/N12-1020`. (cited on p. 104)

Lehmann, Hans M., Caren auf dem Keller, and Beni Ruef (2006). ZEN Corpus 1.0. In Roberta Facchinetti and Matti Rissanen, eds., *Corpus-Based Studies of Diachronic English*, pages 135–155. Bern, Switzerland: Peter Lang. (cited on p. 109)

Levenshtein, Vladimir I. (1966). Binary codes capable of correcting deletions, insertions and reversals. *Cybernetics and Control Theory*, 10(8):707–710. (cited on p. 71)

Liu, Fei, Fuliang Weng, Bingqing Wang, and Yang Liu (2011). Insertion, deletion, or substitution? normalizing text messages without pre-categorization nor supervision. In *Proceedings of the 49th Annual Meeting of the Association for Computational Linguistics: Human Language Technologies*, pages 71–76. Stroudsburg, PA, USA: Association for Computational Linguistics. URL `http://aclweb.org/anthology/P11-2013`. (cited on p. 9)

Lopresti, Daniel and Zhou Jiangying (1997). Using consensus sequence voting to correct OCR errors. *Computer Vision and Image Understanding*, 67(1):39–47. doi: 10.1006/cviu.1996.0502. (cited on p. 34)

Manning, Christopher D., Prabhakar Raghavan, and Hinrich Schütze (2008). *Introduction to Information Retrieval*. Cambridge, UK: Cambridge University Press. URL `http://informationretrieval.org/`. (cited on pp. 12 and 70)

Manning, Christopher D. and Hinrich Schütze (1999). *Foundations of Statistical Natural Language Processing*. Cambridge, MA, USA: MIT Press. (cited on pp. 87 and 88)

Marquilhas, Rita (2012). A historical digital archive of Portuguese letters. In Marina Dossena and Gabriella Del Lungo Camiciotti, eds., *Letter Writing in Late Modern Europe*. Amsterdam, The Netherlands: John Benjamins. (cited on p. 115)

Martineau, France (2004). Un corpus de textes français pour l'analyse de la variation diachronique et dialectale. In *Actes du colloque << L'analyse de données textuelles : De l'enquête aux corpus littéraires >>*. URL `http://www.cavi.univ-paris3.fr/lexicometrica/thema/thema7.htm`. (cited on pp. 111 and 112)

Martineau, France (2008). Un corpus pour l'analyse de la variation et du changement linguistique. *Corpus*, 7. URL `http://corpus.revues.org/index1508.html`. (cited on p. 111)

Martineau, France, Constanta R. Diaconescu, and Paul Hirschbühler (2007). Le Corpus Voies du français : de l'élaboration à l'annotation. In Pierre Kunstmann and Achim Stein, eds., *Le Nouveau Corpus d'Amsterdam. Actes de l'atelier de Lauterbad, 23–26 février 2006*, vol. 34 of *Zeitschrift für französische Sprache und Literatur – Beihefte. Neue Folge (ZFSL-B)*, pages 121–142. Stuttgart, Germany: Steiner. (cited on p. 111)

Mazziotta, Nicolas (2010). Building the syntactic reference corpus of medieval French using NotaBene RDF annotation tool. In *Proceedings of the Fourth Linguistic Annotation Workshop*, pages 142–146. Stroudsburg, PA, USA: Association for Computational Linguistics. URL `http://aclweb.org/anthology/W10-1820`. (cited on pp. 98 and 111)

McGillivray, Barbara, Marco Passarotti, and Paolo Ruffolo (2009). The Index Thomisticus Treebank project: Annotation, parsing and valency lexicon. *Traitement Automatique des Langues*, 50(2):103–127. URL `http://atala.org/IMG/pdf/TAL-2009-50-2-04-McGillivray.pdf`. (cited on p. 114)

Mengel, Andreas and Wolfgang Lezius (2000). An XML-based representation format for syntactically annotated corpora. In *Proceedings of the 2nd International Conference on Language Resources and Evaluation (LREC 2000)*, pages Article 59+. Paris: European Language Resources Association (ELRA). URL `http://www.lrec-conf.org/proceedings/lrec2000/pdf/59.pdf`. (cited on p. 60)

Minozzi, Stefano (2009). The Latin WordNet project. In Peter Anreiter and Manfred Kienpointner, eds., *Latin Linguistics Today. Akten des 15. Internationalem Kolloquiums zur Lateinischen Linguistik*, vol. 137 of *Innsbrucker Beiträge zur Sprachwissenschaft*, pages 707–716. URL `http://www.dfll.univr.it/documenti/Iniziativa/dall/dall234343.pdf`. (cited on p. 115)

Mitton, Roger (1996). *English Spelling and the Computer*. Harlow, UK: Longman. URL `http://eprints.bbk.ac.uk/469/`. (cited on p. 16)

Moon, Taesun and Jason Baldridge (2007). Part-of-speech tagging for middle English through alignment and projection of parallel diachronic texts. In *Proceedings of the 2007 Joint Conference on Empirical Methods in Natural Language Processing and Computational Natural Language Learning (EMNLP-CoNLL)*, pages 390–399. Association for Computational Linguistics. URL `http://aclweb.org/anthology/D07-1041`. (cited on pp. 87, 94, and 95)

Navarro, Gonzalo (2001). A guided tour to approximate string matching. *ACM Computing Surveys*, 33(1):31–88. doi: 10.1145/375360.375365. (cited on pp. 73 and 78)

Needleman, Saul B. and Christian D. Wunsch (1970). A general method applicable to the search for similarities in the amino acid sequence of two proteins. *Journal of Molecular Biology*, 48(3): 443–453. doi: 10.1016/0022-2836(70)90057-4. (cited on p. 78)

Neuefeind, Claes, Jürgen Rolshoven, and Fabian Steeg (2011). Die Digitale Rätoromanische Chrestomathie – Werkzeuge und Verfahren für die Korpuserstellung durch kollaborative Volltexterschließung. In *Multilingual Resources and Multilingual Applications: Proceedings of the Conference of the German Society for Computational Linguistics and Language Technology (GSCL 2011)*, pages 163–168. GSCL, Universität Hamburg. URL `http://www.corpora.uni-hamburg.de/gscl2011/downloads/AZM96.pdf`. (cited on p. 45)

Norman, Jerry (1988). *Chinese*. Cambridge Language Surveys. Cambridge, UK: Cambridge University Press. (cited on p. 102)

Nunberg, Geoffrey (2009). Google's book search: A disaster for scholars. *The Chronicle of Higher Education*. URL `http://chronicle.com/article/Googles-Book-Search-A/48245/` (accessed 2012-06-04). (cited on p. 26)

Och, Franz J. and Hermann Ney (2003). A systematic comparison of various statistical alignment models. *Computational Linguistics*, 29(1):19–51. doi: 10.1162/089120103321337421. (cited on pp. 75, 94, and 117)

O'Rourke, Alan J., Alexander M. Robertson, Peter Willett, Penny Eley, and Penny Simons (1996). Word variant identification in Old French. *Information Research*, 2(4). URL http://informationr.net/ir/2-4/paper22.html. (cited on p. 78)

Ott, Wilhelm (1979). A text processing system for the preparation of critical editions. *Computers and the Humanities*, 13(1):29–35. URL http://www.jstor.org/stable/30207231. (cited on p. 57)

Ott, Wilhelm (2000). Strategies and tools for textual scholarship: the Tübingen System of Text Processing Programs (TUSTEP). *Literary and Linguistic Computing*, 15(1):93–108. doi: 10.1093/llc/15.1.93. (cited on p. 57)

Padró, Lluís, Miquel Collado, Samuel Reese, Marina Lloberes, and Irene Castellón (2010). FreeLing 2.1: Five years of open-source language processing tools. In Nicoletta Calzolari, Khalid Choukri, Bente Maegaard, Joseph Mariani, Jan Odijk, Stelios Piperidis, Mike Rosner, and Daniel Tapias, eds., *Proceedings of the Seventh International Conference on Language Resources and Evaluation (LREC'10)*, pages 931–936. European Language Resources Association (ELRA). URL http://www.lrec-conf.org/proceedings/lrec2010/pdf/14_Paper.pdf. (cited on p. 93)

Paixão de Sousa, Maria C. and Thorsten Trippel (2006). Building a historical corpus for Classical Portuguese: some technological aspects. In *Proceedings of the 5th International Conference on Language Resources and Evaluation (LREC 2006)*, pages 1831–1836. European Language Resources Association (ELRA). (cited on p. 115)

Pantelia, Maria (2000). 'Νοῦς into chaos': The creation of the Thesaurus of the Greek Language. *International Journal of Lexicography*, 13(1):1–11. doi: 10.1093/ijl/13.1.1. (cited on p. 57)

Passarotti, Marco (2010a). Leaving behind the less-resourced status. The case of Latin through the experience of the Index Thomisticus Treebank. In Kepa Sarasola, Francis M. Tyers, and Mikel L. Forcada, eds., *7th SaLTMiL Workshop on Creation and use of basic lexical resources for less-resourced languages*, pages 27–32. URL http://www.lrec-conf.org/proceedings/lrec2010/workshops/W21.pdf. (cited on pp. 86, 89, and 114)

Passarotti, Marco (2010b). Per una *treebank* dell'italiano antico. In Maria Iliescu, Heidi Siller-Runggaldier, and Paul Danler, eds., *Actes du XXVe Congrès International de Linguistique et de Philologie Romanes (CILPR)*, vol. VI, pages 269–278. Berlin, Germany: De Gruyter. doi: 10.1515/9783110231922.6-269. (cited on p. 89)

Paul, Hermann (2007). *Mittelhochdeutsche Grammatik*. No. 2 in Sammlung kurzer Grammatiken germanischer Dialekte. A: Hauptreihe. Tübingen, Germany: Niemeyer, 25th ed. doi: 10.1515/9783110942347.1. (cited on p. 69)

Paulevé, Loïc, Hervé Jégou, and Laurent Amsaleg (2010). Locality sensitive hashing: A comparison of hash function types and querying mechanisms. *Pattern Recognition Letters*, 31(11):1348–1358. doi: 10.1016/j.patrec.2010.04.004. (cited on p. 79)

Pettersson, Eva and Joakim Nivre (2011). Automatic verb extraction from historical Swedish texts. In *Proceedings of the 5th ACL-HLT Workshop on Language Technology for Cultural Heritage, Social Sciences, and Humanities (LaTeCH 2011)*, pages 87–95. Morristown, NJ, USA: Association for Computational Linguistics. URL http://aclweb.org/anthology/W11-1512. (cited on p. 8)

Philips, Lawrence (2000). The Double Metaphone search algorithm. *C/C++ Users Journal*, 18(6): 38–43. URL http://drdobbs.com/184401251. (cited on p. 77)

Pianta, Emanuele, Luisa Bentivogli, and Christian Girardi (2002). MultiWordNet: developing an aligned multilingual database. In *Proceedings of the First International Conference on Global WordNet*, pages 21–25. URL http://multiwordnet.fbk.eu/paper/MWN-India-published.pdf. (cited on p. 115)

Pilz, Thomas (2009). *Nichtstandardisierte Rechtschreibung: Variationsmodellierung und rechnergestützte Variationsverarbeitung*. Ph.D. thesis, Universität Duisburg-Essen. URL http://www.scg.inf.uni-due.de/fileadmin/Veroeffentlichungen/ Pilz-Nichtstandardisierte_Rechtschreibung(2009).pdf. (cited on p. 75)

Pilz, Thomas, Wolfram Luther, Norbert Fuhr, and Ulrich Ammon (2006). Rule-based search in text databases with nonstandard orthography. *Literary and Linguistic Computing*, 21(2):179–186. doi: 10.1093/llc/fql020. (cited on pp. 75 and 82)

Pirkola, Ari, Heikki Keskustalo, Erkka Leppänen, Antti-Pekka Känsälä, and Kalervo Järvelin (2002). Targeted s-gram matching: a novel n-gram matching technique for cross- and monolingual word form variants. *Information Research*, 7(2). URL http://informationr.net/ir/7-2/ paper126. (cited on p. 78)

Piskorski, Jakub, Marcin Sydow, and Karol Wieloch (2009). Comparison of string distance metrics for lemmatisation of named entities in Polish human language technology. In Zygmunt Vetulani and Hans Uszkoreit, eds., *Human Language Technology. Challenges of the Information Society*, vol. 5603 of *Lecture Notes in Computer Science*, chap. 36, pages 413–427. Berlin/Heidelberg: Springer. doi: 10.1007/978-3-642-04235-5_36. (cited on p. 78)

Plamondon, Réjean and Sargur N. Srihari (2000). Online and off-line handwriting recognition: a comprehensive survey. *IEEE Transactions on Pattern Analysis and Machine Intelligence*, 22(1): 63–84. doi: 10.1109/34.824821. (cited on p. 27)

Poesio, Massimo, Eduard Barbu, Egon Stemle, and Christian Girardi (2011). Structure-preserving pipelines for digital libraries. In *Proceedings of the 5th ACL-HLT Workshop on Language Technology for Cultural Heritage, Social Sciences, and Humanities (LaTeCH 2011)*, pages 54–62. Stroudsburg, PA, USA: Association for Computational Linguistics. URL http://aclweb.org/anthology/ W11-1508. (cited on p. 66)

Pollock, Joseph J. (1982). Spelling error detection and correction by computer: Some notes and a bibliography. *Journal of Documentation*, 38(4):282–291. doi: 10.1108/eb026733. (cited on p. 73)

Popat, Ashok C. (2009). A panlingual anomalous text detector. In *Proceedings of the 9ᵗʰ ACM symposium on Document engineering (DocEng '09)*, pages 201–204. New York, NY, USA: ACM. doi: 10.1145/1600193.1600237. (cited on pp. 81 and 82)

Poudat, Céline and Dominique Longrée (2009). Variations langagières et annotation morphosyntaxique du latin classique. *Traitement Automatique des Langues*, 50(2):129–148. URL http://www.atala.org/Variations-langagieres-et. (cited on pp. 90 and 91)

Powell, Tracy and Gordon Paynter (2009). Going grey? Comparing the OCR accuracy levels of bitonal and greyscale images. *D-Lib Magazine*, 15(3/4). doi: 10.1045/march2009-powell. (cited on p. 30)

Pustejovsky, James, Kiyong Lee, Harry Bunt, and Laurent Romary (2010). ISO-TimeML: An international standard for semantic annotation. In Nicoletta Calzolari, Khalid Choukri, Bente Maegaard, Joseph Mariani, Jan Odijk, Stelios Piperidis, Mike Rosner, and Daniel Tapias, eds., *Proceedings of the Seventh International Conference on Language Resources and Evaluation (LREC'10)*. Paris: European Language Resources Association (ELRA). URL http://www.lrec-conf. org/proceedings/lrec2010/pdf/55_Paper.pdf. (cited on p. 60)

Ramel, Jean-Yves, Sébastien Busson, and Marie-Luce Demonet (2006). AGORA: the interactive document image analysis tool of the BVH project. *Second International Workshop on Document Image Analysis for Libraries (DIAL 2006)*, pages 145–155. doi: 10.1109/DIAL.2006.2. (cited on p. 49)

Rayson, Paul, Dawn Archer, Alistair Baron, Jonathan Culpeper, and Nicholas Smith (2007). Tagging the bard: Evaluating the accuracy of a modern POS tagger on Early Modern English Corpora. In Matthew Davies, Paul Rayson, Susan Hunston, and Pernilla Danielsson, eds., *Corpus Linguistics Conference (CL2007)*. Birmingham, UK: University of Birmingham. URL http://ucrel.lancs. ac.uk/publications/CL2007/paper/192_Paper.pdf. (cited on pp. 87, 91, and 92)

Rayson, Paul, Dawn Archer, Scott Piao, and Tony McEnery (2004). The UCREL semantic analysis system. In *Proceedings of the LREC 2004 Workshop on Beyond Named Entity Recognition Semantic Labelling for NLP Tasks*, pages 7–12. Paris: European Language Resources Association (ELRA). URL http://comp.eprints.lancs.ac.uk/922/. (cited on p. 7)

Rayson, Paul, Dawn Archer, and Nicholas Smith (2005). VARD versus Word: A comparison of the UCREL variant detector and modern spell checkers on English historical corpora. In *Proceedings of Corpus Linguistics 2005*. (cited on p. 74)

Rechtsquellenstiftung des Schweizerischen Juristenverbandes, ed. (2007). *Rechtsquellen der Stadt und Herrschaft Rapperswil*, vol. SSRQ SG II/2/1 (XIV. Abteilung: Die Rechtsquellen des Kantons St. Gallen, Zweiter Teil: Die Stadtrechte von St. Gallen und Rapperswil, 2. Reihe: Die Rechtsquellen der Stadt und Herrschaft Rapperswil, Band 1) of *Sammlung Schweizerischer Rechtsquellen*. Basel, Switzerland: Schwabe. Prepared by Pascale Sutter. (cited on p. 18)

Rechtsquellenstiftung des Schweizerischen Juristenverbandes, ed. (2009). *Appenzeller Landbücher*, vol. SSRQ AR/AI 1 (XIII. Abteilung: Die Rechtsquellen der Kantone Appenzell, Band 1) of *Sammlung Schweizerischer Rechtsquellen*. Basel, Switzerland: Schwabe. Prepared by Nathalie Büsser, indexing by Margrit Meyer Kälin. (cited on pp. 63, 64, 66, and 67)

Rehbein, Malte, Torsten Schaßan, and Patrick Sahle, eds. (2009). *Kodikologie und Paläographie im digitalen Zeitalter – Codicology and Palaeography in the Digital Age*. No. 2 in Schriften des Instituts für Dokumentologie und Editorik. Norderstedt, Germany: BoD. URL `http://kups.ub.uni-koeln.de/2939/`. (cited on p. 21)

Reynaert, Martin (2005). *Text-Induced Spelling Correction*. Ph.D. thesis, Tilburg University, Tilburg, The Netherlands. URL `http://ilk.uvt.nl/~mre/TISC.PhD.MartinReynaert.pdf.gz`. (cited on p. 79)

Reynaert, Martin (2008). Non-interactive OCR post-correction for giga-scale digitization projects. In Alexander Gelbukh, ed., *Computational Linguistics and Intelligent Text Processing*, vol. 4919 of *Lecture Notes in Computer Science*, chap. 53, pages 617–630. Berlin/Heidelberg: Springer. doi: 10.1007/978-3-540-78135-6_53. (cited on p. 79)

Reynaert, Martin (2011). Character confusion versus focus word-based correction of spelling and OCR variants in corpora. *International Journal on Document Analysis and Recognition*, 14(2): 173–187. doi: 10.1007/s10032-010-0133-5. (cited on pp. 79, 80, and 81)

Ribarov, Kiril and Caroline Sporleder, eds. (2008). *Proceedings of the LREC 2008 Workshop on Language Technology for Cultural Heritage Data (LaTeCH 2008)*. URL `http://www.lrec-conf.org/proceedings/lrec2008/workshops/W22_Proceedings.pdf`. (cited on p. 127)

Rissanen, Matti (2008). Corpus linguistics and historical linguistics. In Anke Lüdeling and Merja Kytö, eds., *Corpus Linguistics. An International Handbook*, vol. 1 of *Handbooks of Linguistics and Communication Science*, chap. 4, pages 53–68. Mouton de Gruyter. doi: 10.1515/9783110211429.1.53. (cited on p. 101)

Robertson, Alexander M. and Peter Willett (1992). Searching for historical word-forms in a database of 17th-century English text using spelling-correction methods. In *SIGIR '92: Proceedings of the*

15th annual international ACM SIGIR conference on Research and development in information retrieval, pages 256–265. New York, NY, USA: ACM. doi: 10.1145/133160.133208. (cited on pp. 73 and 78)

Robertson, Alexander M. and Peter Willett (1993). A comparison of spelling-correction methods for the identification of word forms in historical text databases. *Literary and Linguistic Computing*, 8(3):143–152. doi: 10.1093/llc/8.3.143. (cited on pp. 76 and 77)

Rogers, Heather J. and Peter Willett (1991). Searching for historical word forms in text databases using spelling-correction methods: Reverse error and phonetic coding methods. *Journal of Documentation*, 47(4):333–353. doi: 10.1108/eb026883. (cited on p. 77)

Rögnvaldsson, Eiríkur and Sigrún Helgadóttir (2008). Morphological tagging of Old Norse texts and its use in studying syntactic variation and change. In Kiril Ribarov and Caroline Sporleder, eds., *Proceedings of the LREC 2008 Workshop on Language Technology for Cultural Heritage Data (LaTeCH 2008)*, pages 40–46. (cited on pp. 90, 92, and 93)

Rögnvaldsson, Eiríkur, Anton K. Ingason, and Einar F. Sigurðsson (2011). Coping with variation in the Icelandic Parsed Historical Corpus (IcePaHC). *Oslo Studies in Language*, 3(2):97–112. URL https://www.journals.uio.no/index.php/osla/article/download/104/202. (cited on p. 113)

Ruge, Nikolaus (2005). Zur morphembezogenen Überformung der deutschen Orthographie. *Linguistik online*, 25:65–83. URL http://www.linguistik-online.de/25_05/ruge.pdf. (cited on pp. 12 and 13)

Sánchez-Marco, Cristina, Gemma Boleda, Josep M. Fontana, and Judith Domingo (2010). Annotation and representation of a diachronic corpus of Spanish. In Nicoletta Calzolari, Khalid Choukri, Bente Maegaard, Joseph Mariani, Jan Odijk, Stelios Piperidis, Mike Rosner, and Daniel Tapias, eds., *Proceedings of the Seventh International Conference on Language Resources and Evaluation (LREC'10)*. European Language Resources Association (ELRA). URL http://www.lrec-conf.org/proceedings/lrec2010/pdf/535_Paper.pdf. (cited on p. 93)

Sánchez-Marco, Cristina, Gemma Boleda, and Lluís Padró (2011). Extending the tool, or how to annotate historical language varieties. In *Proceedings of the 5th ACL-HLT Workshop on Language Technology for Cultural Heritage, Social Sciences, and Humanities*, pages 1–9. Portland, OR, USA: Association for Computational Linguistics. URL http://aclweb.org/anthology/W11-1501. (cited on pp. 87, 93, and 94)

Santos, Diana (2011). Linguateca's infrastructure for Portuguese and how it allows the detailed study of language varieties. *Oslo Studies in Language*, 3(2):113–128. URL https://www.journals.uio.no/index.php/osla/article/view/100/203. (cited on p. 116)

Scheible, Silke, Richard J. Whitt, Martin Durrell, and Paul Bennett (2011a). Evaluating an 'off-the-shelf' POS-tagger on Early Modern German text. In *Proceedings of the 5th ACL-HLT Workshop on Language Technology for Cultural Heritage, Social Sciences, and Humanities*, pages 19–23. Portland, OR, USA: Association for Computational Linguistics. URL `http://aclweb.org/anthology/ W11-1503`. (cited on pp. 87 and 92)

Scheible, Silke, Richard J. Whitt, Martin Durrell, and Paul Bennett (2011b). A gold standard corpus of Early Modern German. In *Proceedings of the 5th Linguistic Annotation Workshop (LAW V)*, pages 124–128. Stroudsburg, PA, USA: Association for Computational Linguistics. URL `http://www.aclweb.org/anthology/W11-0415`. (cited on p. 100)

Schiller, Anne, Simone Teufel, Christine Stöckert, and Christine Thielen (1999). Guidelines für das Tagging deutscher Textcorpora mit STTS (kleines und großes Tagset). Tech. rep., Universität Stuttgart, Universität Tübingen, Stuttgart, Germany. URL `http://www.ims.uni-stuttgart. de/projekte/corplex/TagSets/stts-1999.pdf`. (cited on p. 91)

Schmid, Helmut (1994). Probabilistic part-of-speech tagging using decision trees. In *Proceedings of the International Conference on New Methods in Language Processing*, pages 44–49. (cited on pp. 14, 89, and 90)

Schmid, Helmut (1995). Improvements in part-of-speech tagging with an application to German. In *Proceedings of the ACL SIGDAT-Workshop*, pages 47–50. (cited on p. 92)

Schneider, Gerold (2008). *Hybrid Long-Distance Functional Dependency Parsing*. Ph.D. thesis, Universität Zürich, Zurich, Switzerland. (cited on p. 99)

Schneider, Gerold (2011). *Pro3Gres Technical Documentation*. University of Zurich, Institute of Computational Linguistics, Zurich, Switzerland. URL `http://www.cl.uzh.ch/research/ techreport/TR_2011_02.pdf` (accessed 2012-06-30). (cited on p. 99)

Schneider, Gerold (2012). Adapting a parser to historical English. In Matti Rissanen Jukka Tyrkkö, Terttu Nevalainen and Matti Kilpiö, eds., *Proceedings of the Helsinki Corpus Festival*. To appear. (cited on pp. 99 and 100)

Schreibman, Susan, Ray Siemens, and John Unsworth, eds. (2004). *A Companion to Digital Humanities*. Oxford, UK: Blackwell. URL `http://digitalhumanities.org/companion`. (cited on p. 6)

Sharoff, Serge (2006). Creating General-Purpose Corpora Using Automated Search Engine Queries. In Marco Baroni and Silvia Bernardini, eds., *Wacky! Working Papers on the Web as Corpus*. Bologna: GEDIT. (cited on p. 25)

Siemund, Rainer and Claudia Claridge (1997). The Lampeter corpus of early modern english tracts. *ICAME Journal*, 21:61–70. URL `http://icame.uib.no/ij21/lampcorp.pdf`. (cited on p. 109)

Skjrholt, Arne (2011). More, faster: Accelerated corpus annotation with statistical taggers. *Journal for Language Technology and Computational Linguistics*, 26(2):151–163. URL `http://www.jlcl.org/2011_Heft2/7.pdf`. (cited on p. 90)

Smith, Temple F. and Michael S. Waterman (1981). Identification of common molecular subsequences. *Journal of molecular biology*, 147(1):195–197. doi: 10.1016/0022-2836(81)90087-5. (cited on p. 78)

Sojka, Petr and Radim Hatlapatka (2010). Document engineering for a digital library: PDF recompression using JBIG2 and other optimizations of PDF documents. In *Proceedings of the 10th ACM symposium on Document engineering*, DocEng '10, pages 3–12. New York, NY, USA: ACM. doi: 10.1145/1860559.1860563. (cited on p. 31)

Souvay, Gilles and Jean-Marie Pierrel (2009). LGeRM: Lemmatisation des mots en Moyen Français. *Traitement Automatique des Langues 50, 2 (2009) 21*, 50(2):149–172. URL `http://halshs.archives-ouvertes.fr/halshs-00396452/`. (cited on pp. 96 and 97)

Spencer, Matthew and Christopher J. Howe (2004). Collating texts using progressive multiple alignment. *Computers and the Humanities*, 38(3):253–270. doi: 10.1007/s10579-004-8682-1. (cited on p. 35)

Sporleder, Caroline, Antal van den Bosch, and Kalliopi Zervanou, eds. (2011). *Language Technology for Cultural Heritage: Selected Papers from the LaTeCH Workshop Series*. Berlin/Heidelberg: Springer. doi: 10.1007/978-3-642-20227-8. (cited on p. 117)

Sporleder, Caroline and Kalliopi Zervanou, eds. (2010). *Proceedings of the ECAI 2010 Workshop on Language Technology for Cultural Heritage, Social Sciences, and Humanities (LaTeCH 2010)*. URL `http://ilk.uvt.nl/LaTeCH2010/LPF/ws16.pdf`. (cited on p. 128)

Sproat, Richard (2000). *A Computational Theory of Writing Systems*. Studies in Natural Language Processing. Cambridge University Press. URL `http://www.cslu.ogi.edu/~sproatr/newindex/wsbook.pdf` (accessed 2012-06-13). (cited on p. 53)

Stehouwer, Herman and Menno van Zaanen (2010). Finding patterns in strings using suffixarrays. In *Proceedings of the 2010 International Multiconference on Computer Science and Information Technology (IMCSIT 2010)*, pages 505–511. New York, NY, USA: IEEE. URL `http://ieeexplore.ieee.org/xpls/abs_all.jsp?arnumber=5679928`. (cited on p. 78)

Stein, Achim (2002). Étiquetage morphologique et lemmatisation de textes d'ancien français. In Pierre Kunstmann, France Martineau, and Danielle Forget, eds., *Ancien et moyen français sur le Web : enjeux méthodologiques et analyse de discours (Actes du colloque organisé à Ottawa en octobre 2002)*, pages 273–284. Ottawa: Les Éditions David. URL `http://www.uni-stuttgart.de/lingrom/stein/forschung/altfranz/afrlemma.pdf`. (cited on p. 96)

Stein, Achim (2007). Resources and tools for Old French text corpora. In Toshihiro Takagaki, Nobuo Tomimori, and Yoichiro Tsuruga, eds., *Corpus-Based Perspectives in Linguistics*, vol. 6 of *Usage Based Linguistic Informatics*, pages 217–229. Amsterdam/Philadelphia: John Benjamins. (cited on p. 89)

Stein, Achim (2008). Syntactic annotation of Old French text corpora. *Corpus*, 7:157–171. URL http://corpus.revues.org/index1510.html. (cited on pp. 98 and 110)

Strunk, Jan (2003). *Information retrieval for languages that lack a fixed orthography*. Seminar paper, Stanford University, Stanford, CA, USA. URL http://www.linguistics.ruhr-uni-bochum.de/~strunk/LSreport.pdf. (cited on p. 9)

Taavitsainen, Irma and Päivi Pahta, eds. (2010). *Early Modern English Medical Texts: Corpus description and studies*. Amsterdam, The Netherlands: John Benjamins. (cited on p. 109)

Taavitsainen, Irma, Päivi Pahta, and Martti Mäkinen (2005). *Middle English Medical Texts*. Amsterdam, The Netherlands: John Benjamins. (cited on p. 109)

Taghva, Kazem, Tom Nartker, Allen Condit, and Julie Borsack (2001). Automatic removal of "garbage strings" in OCR text: An implementation. In *Proceedings of the 5th World Multi-Conference on Systemics, Cybernetics and Informatics*. (cited on p. 81)

TEI Consortium, ed. (2007). *TEI P5: Guidelines for Electronic Text Encoding and Interchange*. Charlottesville, VA, USA: TEI Consortium. URL http://www.tei-c.org/Guidelines/P5/. (cited on pp. 60, 62, and 64)

Telljohann, Heike, Erhard W. Hinrichs, Sandra Kübler, Heike Zinsmeister, and Kathrin Beck (2009). Stylebook for the Tübingen treebank of written German (TüBa-D/Z). Tech. rep., Universität Tübingen, Seminar für Sprachwissenschaft. URL http://www.sfs.uni-tuebingen.de/resources/tuebadz-sty-2009.pdf (accessed 2011-07-17). (cited on p. 21)

Terrades, Oriol R., Alejandro H. Toselli, Nicolas Serrano, Verónica Romero, Enrique Vidal, and Alfons Juan (2010). Interactive layout analysis and transcription systems for historic handwritten documents. In *Proceedings of the 10th ACM symposium on Document engineering*, DocEng '10, pages 219–222. New York, NY, USA: ACM. doi: 10.1145/1860559.1860607. (cited on p. 49)

Thesaurus Linguae Graecae (2011). *The TLG Beta Code Manual 2011*. Thesaurus Linguae Graecae, Irvine, CA, USA. URL http://www.tlg.uci.edu/encoding/BCM2011.pdf. (cited on p. 56)

Tiedemann, Jörg (2011). *Bitext Alignment*, vol. 14 of *Synthesis Lectures on Human Language Technologies*. San Rafael, CA, USA: Morgan & Claypool. doi: 10.2200/S00367ED1V01Y201106HLT014. (cited on p. 117)

Tsunakawa, Takashi, Naoaki Okazaki, and Jun'ichi Tsujii (2008). Building bilingual lexicons using lexical translation probabilities via pivot languages. In Nicoletta Calzolari, Khalid Choukri, Bente Maegaard, Joseph Mariani, Jan Odijk, Stelios Piperidis, and Daniel Tapias, eds., *Proceedings of the Sixth International Conference on Language Resources and Evaluation (LREC'08)*. European Language Resources Association (ELRA). URL `http://www.lrec-conf.org/proceedings/lrec2008/pdf/423_paper.pdf`. (cited on p. 85)

TUSTEP Manual (2012). *TUSTEP: Handbuch und Referenz*. Universität Tübingen, Zentrum für Datenverarbeitung, Tübingen, Germany. URL `http://www.tustep.uni-tuebingen.de/pdf/handbuch.pdf` (accessed 2012-06-12). (cited on p. 57)

The Unicode Consortium (2012). *The Unicode Standard, Version 6.1.0*. Mountain View, CA, USA: The Unicode Consortium. URL `http://www.unicode.org/versions/Unicode6.1.0/`. (cited on pp. 54 and 55)

Vale, Oto, Arnaldo Candido Jr., Marcelo Muniz, Clarissa Bengtson, Lívia Cucatto, Abner Batista, Maria C. Parreira, Maria T. Biderman, and Ra Aluísio (2008). Building a large dictionary of abbreviations for named entity recognition in Portuguese historical corpora. In Caroline Sporleder and Kiril Ribarov, eds., *Proceedings of the LREC 2008 Workshop on Language Technology for Cultural Heritage Data (LaTeCH 2008)*, pages 47–54. (cited on p. 116)

van Reenen, Pieter and Maaike Mulder (2000). Un corpus linguistique de 3000 chartes en moyen néerlandais du 14e siècle. In Mireille Bilger, ed., *Corpus, méthodologie et applications linguistiques*, pages 209–217. Paris: Champion/Presses Universitaires de Perpignan. (cited on p. 105)

Volk, Martin, Noah Bubenhofer, Adrian Althaus, Maya Bangerter, Lenz Furrer, and Beni Ruef (2010). Challenges in building a multilingual Alpine heritage corpus. In Nicoletta Calzolari, Khalid Choukri, Bente Maegaard, Joseph Mariani, Jan Odijk, Stelios Piperidis, Mike Rosner, and Daniel Tapias, eds., *Proceedings of the Seventh International Conference on Language Resources and Evaluation (LREC'10)*, pages 1653–1659. European Language Resources Association (ELRA). URL `http://www.lrec-conf.org/proceedings/lrec2010/pdf/110_Paper.pdf`. (cited on p. 45)

Volk, Martin, Lenz Furrer, and Rico Sennrich (2011). Strategies for reducing and correcting OCR errors. In Caroline Sporleder, Antal Bosch, and Kalliopi Zervanou, eds., *Language Technology for Cultural Heritage*, Theory and Applications of Natural Language Processing, chap. 1, pages 3–22. Berlin/Heidelberg: Springer. doi: 10.1007/978-3-642-20227-8_1. (cited on pp. 34, 38, 39, and 40)

von Ahn, Luis, Benjamin Maurer, Colin McMillen, David Abraham, and Manuel Blum (2008). reCAPTCHA: Human-based character recognition via web security measures. *Science*, 321(5895): 1465–1468. doi: 10.1126/science.1160379. (cited on pp. 45 and 48)

Wagner, Robert A. and Michael J. Fischer (1974). The String-to-String correction problem. *Journal of the ACM*, 21(1):168–173. doi: 10.1145/321796.321811. (cited on p. 78)

Wilcock, Graham (2009). *Introduction to Linguistic Annotation and Text Analytics*. No. 3 in Synthesis Lectures on Human Language Technologies. San Rafael, CA, USA: Morgan & Claypool. doi: 10.2200/S00194ED1V01Y200905HLT003. (cited on pp. 60 and 87)

Winter, Thomas N. (1999). Roberto Busa, S.J., and the invention of the machine-generated concordance. *The Classical Bulletin*, 75(1):3–20. URL http://digitalcommons.unl.edu/classicsfacpub/70/. (cited on p. 101)

Wong, Kam-Fai, Wenjie Li, Ruifeng Xu, and Zheng-sheng Zhang (2009). *Introduction to Chinese Natural Language Processing*, vol. 4 of *Synthesis Lectures on Human Language Technologies*. San Rafael, CA, USA: Morgan & Claypool. doi: 10.2200/S00211ED1V01Y200909HLT004. (cited on p. 99)

World Wide Web Consortium (2004). XML Schema Part 1: Structures. URL http://www.w3.org/TR/xmlschema-1/ (accessed 2011-04-17). (cited on p. 61)

World Wide Web Consortium (2010). Cascading Style Sheets Level 2 Revision 1 (CSS 2.1) Specification. URL http://www.w3.org/TR/CSS2/ (accessed 2011-04-17). (cited on p. 65)

Wright, Joseph (1917). *A Middle High German Primer*. Oxford, UK: Clarendon. URL http://www.gutenberg.org/ebooks/22636. (cited on p. 13)

Wu, Sun, Udi Manber, Gene Myers, and Webb Miller (1990). An O(*NP*) sequence comparison algorithm. *Information Processing Letters*, 35(6):317–323. doi: 10.1016/0020-0190(90)90035-V. (cited on p. 72)

Xiang, Xuyu, Dafang Zhang, and Jiaohua Qin (2007). A new algorithm for the longest common subsequence problem. In *Computational Intelligence and Security Workshops (CISW 2007)*, pages 112–115. New York, NY, USA: IEEE. doi: 10.1109/CISW.2007.4425458. (cited on p. 73)

Xue, Zhenzhen, Dawei Yin, and Brian D. Davison (2011). Normalizing microtext. In *Analyzing Microtext: Papers from the 2011 AAAI Workshop*, vol. WS-11-05 of *AAAI Workshops*, pages 74–79. Palo Alto, CA, USA: AAAI. URL http://www.aaai.org/ocs/index.php/WS/AAAIW11/paper/view/3987. (cited on p. 9)

Zeldes, Amir, Julia Ritz, Anke Lüdeling, and Christian Chiarcos (2009). ANNIS: A search tool for multi-layer annotated corpora. In *Proceedings of Corpus Linguistics 2009*. URL http://www.linguistik.hu-berlin.de/institut/professuren/korpuslinguistik/mitarbeiter-innen/amir/pdf/CL2009_ANNIS_pre.pdf. (cited on p. 112)

Author's Biography

MICHAEL PIOTROWSKI

Michael Piotrowski is head of the Digital Humanities research group at the Leibniz Institute of European History in Mainz, Germany. Before this, he worked as a postdoc researcher with the Law Sources Foundation of the Swiss Lawyers Society and was an adjunct lecturer at the Institute of Computational Linguistics of the University of Zurich, Switzerland. He received his doctoral degree in Computer Science in 2009 from Otto von Guericke University Magdeburg, Germany. He also holds an M.A. in Computational Linguistics, English Philology, and Applied Linguistics from Friedrich-Alexander University Erlangen-Nuremberg, Germany. His main research interests are language technology for historical texts, document engineering, interactive editing and authoring aids, and e-learning technology.

Printed in the United States
by Baker & Taylor Publisher Services